Race-Conscious Caring in Educational Leadership

Race-Conscious Caring in Educational Leadership

A Narrative Ethics

Michael G. Gunzenhauser, Osly J. Flores,
and Michael W. Quigley

Teachers College Press
Teachers College, Columbia University

Published by Teachers College Press,® 1234 Amsterdam Avenue, New York, NY 10027

Front cover by Edwin Kuo Design. Images by Carl D. Master and Bovall, both via Shutterstock.

Portions of this text appeared in earlier versions in the following articles, and excerpts appear here courtesy of Sage Publications:

Flores, O. J. (2018). (Re)constructing the language of the achievement gap to an opportunity gap: The counternarratives of three African American women school leaders. *Journal of School Leadership, 28*(3), 344–373.

Flores, O. J., & Gunzenhauser, M. G. (2021). Justice in the gaps: School leader dispositions and the use of data to address the opportunity gap. *Urban Education, 56*(2), 261–288.

Gunzenhauser, M. G., Flores, O. J., & Quigley, M.W. (2021). Race-conscious ethics in school leadership: From impersonal caring to critical responsibility. *Teachers College Record, 123*(2), 1–40.

Gunzenhauser, M. G., Flores, O. J., & Quigley, M. W. (2024). Race-conscious caring for anti-racist leadership: A narrative ethics for cultivating communal responsibility. *Journal of School Leadership, 34*(1), 3–25.

Portions of this text appeared in an earlier version in the following article, and excerpts appear here courtesy of Taylor and Francis:

Flores, O. J., & Gunzenhauser, M. G. (2019). The problems with colorblind leadership revealed: A call for race-conscious leaders. *International Journal of Qualitative Studies in Education, 32*(8), 963–981.

Library of Congress Cataloging-in-Publication Data is available at loc.gov

ISBN 978-0-8077-8742-7 (paper)
ISBN 978-0-8077-8743-4 (hardcover)
ISBN 978-0-8077-8326-9 (ebook)

Printed on acid-free paper
Manufactured in the United States of America

Contents

Preface

In her commencement address to the 1988 graduates of Sarah Lawrence College, Toni Morrison (2019) embedded a statement about the meaning and value of education:

> And by education I do not mean hobbling the mind, but liberating it; by education I do not mean passing on monologues, but engaging in dialogues. Listening, assuming sometimes that I have a history, a language, a view, an idea, a specificity. Assuming that what I know may be useful, may enhance what you know, may extend or complete it. My memory is as necessary to yours as your memory is to mine. (p. 71)

Learning from others is a fundamental, relational human activity, and the urgency Morrison accords to it speaks to our times when competing visions of the meaning and value of education are very much on the minds of educators and parents who dream of an expansive future for their children. Educational leaders have the daunting responsibility and incredible opportunity to create schools that, in Morrison's words, "produce humane human beings" and to "refuse to continue to produce generation after generation of people trained to make expedient decisions rather than humane ones" (p. 71).

As educators and educational scholars, we strive to create rich and humane educational opportunities for all children. With ample evidence that schooling in the United States is marked by systemic inequities in opportunities, we have come together to focus on the role of the educational leader in eradicating those inequities. We believe the school leader has a powerful role in creating spaces for more equitable educational experiences, in guiding teachers to build their capacity to serve all children, and in collaborating with communities and other leaders to take collective responsibility for all children.

We have sought to develop an educational leadership ethics that would be up to the task. In this book, we place special emphasis on children of color, whose disparate educational opportunities have led to the accumulation of an educational debt (Ladson-Billings, 2006). Building a model for race-conscious caring, we remake leadership ethics to focus on racial equity, incorporating four components—race consciousness, critical caring, justice leadership, and ethical praxis. This book names and explains this model for the first time. It is a model of professional ethics drawing from two ethical traditions—caring ethics and narrative ethics—that give new life to the study of equity leadership. We hope to inspire practicing leaders and those aspiring to be leaders to engage in the complementary processes of narrating their own moral narratives and witnessing the moral narratives of others—true to Morrison's call for an education that engages in dialogue and to her exhortation about the urgency of an education for liberation.

Our model considers the perspectives of practicing school leaders, both those who exemplify race-conscious caring and those who fall short on various dimensions. The model of race-conscious caring addresses three perpetual problems they have faced in their leadership practice—race-evasiveness, impersonal caring, and systemic gaps in educational opportunity. These perpetual problems have been neither resolved nor replaced by any of the developments in schools or the wider political discourse in the recent past. Instead, the need for greater capacity for race-conscious caring has become more intense. The school leaders' varied views are presented to show the scale and texture of these key problems and suggest ways all leaders can develop their capacity.

We began working on *Race-Conscious Caring* before the COVID-19 pandemic, before the murder of George Floyd, before the renewed interest in antiracist scholarship, and before the subsequent backlash against critical race theory and anything carrying the label of diversity, equity, and inclusion. During this time, the need for a book like *Race-Conscious Caring in Educational Leadership* has become even more urgent. Changing political discourse has pushed and pulled school leaders in various directions, evidence of the persistent contention over the desire for greater equity in schools and society.

We collaborated on this book as three scholars from different disciplines in education. Mike Gunzenhauser is a philosopher of education and a qualitative methodologist. Osly Flores is an educational leadership scholar. Michael Quigley is an educational sociologist. Our common interests are in equity leadership, antiracist practice, and educational preparation that leads to stronger educators and school leaders for children of color. Our various interests from our subdisciplines have come together in this book in unique and enriching ways. Osly designed the original study that became the book. He interviewed 22 school leaders in Southwestern Pennsylvania about their equity leadership. From our analysis of the data over several years, we identified individual components of equity leadership, and then for this book we developed our framework that brings together all of the elements into a single model.

We also get into some complications and implications of the work, focusing on efforts we have undertaken to put these ideas into practice in our graduate courses, our educator preparation curricula, consultancies, and professional development sessions. We have come to understand that all three of us are most interested in working with school leaders who seek to be better equity leaders—leaders who recognize the significance of race, racism, and racial identity in the lives of children of color and who wish to build their own capacity to promote equity. This book is unique in that our route toward equity leadership is professional ethics. We draw on the significance of caring as the basis for professional ethics and the power of narrative ethics—both for critical self-reflection on one's own moral narrative and for witnessing the moral narratives of others whose experiences differ from one's own. At the end of Chapter 5 is an exercise leaders can complete to build their own moral narratives. Readers can complete that exercise now—several school leaders have tried it and found it useful. Readers will get more out of the exercise after reading the whole book.

For their thoughtful participation in the interview study, we are grateful to our 22 respondents. Their candor greatly helped us identify the key issues facing school leaders as they struggle with the demands of accountability policy, standards-based reform, and institutionalized educational inequities. The examples of ethical praxis from the strongest race-conscious leaders, as well as the developing strengths of leaders attempting to build their capacity for equity leadership, provide guidance on what's possible and how all leaders can move beyond good intentions and enrich their practice. We are also grateful to the various partners who have worked with us on equity leadership projects, including Angela Allie and Eboni Zamani-Gallaher. Diane Kirk, Jerry Longo, and Charlene Trovato helped recruit initial respondents. Rebecca Taylor and Stacy Otto read our initial book proposal and helped us make our ideas clearer and more cohesive. Leigh Patel provided key input at a pivotal point in our conceptual development. Brian Ellerbeck provided essential guidance on the structure and scope of the book. Joshua Childs was an early partner in the initial work. New research partners Sierra Stern and Keanna Cash reviewed portions of the book and helped us think about our project in new ways. Colleagues Oscar Patrón, Oscar Medina, Gretchen Givens Generett, and Linda DeAngelo have been constant thought partners. Cameron Barnett and Lori Delale-O'Connor provided key inspiration as we were finishing the book. School leaders Thomas Koulentes, Eileen McMahon, and Yvonne Tsagalis graciously provided feedback on the moral narrative exercise in Chapter 5. Editors Brian Ellerbeck and Nancy Mandel provided essential encouragement and helped us be clearer. Our families have provided support and encouragement throughout the process. Thank you all for contributing to this work. The educational experiences of the children in our families—our children, grandchildren, and niblings—have provided continual inspiration for the urgency of the project.

CHAPTER 1

What Does It Mean to Be a Caring Leader?

What does it mean for a school leader to be caring and just? What does it mean to work against the power of racism? Throughout the education sector, educators and leaders are being challenged by students and communities to place racial differences and awareness of racism at the center of their practice. At the same time, some parents and policymakers are pressuring schools to cut back their diversity, equity, and inclusion efforts. Quite often, leaders stumble, failing to understand and respond to the needs and interests of their students, their students' families, and the larger communities they serve.

In this book, we argue that in order to lead a school in equitable and antiracist practice, a leader most fundamentally needs a leadership ethics built on *race-conscious caring*—an ethical praxis grounded in race consciousness, critical caring, and justice leadership that provides a critical and reflective vision of what education can mean for children of color. In this chapter, we briefly define each of these components and how they combine in a vision of ethical praxis. We acknowledge that developing race-conscious caring requires a lot of work. Ethics is always work, and it takes more than good intentions. Developing a professional practice that centers others and their concerns is a lifelong project, drawing from one's history, moral commitments, values, and connection to communities.

To make the case for race-conscious caring, we explore the major themes from our study of school leaders in the metropolitan Pittsburgh area in Southwestern Pennsylvania. In an interview study, we asked 22 school leaders about their educational visions and how they enact their visions to serve their particular student populations. We also asked about their perspectives on the experiences of children of color in their districts and their use of data to address educational inequities. To better understand the variation in perspectives about leadership for equity in our area, we drew from a sample of schools throughout the county. We analyzed the interview data from multiple angles to depict the leaders' perspectives in relation to their equity practices. From that analysis, we built our theory of race-conscious caring over several years. This ethical praxis is evident in some leaders rather fully and in most others incompletely. In the Appendix, we describe our research methods in full detail.

STUDENTS DEMANDING CHANGE

We argue that developing and maintaining a race-conscious caring ethics is central to every school leader's practice. It is needed in all school communities, whether or not the school enrolls large numbers of students of color. The words of students reflecting on their school experiences make that need clear.

In June 2020, graduating senior William Generett III called out his high school, an affluent and well-resourced school in the suburbs of Pittsburgh, for systematically evading the issues students of color face (Generett, 2020). As a Black[1] student at Fox Chapel Area High School, Generett cocreated the school's first Black Student Union, which drew members from among the overall student body. In an essay expressing his response to the murder of George Floyd in May 2020 under the knee of a Minneapolis police officer, Generett explains the challenges of growing up Black in a predominantly white community:

> Most of my white peers are not capable of having a real conversation regarding race and police brutality. It is very lonely to be smart and Black in Fox Chapel. In a school that does not actively try to fight racism, kids of color constantly have to defend ourselves and what we stand for. (Generett, 2020, para. 2)

Naming his school as "not actively try[ing] to fight racism," Generett voices the concern we have for this book: challenging school leaders to act with intention against racism.

In a subsequent essay, Fox Chapel classmate J. Oliver Choo (2020, June 18) said of Generett, "While he has campaigned against racial inequity for years, his work is finally being reciprocated by a massive wave of response" (para. 10). Choo followed with his own story of his experience as an Asian American student in the same high school and his disgust with his classmates for their overt displays of racism toward him and other Asian American students. Choo adds this about school leaders:

---

1. In this text, we follow the rationale of Michael Dumas (2016) in capitalizing Black but not white. Dumas makes a distinction between Black as a chosen identity of people (many of whom are African American) with shared history and experience and white as a social construct which "does not describe a group with a sense of common experiences or kinship outside of acts of colonization and terror" (p. 13). Dumas presents the term blackness in lowercase to signify blackness as "a social construction of racial meaning, much as whiteness" (p. 13).

> I suppose that the school administrators may have been unaware of this pervasive culture of racial insensitivity—despite the fact that I have both experienced and observed the use of offensive language with faculty present. In any case, the onus should not fall on victims to report incidents that are often too personal, too intimate and too painful to put into words. The burden should fall on perpetrators to reform their own destructive behavior and on school leaders to aggressively eradicate it. (Choo, 2020, para. 10)

Following on Generett's naming of the lack of race-conscious leadership, Choo highlights the specific inaction by school leaders when racist incidents happen.

Choo and Generett were among the more than 800 students and alumni of the school pushing for change in the district, who in the summer of 2020 petitioned the school board to address racism in the school proactively in light of a series of Instagram postings of photos and videos laced with racial epithets. Local media outlet Public Source published their essays and reported on the developments at Fox Chapel Area High School: "The videos that started circulating recently showed Fox Chapel students using the n-word, in one case, shouting it at a house party while students were dancing" (Morrison, 2020, para. 2). Later that month, in response to the petition, the district's board of directors adopted a resolution that recognized the racism of these and other actions and resolved to address racism through curriculum, hiring practices, and policy review. The resolution reads in part:

> NOW, THEREFORE BE IT RESOLVED that the Fox Chapel Area School Board, unequivocally stands firm in its collective responsibility to foster an equitable and inclusive environment for every student, staff member, parent, and community member. We commit to use our role as school board directors to recognize, respond, and speak out against injustice and racial inequity in our school community. (Fox Chapel Area School District, 2020, June 29, p. 2)

The work in the Fox Chapel Area School District continues. While district leaders have pursued new professional development in equity and inclusion, they have faced backlash. A school board candidate running on a platform to repeal the June 2020 resolution lost in a November 2021 election. During his campaign, he made claims, repeated throughout the area, about the district indoctrinating teachers and students and making white people feel bad. Organized disruptions of school board meetings, evident throughout the nation amid the third and fourth waves of COVID-19 infections, took place in several Fox Chapel school board meetings and in other districts in southwestern Pennsylvania (Goldstein, 2021).

About 17 miles from Fox Chapel sits McKeesport Area Senior High School, where in July 2019 students resolved a lawsuit against their school district with an agreement allowing them to establish a Black Student Union

(Cook, 2019). Beginning in August 2018, the student group sought to create a space in which students could discuss their concerns about racial inequities at their school, particularly in the form of disparities in discipline of students of color, as documented in data reported to the Pennsylvania Department of Education (Herring, 2019a, 2019b; McKinney, 2019).

In the lawsuit filed in early April 2019, the students cited unaddressed racial comments by teachers and a particular teacher's physical aggression (McKinney, 2019). In the months-long effort to resolve the situation, the McKeesport superintendent publicly argued against the creation of the organization, positioning it as divisive and not the true intentions of the students, but instead the work of a political rival agitating against him (Herring, 2019a). According to students, the superintendent advocated for a larger group, assembling a mixed-race group of students to encourage the creation of a McKeesport Student Union rather than a Black Student Union (Herring, 2019b).

Prior to the settlement, 9th-grader TyNeshia Bowling spoke to a public radio reporter about her experience:

> So far, I have learned that a lot of people don't get a lot of things that we go through—and some people don't want to get it. They don't want to hear about it. That's probably one of the reasons why they're trying to shut it down and not talk about anything. That's why I think we should have a black student union: to talk about everything. (Herring, 2019b, para. 44)

The lawsuit was settled on First Amendment and Equal Access Act grounds, with the district agreeing to the group's formation and the group agreeing to limit its leadership to student members, excluding the community groups the students wished to consult as mentors (Cook, 2019). In her blog post in the Duquesne University law journal, *Juris Magazine*, Samantha Cook wrote that the superintendent "was within his rights as a superintendent to set such limitations on access to nonstudents . . . However, it was a misstep or serious oversight for the district to evade the formation of the student group in the first place" (para. 6).

Another legal action in the Pittsburgh metropolitan area arose from incidents in 2021 in the Norwin School District, a district that serves suburban and rural communities. The district came to a resolution in 2024 with the U.S. Department of Education's Office of Civil Rights (OCR) concerning complaints that the district allowed a "racially hostile environment to exist" (Haviland, 2024, para. 1). The incidents highlighted by the OCR report included several instances of students using racially offensive language on social media. The OCR documented a classroom incident in which a white student told a Black student to "go pick cotton" and another incident in which a student wrote the n-word on an online Google classroom homework assignment.

Another significant incident occurred during the school's Homecoming week. October 11, 2021, was designated "'Merica Monday," when high school students were invited to wear red, white, and blue, and two students wore Confederate attire. The OCR determined this led to a racially hostile environment in the school, as reported by students, staff, parents, and community members. A Black female student named Kalea Armstrong, a junior at the time of the incident, shared with the local television news her shock to see the two students prominently wearing Confederate attire:

> Some people were just wearing red, white, and blue. I think when you put the Confederate flag on, which is a symbolism of racism from the South, it's jaw-dropping. . . . I was infuriated. I went down to the principal's office [and] talked to him in the office. It brought me to tears. [The principal] said that they are going to work on the situation and that they are calling the students down to the office, that he feels for me, and that he will try to do anything to make it better. (Borrasso & Smith, 2021, paras. 4, 6)

The school administrators spoke with the two students and their parents. They had the two students remove their attire. In interviews with OCR officials, the high school principal "did not believe that the October 11 incident was an incident of racial harassment, but rather, an isolated dress code violation," and the assistant principal "did not believe this was an incident of racial harassment, although he acknowledged that the incident likely bothered students" (Haviland, 2024, para. 32). With these actions, school leaders attempted to explain away the intentions of the two students, despite ample evidence of prior engagement in racial harassment.

OCR supervisory attorney Christina Haviland (2024) documents the OCR's analysis:

> [A]lthough the District was made aware of severe and pervasive incidents of racial harassment, the District failed to evaluate whether the incidents created a racially hostile environment for students, failed to recognize some incidents as race-based harassment, minimized the conduct including in a press release as well as in correspondence to the School Board and with parents, and generally failed to take action reasonably designed to redress the racially hostile environment or mitigate its effects on students and the larger community. The evidence suggests that the District's failure to take reasonable steps to eliminate the hostile environment was rooted—in part—in its misunderstanding of its obligation to consider whether incidents that occur on social media, even if off campus, create or contribute to a racially hostile environments for students. (p. 10)

In short, Norwin district and school leaders downplayed, ignored, and passively responded to racialized issues. Norwin and OCR officials agreed to an extensive list of reforms to remedy the hostile racial environment and improve the culture of the district (Forstadt, 2024; Haviland, 2024).

PITTSBURGH AS A SITE FOR RACE-CONSCIOUS CARING

Understanding these stories calls for an explanation of the organization of public schooling in Southwestern Pennsylvania. These school districts are located in a single metropolitan area, but their demographic compositions are quite different. In Allegheny County, there are 43 separate school districts for a population of 1.25 million total persons and about 230,000 persons under 18 (U.S. Census Bureau, 2020). In a county recorded in the 2020 census as 75.7% white, 13.1% Black, 5.3% multiracial, 4.7% Asian, 2.7% Latina/o, and 0.2% Native American, school districts vary tremendously in the percentages of children of color enrolled in their schools. Fox Chapel Area School District has some socioeconomic diversity but is relatively wealthy and predominantly white. In 2019, Fox Chapel Area High School was 84% white, 8% Asian, 4% Black, 3% Latina/o, and 1% two or more races, with 16% qualifying for free or reduced-price lunch (National Center for Educational Statistics [NCES], 2019). McKeesport Area School District is much more racially and culturally diverse and serves a greater percentage of children living in poverty. In 2019, McKeesport Area Senior High School was 46% white, 41% Black, 11% two or more races, and 1% Latina/o, with 76% qualifying for free or reduced-price lunch (NCES, 2019). Both school districts sit in Allegheny County, an urban county that includes the city of Pittsburgh. Norwin School District sits in neighboring Westmoreland County, encompassing some suburban areas, some small towns, and a large rural area. In the 2022–2023 school year, Norwin High School enrolled 92% white, 3.4% multiracial, 2% Asian, 1.5% Black, 1.5% Latina/o, and 0.1% Native American students, and 25% of students qualified for free or reduced-price lunch.

As the contrasts among these school districts suggest, districts in the Pittsburgh metropolitan area vary widely in the percentage of students of color enrolled. The districts also vary in tax base, socioeconomic status, and per-pupil expenditure. Schools in close proximity to each other in the Pittsburgh area vary tremendously in their capacity to support students of color, to address racial difference, and to promote educational equity and justice. This variation repeats in many communities throughout the United States. Providing the structures and conditions for all children to flourish should be a significant shared goal for public education anywhere in the United States. However, the evidence makes it clear that those are neither the norms nor the apparent priorities of public education.

A 2019 report by local media outlet Public Source revealed that five Allegheny County school districts had "double-digit racial achievement gaps in every school" in their districts in the 2017–2018 school year (Niederberger, 2019, para. 7). Some schools in the largest district, Pittsburgh Public Schools, reported "gaps exceed[ing] 40 percentage points at some grade levels" (para. 11). When asked by Public Source, the superintendent of Northgate School District described how she and her curriculum director found a hidden example of institutional racism in the district's achievement data (Niederberger et al., 2019). In analyzing a 21-percentage-point gap in middle and high school students' math proficiency between its white (42.2% proficiency) and Black students (20.8% proficiency), the leaders noticed the differential tracking of white and Black students into math tracks in middle school, which set white and Black students on different trajectories toward math achievement in high school. Of note is that the Northgate superintendent was one of the very few school leaders willing to talk about institutional racism with Public Source.

The stories from these Pittsburgh area schools suggest that much needs to be done to improve educational equity, and much is needed from school leaders for more responsible and caring engagement with issues of race and racism. Moreover, as the demographic and school performance data suggest, inequities in resources and capacity for change are strongly evident, even in single metropolitan areas. In addition, the student voices reported in local media show the clear demand for more proactive, race-conscious leadership. In this book, we dig deeply into the variation of capacity in the region to build a model of race-conscious caring. We show what race-conscious leadership looks like in practice and how and why it is lacking in so many settings and among so many school leaders. In the variation of experiences and abilities, there are opportunities to foster improvement.

As an ethical praxis, race-conscious caring necessitates continual and critical reflection and active practice. It requires paying close attention to and valuing the experiences of children and families from varied backgrounds. It requires acknowledging one's limitations of exposure and experience across different races and ethnicities. It also requires opening oneself up and desiring to learn about the histories and perspectives of those in one's school community. Especially for those with limited experience across differences, race-conscious caring requires engaging in a narrative process—reading and listening to the experiences of people who are different from oneself and narrating one's own life as a historically, racially, and otherwise socially positioned ethical person. These are processes we model throughout the book.

We believe school leaders play an essential role in creating structures and conditions that promote the flourishing of all students, and we believe it is important to focus on the school leader as a significant locus of change. The Pittsburgh context is particular and interesting, but the conditions and issues are not unique. As readers proceed through the following chapters, we invite them to imagine how the particular histories of their communities and the particular needs and interests of the students they care about are significant for the work leaders need to do for educational equity—whether they are existing or aspiring school leaders, leadership faculty, policy makers, or other members of educational communities interested in having a role in educational equity. As we argue in this book, stronger educational leadership grounded in race-conscious caring should be fundamental to all leaders' practice and in all settings.

EQUITY, JUSTICE, AND ANTIRACISM IN SCHOOL LEADERSHIP

In our current time, it is vital that school leaders engage in practices that lead to greater equity in schools. Racism is one of the main barriers to equity, and as we explain in depth below, it contributes to nearly every aspect of the educational experience, parceling out opportunities and experiences differentially and systematically. Systematic attacks on diversity, equity, and inclusion in schools reflect antagonism toward progress achieved in making institutions more accessible, fair, and effective for children of color. But progress has been tenuous and not systematic. As faculty preparing school leaders, we are focused on the roles that leaders play in cultivating change, and we are very interested in building the capacity of school leaders to address the differential educational experiences of children of color. The stories of those differential experiences are partially told in the data about student performance on standardized testing, and they are more accurately depicted by the variation in opportunities that students have (Darling-Hammond, 2010, 2013; Orfield & Jarvie, 2020). They are also told in the firsthand accounts of students like William Generett III, J. Oliver Choo, TyNeshia Bowling, and Kalea Armstrong; histories of racial segregation and subjugation (Orfield, 2013; Orfield & Frankenberg, 2014; Rutan & Glass, 2017; Trotter & Day, 2010); and numerous other stories of the educational experiences of students of color struggling to be recognized by their school leaders. Even in school districts where differential achievement is not recorded (or the percentage of students of color is so small that the state does not require schools to disaggregate data and report it publicly), attention to race, racial difference, and racism is sorely needed. Attention that is caring and responsive is essential.

In this book we share what we have learned about race-conscious caring from both its presence and absence among the leaders we studied. We break the concept into several thematic components. We show how these themes are evident in the most race-conscious leaders and how shades and variations in these components are evident across our sample. Based on our analysis of the interview data and our consideration of a broad literature in professional ethics and equity leadership, we build a rationale for a leadership ethics of genuine caring that is race-conscious, culturally sustaining, and collectively responsible. We argue that race-conscious caring is vital for school leaders to create and sustain more equitable educational spaces. All leaders would benefit from critical self-reflection about their experiences with racial difference, the development of their capacity for engaging diverse communities, and the cultivation of a strong sense of responsibility for the educational experiences of all students.

We have found it important to understand when race-conscious caring is not evident and how and why that might be the case. We describe key barriers: color-evasiveness, impersonal caring, and rational/technical concern for test scores—perspectives quite popular among the school leaders we interviewed. These perspectives often seem to arise from good intentions; we show how they in fact perpetuate inequities in educational experiences for children of color. Good intentions even seem to get in the way of change, as these perspectives persist because of leaders' lack of experience and the lack of challenges to their good intentions. The result is inaction. Many principals, especially white principals in schools with a small percentage of students of color, maintain a color-evasive perspective and "impersonal caring" (Code, 1995), with abstract and technical concern for student performance. In contrast, principals with race-conscious attitudes care for children of color differently; they exercise *critical caring*, denoted by more marked elaboration of *collective responsibility*, a moral sense of purpose that stretches to the education of all children and the quality of everyone's education.

As the book progresses, we explain each thematic component of race-conscious caring—race consciousness, critical caring, justice leadership, and ethical praxis—as a leadership ethics model. We explore the implications of race-conscious caring and propose ideas for building school leader capacity. We want school leaders to interrogate their preexisting notions of caring and challenge themselves fundamentally about their assumptions of what it means to care for children, families, and communities that are underserved, marginalized, racialized, and minoritized. While good intentions are a good place to start, we need leaders to be much more than well-intentioned. They need to take the risks that will be involved in building their knowledge and experience to get past good intentions and onto a more critical, ethical praxis. We believe it will be important for school leaders to do this work *relationally*—with their communities and with other school leaders. What we mean by *relational* is that all school leaders can learn many lessons from the ethical practices of colleagues who have more extensive experiences with racial difference and who draw from their histories and racial identities to be strong community advocates and culturally responsive leaders. Without critical reflection and engagement in communities of care with colleagues with distinctly different ethical frames, leaders are likely to fall back upon color-evasive perspectives that may be well-meaning but are largely ineffective for promoting more equitable educational experiences for children.

RACE-CONSCIOUS CARING AS LEADERSHIP ETHICS

To develop these ideas, we bring together several areas of scholarship to analyze our interview data, situate it in a local context, and derive implications for school leaders and educators more broadly. Recently, researchers have identified a need to link educators' experience of race and ethnicity and their experience of caring (Louis et al., 2016). Authors have also expanded the meta-ethical bases for these discussions, putting into use broader and more recent ethical theory, specifically drawing from critical, feminist, and critical race theory (for example, Bass, 2009, 2012, 2016, 2020; Rivera-McCutcheon, 2021; Touré & Thompson Dorsey, 2018; Witherspoon & Arnold, 2010).

In this book, we make sense of the work of race-conscious school leaders and of those who aspire to greater equity leadership but whose perspectives limit their success. We show how and why leaders fall short, in contrast to more race-conscious leaders, to help readers be reflective about their own work, the gaps in opportunity that are evident in schools, and the extensive learning needed for today's educational leaders. Throughout our work on this project of investigating school leaders for equity, we have stressed the need to build capacity in school leaders throughout the education sector, and so it has been important to us to piece together how exactly capacity falls short so we can see where avenues can be opened up to expand capacity. Our work has led to an approach to ethical praxis that is challenging but essential for every school leader and in every context. In what follows, we introduce the reader to the four components of race-conscious caring leadership: (1) *race consciousness,* (2) *critical caring,* (3) *justice leadership,* and (4) *ethical praxis*. Figure 1.1 suggests how these key concepts relate to each other.

The model for race-conscious caring emerges from data analysis and engagement with the relevant ethical theory and leadership research. The book provides examples of each component of the model. In Figure 1.1, race consciousness appears at the top of the model as a vital beginning point, complemented by critical caring and justice. These three combine to contribute to the holistic practice of ethical praxis, the enactment of narrative ethics in leadership practice. In subsequent chapters, we detail each of these concepts and draw examples from our interview study to connect race-conscious leadership ethics to practice. This is a fully asset-based approach to countering racism in schools and speaks fundamentally to the kinds of ethical persons leaders should be.

Race Consciousness

Race consciousness is centered on the significance of race as a social construct with historic (Morrison, 1992), legal (Bell, 2004), and philosophical import (Mills, 1998). We start with the assumption that race and racism

Figure 1.1. Race-Conscious Caring Leadership

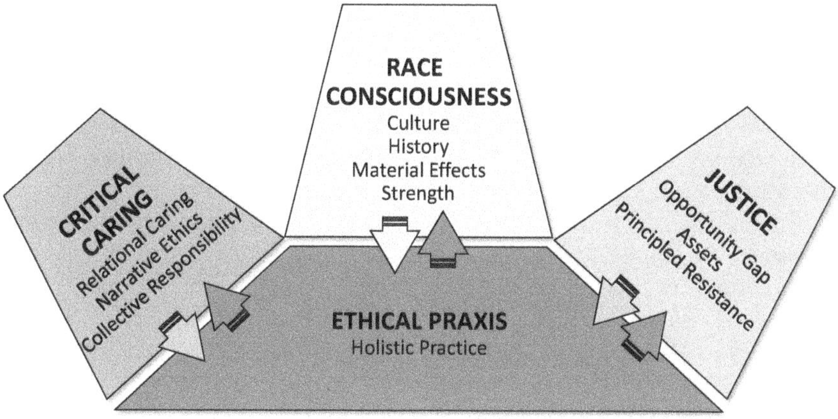

have material effects on the lives of real persons. Further, race is a source of strength, resistance, and moral value as a component of individual and group identity. Consciousness of the relevance of race to educational practice invites dispositions of inquiry and attentiveness, humility and respect. Race consciousness works against its opposite, color-evasiveness, the popular and problematic cultural practice of intentionally avoiding the historical reality of racism and the significance of race and racism in everyday life (Annamma et al., 2017).

Color-evasiveness is a concept developed by Subini Annamma and her colleagues (2017) to expand the implicitly ableist concept of "color blindness." Eduardo Bonilla-Silva (2014) has shown how members of the dominant culture systematically avoid the significance and importance of race and racism in their personal and professional lives. Rather than being passively "color-blind," being color-evasive means enacting intentional strategies, positioning oneself as powerful and morally justified (Annamma et al., 2017). In contrast, race consciousness is characterized by several components, introduced below. These are the features of race consciousness we see as especially relevant to leadership ethics: the cultural significance of race and racism, the historical importance of race and racism, the material effects of racism, and the sources of strength, resistance, and moral value in racialized identity.

Cultural Significance. An initial component of race consciousness is acknowledging the cultural significance of race. Racial difference has been fundamental to constructing what cultural actors describe as a desirable, moral, and educated person. A key project of the Progressive era in the early 20th century was establishing what philosophically and psychologically constitutes an independent, thinking, scientific person (Dewey, 1938; Thorndike, 1914), and a good deal of attention was focused on how modern persons think and act. As Toni Morrison (1992) has argued, racial difference—and especially a contrast between white and Black—has held a key place in the American cultural imagination. In her touchstone work on the subject, *Playing in the Dark: Whiteness and the Literary Imagination,* Morrison writes about the role of race in canonical American literature for the construction of self, agency, and goodness. As we explain in greater detail in Chapter 2, the cultural import of race is pervasive in our ideas about education and ethics.

Historical Importance. Race and racism figure prominently in the development of United States history, as in its literature. National history matters; further, as Muhammad Khalifa (2018) argues, the local histories of communities are particularly relevant for those leading public schools. Parents and other community members draw from their understanding of history to make meaning of their children's experiences in public schools. Conditions that seem immutable have histories. In this book, the history of race in Pittsburgh and Allegheny County, in particular, are significant for understanding the larger context of schools, particularly the history of struggle for equitable resources, employment of Black teachers, and residential segregation. This local history follows many of the patterns of the racial history of the United States overall. As significant as industrialization and union organizing have been for the city and region, we must recognize how deeply racialized that history is and how it has affected the industrial and educational workforces, the life chances of racialized children, and educational opportunities (Trotter & Day, 2010). Similarly, the region's relatively small percentage of persons identifying as Asian, Asian American, Latina/o, and Native American reflects settler colonialism, historical migration patterns, and exclusionary practices.

Material Effects. Echoing national trends, the history of race and racism in the Pittsburgh region has led to disparities in wealth, health, and educational access and to the maintenance of racialized housing borders and school district boundaries (Trotter & Day, 2010). Pittsburgh remains the largely racially segregated city it was throughout the 20th century, with the integration of neighborhoods appearing noticeably in very recent census data (Center for Race and Social Problems [CRSP], 2015). As documented through history, racism causes measurable economic and health disparities as it minoritizes and marginalizes people. Disparities in access to child care, measured proficiency in reading and math, graduation rates, and educational attainment are evident in CRSP's analysis of the 2010 census. In economic terms, disparities are found in the median value of assets, poverty, unemployment, median income, and homeownership. In public health, disparities are found in measures such as infant mortality, the prevalence of diabetes and cardiovascular disease, and rates of HIV infection. These measurable effects combine into an experience of systematic marginalization, in schools as in the larger system of subjugation of which they are part. All of these material effects contribute to the experiences of students. School leaders need to know about the material effects of racism in the larger culture and in their communities. They need an appreciation of their potential role in changing material conditions, in their practice, and in collaboration with outside organizations and agencies.

Strength, Resistance, and Moral Value. At the same time, we understand that focusing only on historically situated disparities runs the very real risk of undermining the strength, resistance, and moral value embedded in communities of color. Cultural assets and continual resistance to domination and annihilation have kept communities of color alive and thriving for centuries. In particular, the historical strengths of the African American community in Pittsburgh are especially significant for the establishment of race consciousness. While this book is not relevant only to the Pittsburgh area, we share details from the communities our data comes from so that readers can appreciate a phenomenon in context and so they can connect what is happening in Pittsburgh to their own local histories and conditions. As is true throughout the United States, the long history of struggle for access to educational and economic opportunity is a tremendous resource for leaders looking to continue the work of racial equity in the region (Trotter & Day, 2010). The explosion of arts activity in the historically Black Hill District of Pittsburgh has contributed greatly to Black and African American cultural identity. The development of civic, religious, athletic, and political organizations in Black communities in Pittsburgh has created narratives of success and resistance that are evident throughout the region today. At the same time, they might not be recognized by leaders who habitually ignore history and the significance of race.

Race consciousness has been evident in the work of various researchers in educational leadership, notably in the area of culturally responsive school leadership (Briscoe & Khalifa, 2015; Khalifa, 2018; Khalifa et al., 2013; Theoharis & Haddix, 2011) and studies of leaders of color (Brooks & Arnold, 2013; Dillard, 1995; Gooden, 2012; Rivera-McCutcheon, 2021). Race consciousness in leadership involves several features. At its most basic, leaders acknowledge racial identity as a significant source of strength in the construction of the selves of their students (Carter, 2009). Racial difference and specific racial history are, in other words, sources of interest, celebration, and knowledge. Racial identity is an asset and a gateway to additional assets that commonly are systematically devalued, particularly in schools.

Race consciousness is an active position. It requires a strategy, constant learning, and principled resistance to the status quo, and we must recognize that color-evasiveness seems to be the default perspective for most school leaders. In other words, if race can be evaded, most parents, students, and teachers will be glad to follow along and allow it to continue to be evaded, and the larger dominant culture will support that evasion. Therefore, leaders need to be critically self-reflective in their practice and guide their teachers to be likewise. Chapter 2, which focuses on race consciousness, shows the variation in color-evasiveness and race consciousness found in the words of school leaders. Some leaders have created cultures within their schools that foster continual teacher learning and self-reflexivity in service to all students' needs and interests. As we explain in Chapter 2, race consciousness contributes to leadership practices that attend to the needs and interests of students of color.

Critical Caring

The second theme of race-conscious caring is critical caring. For this component of critical caring, discussed in Chapter 3, we recognize and bring together the importance of relational caring, narrative ethics, and collective responsibility. These elements make up our critical caring ideal. We place our work in the relational ethics tradition that emerged in the work of educational psychologist Carol Gilligan (1979, 1982) and educational philosopher Nel Noddings (1984). Noddings elaborated a feminine ethics of caring from the phenomenological experience of (mostly) women, whose ethical motivations and practices were not appropriately captured in the dominant ethical theory at the time.

Educational theorists have, over the last few decades, developed a picture of the caring leader, drawing from caring theory and related ideas about the centrality of moral leadership in educational practice (Fullan, 2011; Sergiovanni, 2009; Starratt, 1991, 2004). Caring has been integrated into ethical leadership models for several decades (Beck, 1994; Shapiro & Gross, 2013; Starratt, 1991, 2004; Stefkovich & Begley, 2007). More recent work has responded to critiques of caring theory as limiting and culturally situated. As suggested by work in race-conscious school leadership research (Bass, 2009, 2012, 2016, 2020), knowing how to care for all children is not systematically evident in school leaders (Khalifa et al., 2016; Louis et al., 2016); blame-the-victim discourses and deficit orientations that rely upon pervasive, negative stereotypes are common (Bass, 2020).

Relational Caring. The first component of critical caring is genuine, relational caring. Early work by Noddings (1984) on the ethics of caring and Lorraine Code (1995) on moral epistemology (among others) shows the importance of moving beyond empty gestures of caring (what Code refers to as "impersonal caring") to practices that direct the ethical carer to learn from the experiences and perspectives of others. Unable to become engrossed in relation, due to their evasion of the significance of race (specifically the experience of racism and its collective resistance) in the lives of children, impersonal carers cannot think and act past their presuppositions about how students feel, how to care about them, and how students should respond to caring (presuppositions which may be well intended but are uninformed).

Using Noddings' (1984) language, this is a complex example of the failure of a carer, a "one-caring," to engage in the motivational displacement that is so significant to caring. The more genuine caring needed cannot be completed unless the motivations of the cared-for are honored and supported. While the motivation to care for a racialized student may be sincere, caring remains abstract because the one-caring has not done the work needed to build a genuine relationship with the student (Fraser-Burgess et al., 2021; Lopez-Kershen, 2018; Valenzuela, 1999). Without a strong relation backed by considerable knowledge (such as the history of racism and its resistance), caring cannot be received by the cared-for, and the relation between the educator and student is compromised.

Narrative Ethics. The second component of critical caring is narrative ethics, an alternative approach to learning and expressing the good, the good life, and right action (Coles, 1989; Green, 2004). Rather than sticking with an abstract, theoretical approach, emphasis in narrative ethics is placed on life stories that explain how ethical choices draw from and enhance one's history, character, priorities, and life aims. In addition, rather than becoming stuck in reasoning through competing abstract principles, the ethical actor considers their place in relation to others. While all of those components are important to various other approaches to ethics, in narrative ethics specific value is placed on coherence, contextual understanding, and moral imagination, which applies to the narrative's author as well as the reader.

Moreover, narrative ethics has a long tradition, particularly among subjugated persons struggling to survive, thrive, and assert their humanity in an unjust and inequitable world. It is particularly well represented in activist and civil rights struggles and is well grounded in African American literary and philosophical traditions (Walker & Snarey, 2004). As an approach to ethics, it draws universally applicable theories about right action from the lives of individuals and/or from the imagined lives of literary figures (Welch, 1990). This is an older, aesthetic form of knowing (Green, 2004), which some ethics educators have turned to in recent years as an approach to ethics instruction in graduate programs (Nash & Jang, 2016). We believe narrative ethics is a way of helping committed professionals enact a praxis of equity and justice in ways that are morally meaningful to their journeys as individuals and members of shared communities. We argue it is crucial to learn from the moral leadership journeys of other race-conscious caring leaders and to systematically explore one's own moral narrative.

Collective Responsibility. The third component of critical caring is collective responsibility. Responsibility for individual student learning and flourishing has long been an important part of school leadership theory (Sirotnik, 2004; Starratt, 2004; Strike, 2006). In our formulation, we make some key distinctions about what responsibility should look like. Echoing the work of philosopher Gert Biesta (2004), responsibility and accountability should not be conflated, the former needing to be based upon the primary relation between educator and student. As Biesta argues, a bent toward managerial accountability erodes relationships of responsibility in schools (between and among students, parents, and teachers), because of the primacy accorded to the school's accountability to the state for test scores.

Similarly, responsibility should not be understood as a solely individualized obligation (Fielding, 2001; Furman, 2004). Compared to the competitive conditions instilled through high-stakes accountability policies that have made being a school leader a high-stakes and pressurized venture, collective responsibility for children looks different in practice. Collective responsibility is drawn from historically grounded, community-centered orientations toward uplift of children (Walker & Snarey, 2004), and leaders need to learn from these traditions to foster collective responsibility. Collective responsibility requires cooperation between schools and school districts and between schools and communities, which is not the norm for educational practice in general.

As we explain in Chapter 3, critical caring can be found in how some respondents narrate their ethical leadership. For some school leaders, race consciousness combines with a collective sense of responsibility and genuine, informed caring relationships with their students and communities and distinctly different language around the building of caring relationships. In many of our other respondents' approaches to caring, we see instead the absence of critical caring. Many principals, especially color-evasive principals in schools with a small percentage of students of color, evidence impersonal caring (Code, 1995). Across the sample of respondents, we reveal the existence of four thematic variations in caring: community-based caring, tough love/tough luck caring, color-evasive caring in what we are calling "fortunate communities," and caring with responsiveness. From a philosophical standpoint, the views are meaningfully distinct, and while these themes sometimes overlap in the perspectives of our participants, for the most part, they are found in particular individuals.

Justice Leadership

The third theme of our race-conscious caring ethics is the social frame leaders need to understand their role in context. An orientation toward justice leadership means having a strengths-based critical consciousness about educational inequity. It is a set of attitudes and dispositions toward children, seeing children and families as possessing strengths and abilities routinely suppressed and ignored by social institutions and social arrangements, especially schools. We characterize justice leadership as a set of dispositions regarding the opportunity gap, student assets, and principled resistance. These attitudes and dispositions lead to responsive practices that build upon the strengths of students of color and other marginalized students and provide greater opportunity. As we present this component, we also explain the variation in orientations to the differential educational experiences of students in their care that school leaders exemplified. While some leaders can read social structures and develop strategies to adapt and resist or change them, others ignore social structures, reinforcing deficit perspectives, attributing blame to subjugated students, families, and communities, and avoiding racially diverse settings.

Opportunity Gap. When differential educational outcomes are described as an "achievement gap," what typically follows are recommendations for individualized interventions to narrow the gap, rather than attending to the structural and cultural arrangements that have effectively produced differential educational opportunities (Carey, 2014; Ladson-Billings, 2006; Milner, 2012, 2020). Such individualized interventions lean toward deficit thinking about students and families. Described alternately in the research literature as an "opportunity gap" (Carter & Welner, 2013) or an "educational debt" (Ladson-Billings, 2006), these shifts in terms move focus to societal, school, and community inputs and structures. As researchers have shown, educational policies that address such issues as discipline (Carter et al., 2017), achievement (Carey, 2014), and school choice (Thompson Dorsey & Roulhac, 2019) reproduce educational inequality through systematically differential opportunities. This more recent research reinforces prior work about the differential educational opportunities generated by high-stakes accountability (Kantor & Lowe, 2013), housing segregation (Orfield, 2013), differential teacher quality (Darling-Hammond, 2013), and within-school tracking (Oakes, 2005, 2008).

In light of the inequitable tendencies of policies that place pressure on school leaders, in this book we offer evidence of leaders with an "opportunity gap" orientation who articulate a structural analysis of inequality. Leaders with an opportunity gap orientation know what they are up against and can name specific strategies that resist pressures to limit horizons for their students. These leaders name the specific instances when policy frames educational experiences in limiting ways, when practices propagated by teachers and others actively reinforce differential opportunity, and when conditions perpetuate differential access to high-quality teaching and culturally sustaining curriculum and instruction.

Assets. As we have already implied, an asset-based disposition toward children of color counters the pervasive interpretation of students of color and students living in poverty as lacking the cultural capital to succeed in schooling (Yosso, 2005). The language of deficit and disadvantage positions children as outsiders and others who require the guardianship and protection of the state. Serving the underserved is then a duty for interventionists keen on filling perceived voids of knowledge and experience. In contrast, an asset-based perspective draws from the knowledges of children and families, their interests, and their capabilities. What Yosso calls "community cultural wealth" is a source of strength and transformation. It is a disposition toward learning from and with school communities, rather than imposing external standards and measures of value, such as standardized measures of achievement normed on dominant populations and accountability schemes that reify such measures and proliferate damaging educational practices.

Principled Resistance. School leaders for more than two decades have had to respond to external pressures to ensure that their students perform well on standardized tests, and leaders in targeted schools (those least likely to do well on standardized tests) feel the pressure acutely (as foretold by Carnoy et al., 2003). Leaders often respond to that pressure not by building capacity but by chasing curriculum fixes or working harder at what they are already doing (Carnoy et al., 2003). However, some leaders respond with a justice disposition, an important foundation to social justice leadership (Murphy, 2003; Murphy & Shipman, 1999). Rather than converting external pressure into internal pressure for test score improvement, a justice orientation needs principled resistance to pressures that would harm or hinder children's educational experiences. Such a disposition requires clarity of purpose and intent in educating children of color and children living in poverty, offering culturally sustaining and enriching curriculum, and guiding teachers' capacity building for responsive practice (Khalifa, 2018).

Leaders who demonstrate a justice orientation can better enact responsibility for student learning (as opposed merely to accountability for student test scores). As we explain in Chapter 4, this strengths-based critical consciousness is evident in resistance to demands that leaders deem unjust for their students. Moreover, it enables models of responsibility for student education experiences in practices such as equity training, detracking, and family outreach.

Ethical Praxis

Ethical praxis, the fourth theme of race-conscious leadership ethics, means enacting race-conscious leadership ethics as an embodied practice. This component makes use of all three previous components to suggest what race consciousness, critical caring, and strengths-based structural analysis look like holistically. So far, we have named the main themes of race-conscious caring leadership, each with its sub-components—three main concepts and ten sub-components. We are not presenting these as a checklist of dispositions and behaviors. Instead, they come together uniquely in holistic practices that specific leaders engage in as ethical praxis (as suggested by Figure 1.1).

Aspects of these practices are evident throughout the literature on culturally responsive teaching, transformative leadership, and critical pedagogy. The ethical praxis we reveal centers on how school leaders recognize race and interrogate and interrupt such issues as scripted curricula, special education representation, differential discipline, absenteeism, teacher quality, deficit mindsets, and white privilege.

Exploring ethical praxis as a holistic practice demonstrates how narrative ethics can work. In Chapter 5, extended narratives from two school leaders capture how they draw from their personal histories, ethical commitments, and educational visions. These leaders enact race-conscious caring in their own unique ways and unique settings. They exercise communal responsibility, bringing together caring and justice. Reading and listening to how other leaders narrate their ethical lives provides an opportunity for school leaders to appreciate where race-conscious leaders' ethics and practice come from and should inspire them to narrate their own ethical lives. Leaders need networks to engage in mutual learning. Attending to the stories of their peers is an act of witnessing. Leaders can then reflect upon their background and experiences, their ethical commitments, and the possible lacks in their capacity. At the end of Chapter 5, we provide a framework to guide leaders on creating their own moral narratives. They may then be better positioned to reach out to build a collective community and create more ethical and socially just educational experiences for all children.

AN ETHICS FOR OUR TIME

The Brookings Institution describes the United States as being in the midst of a "diversity explosion" that changes the country's racial composition (Frey, 2015). As William Frey acknowledges, the United States has endured a long history of blatant discrimination in educational opportunities for children of color. As this change occurs, Frey argues, those in power need to pay greater attention to the needs and interests of those who have been systematically denied opportunity. Commenting on this same demographic transformation, Kfir Mordechay and Gary Orfield (2017) argue for the need for concrete policy and practices. Acknowledging the lack of systematic progress in national civil rights policy (and indeed, systematic reversal of progress toward greater educational equity), there is an urgent need to attend to policies and practices for greater equity in schools.

An undercurrent of the Brookings Institution report is that many people consider the diversity explosion as something to be feared, dreaded, or controlled. Indeed, "explosion" is an eye-catching word that fits a frame of control. In contrast, we argue that a new ethical orientation to difference—a transformation into a caring, race-conscious, ethical praxis—is required to support the work of equity and justice. While this is a necessarily larger cultural project, we emphasize the role a school leader can play in this transformation. As a group of three authors, our focus for the last several years in our individual and collective teaching, scholarship, and professional practice has been on conveying the value of critical reflection on ethical caring, race consciousness, and leading for increasingly diverse communities of children and families in K–12 schools. We find leaders are coming to understand the need for new ways of encountering their practice, so the time is right for rethinking how ethics contributes to equity and justice practice.

The time is right for leaders to move past their good intentions and comfortable notions of caring. As we show throughout the book, leaders need to expand their understanding of others and their capacity for caring. We suggest these need to happen not through more abstract approaches to ethical theory, but through narrative ethics, which provides greater opportunity for new learning and engagement across different experiences. We believe narrative ethics can expand the capacity for equity leadership through critical self-reflection, networks of support for race-conscious practice, and learning from the narrated lives of others.

Throughout the rest of the book, we explore these components of race-conscious leadership ethics and provide examples from the school leader interviews. Chapter 2 explains what we mean by race consciousness and explores the prevalence and allure of color-evasiveness among school leaders. We show how the evasion of race and racism contributes to dispositions toward students and teachers and we reflect on how those dispositions seem to translate into leadership practices. Ethics is the subject of Chapter 3, which describes race-conscious leadership in relation to ethical theory and scholarship on moral leadership. We develop the concept of critical caring, explaining how school leaders approach caring in different ways. In Chapter 4, we explore in more detail what it means to have a justice orientation. Key features of the justice orientation include dispositions toward opportunity gaps, a critical consciousness, and assets. We break down responses to differential achievement scores among leaders' student population and explore the deeper meanings of approaches that look for technical fixes to achievement gaps.

The narratives of the most race-conscious leaders in our sample are the source of inspiration for Chapter 5 on ethical praxis. Conveying moral narratives from two race-conscious caring leaders, we place their leadership in the context of their past experience and their views about moral leadership and the meaning and value of education. We show the value of narrative ethics for conveying a holistic understanding of the views and practices of race-conscious leadership ethics. At the end of Chapter 5, we present an exercise for school leaders to create their own moral narratives, drawing from their background beliefs, moral communities, and ethical principles (Nash & Jang, 2016). In Chapter 6, we address how we bring these components together in our experiences with professional development and leadership preparation. We explore the particular challenges and opportunities associated with adopting race-conscious leadership ethics as a framework for fostering greater equity leadership. Chapter 7 provides implications of our work for professional practice. We return to some of the quandaries we have addressed along the way and offer direction for how to think and work through challenges using race-conscious leadership ethics. The book ends with a methodological appendix describing the research methods for the study.

CHAPTER 2

Race Consciousness

Figure 2.1. Race Consciousness

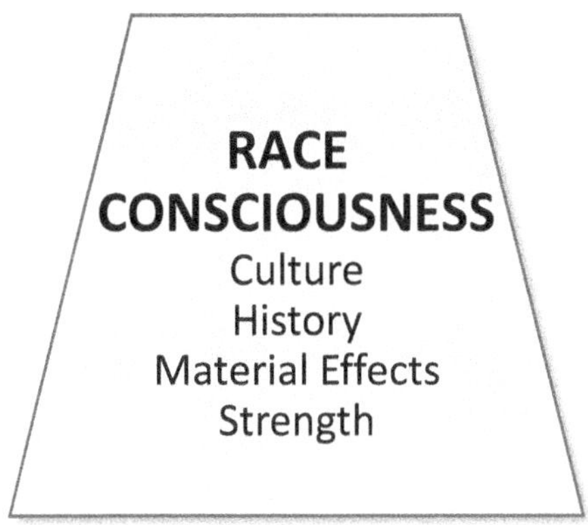

Evading race and racism, a common practice among school leaders, limits a leader's practice and serves to perpetuate the effects of racism in schools. Why the practice is so common may be explained by the perspectives of Jack Maddon, a white male principal in a suburban elementary school. At the time of his interview, he had been principal for 8 years. That year, about 10% of the students in his school were Black, and about 50% qualified for free or reduced-price lunch. His school's percentages were higher than those of the other elementary schools in his predominantly white and affluent district. In his interview, Maddon highlighted some notable experiences with students' parents. Some parents, especially wealthy parents, pressure him to place their children in the gifted program; other parents argue with him about the school's discipline policy and practices. Despite pushback from some parents on how he implements the discipline policy, he remained confident that his approach was fair, and he believed his consistency demonstrates his support for teachers.

Maddon shares that in certain discipline disputes he has been called "racist" by parents of children of color:

> I have been called a racist, and things like that . . . and I always tell [parents], I'm not the racist, because it has nothing to do with race, it has everything to do with behavior, and how [students] act, and the consistency. . . . So, I mean, I used to be offended by it, but I don't get offended by it anymore, because that's just the way they are, and that's the way they grew up, and they don't trust education much, and they don't trust anyone very much.

His detached response is to assert that he knows he is not racist. Maddon demonstrates what we call deflecting rather than engaging in critical self-reflection about the structures or practices in his school that may lead to claims by parents of color that he was being racist. As Tatum (1998) suggests, being called a racist does not make the allegation accurate, yet "it is always important to consider that it might be" (p. 47).

In this quotation, Maddon construes "racist" as a binary term applicable to his identity as an individual. In this view, one is either racist or not; Maddon clearly thinks he is not, and while he used to be concerned about being perceived as racist, he is no longer troubled by that appellation. Maddon rejects parents' racist identification of him and chooses to deflect their complaints, rather than seeing racism not only as endemic to society, but something that everyone needs personally to acknowledge and deal with, given how racism works constantly through institutionalized acts of power continually to subjugate others (Briscoe & Khalifa, 2015; Collins, 2000). Maddon interprets "racist" as an epithet signaling not racist treatment but families' deficient perspectives ("that's just the way they are"), and his belief is that families' perspectives are grounded in experiences external to his school.

With his statements, Maddon thereby callously rejects their experience and casually rejects his role in the institutional operations of racism. Furthermore, his ambiguous response to such parents—"I'm not the racist"—can be interpreted in a few ways. Perhaps he means the parent calling him racist is "the racist," or he may be reserving that appellation for some other kind of racist behavior he deems malicious and intentional. However he means it, Maddon chooses to not be offended by the epithet anymore and moreover refuses the opportunity to take on the parents' perspective. In short, he ignores issues of race and racism as they relate to school discipline. He instead breeds a kind of callous victimhood that excuses his own careless race-evasive racism.

In Chapter 7, we recommend strategies for leaders to disrupt how racism works through them—to de-emphasize their feelings of personal offense in such situations and instead take responsibility for conditions and structures that will work against racism. For now, we want to point out that Maddon's deflective approach limits at least three opportunities: (a) to learn more about the community's and parents of color's perspectives, (b) to understand his role within a larger system of racial subjugation, and

(c) to question his complicity in a system in which he could participate differently. Some detailed analysis of school policies that appear on the surface to be race-neutral shows them to be distinct across racial lines (Briscoe & Khalifa, 2015). When they evade race and racism, leaders show their lack of capacity to initiate race-conscious responses. Leaders who perpetuate differential power relations thereby waive their opportunity to contribute to transformative change and abnegate their responsibility as ethical leaders.

THE NEED FOR RACE CONSCIOUSNESS

Since Maddon's interview in 2014, the need for school administrators to confront educational inequities and racialized incidents in U.S. schools has become even more apparent. The recent outcry for increased racial awareness in education can be attributed to the United States's slow trajectory in acknowledging how meticulous avoidance of race and racism perpetuates systemic inequalities. Beginning in 2015, national education leadership standards for the first time included attention to racial bias and culturally responsive practices (National Policy Board for Educational Administration, 2015), reflecting an expanding research base among leadership scholars who have paid increasing attention to education for social justice. Earlier versions of national leadership standards sidestepped race and racism, instead promoting race-neutral practice and, as a result, turning deficit-based perspectives upon children and families of color (Davis et al., 2015). Time is undoubtedly overdue for purposeful and deliberate placement of race consciousness at the heart of leadership practice.

In this chapter, we examine school leaders who demonstrate race consciousness, those who demonstrate race-evasiveness, and those who combine or vacillate between these two perspectives. We call upon our interview data to demonstrate how school leaders express race consciousness and race-evasiveness in varying degrees, we explain the values associated with these expressions, and we explore the linkage between leaders' beliefs and their stated practices. We first offer an important caveat: Race consciousness and race-evasiveness are not binary concepts. Race consciousness and race-evasiveness can combine in many iterations leading to a range of practices, so care should be taken in drawing conclusions about the values of individual school leaders. Our analysis and the model we propose focus on leaders' expressed views in interviews; we take into account only those practices they mention in their interviews. In our analysis we draw from the range of possible perspectives. We understand these leaders to have broader and likely more conflicting perspectives than those shared with us during data collection (DeMatthews et al., 2021; Ryan, 2003). Indeed, readers may find themselves and their perspectives occupying multiple categories.

Before proceeding, we define race-conscious school leadership: *A race-conscious school leader recognizes the significance of race and racism in culture, history, and the material lives of people and takes a strengths-based approach with students of color and families* (see Figure 2.1). Race-conscious leaders challenge and interrupt marginalization whether students of color make up 2% or 98% of their school's population. In this chapter, we first define race-evasiveness and race consciousness in more detail. Then, drawing from our interview data, we present a model of their expression through a series of rings within three major bands (race-evasiveness, recognition, and race consciousness). Along the way we explain the perspectives about race-evasiveness and race consciousness of our 22 interviewees, we describe deficiencies and inconsistencies in leader perspectives, and we identify missed opportunities for growth and self-reflection.

RACE-EVASIVENESS

Color-evasive ideology became a prominent racial ideology during the post–Civil Rights era of the 1960s under the banner of "colorblindness" (Annamma et al., 2017; Bonilla-Silva, 2014; Bonilla-Silva et al., 2003; Forman & Lewis, 2015). The ideology picked up steam in the backlash to social programs in the 1980s. It led to the embrace of a supposed "post-racial" moment with the election of President Barack Obama in 2008 (Hannah-Jones, 2016) and pervades resistance to ongoing demands for racial reckoning. Some researchers argue that the evasion of race and racism in educational practice connects to the long historical legacy of the U.S. Supreme Court's interpretations of the constitutionality of preferential treatment based upon race (Annamma et al., 2017). Avoiding answering questions about race and racism is the result of the denial of the history of racism and white supremacy, disconnecting one's actions from the structures of domination that operate to privilege actors who deny the continual effects of racism.

Sociologist Eduardo Bonilla-Silva, across several editions of *Racism Without Racists* (2014), explained the color-blind ideology and showed how members of the dominant culture systematically avoid the significance and importance of race and racism in their personal and professional lives. More recently, Subini Annamma and her colleagues (2017) expanded on the concept of colorblindness beyond its ableist roots and labeled it more accurately an active process of evasion. Rather than being passively "color-blind," those who evade race and racism strategically enact their color-evasiveness and position themselves as both powerful and morally justified:

> Those espousing a color-blind racial ideology are individually positioned as racially enlightened while simultaneously reproducing power and inequity in a

> system of white supremacy. It is the systemic violence of racism that impacts our daily lives, not just through individuals but also through institutions. The racial ideology of color-evasiveness allows for an understanding that this failure to address material conditions is not passive, but purposeful. (Annamma et al., 2017, p. 154)

Those embracing colorblindness explicitly claim moral justification for their evasion and moral superiority. They also position themselves as not responsible for the material conditions of racism that exist before their eyes.

Annamma et al. (2017) further articulate the power and extensiveness of color-evasiveness by using a critical disability studies (DisCrit) perspective to move beyond the ableist language implied by "color blindness," implicitly associating the disability of blindness with an undesirable personal quality. It further exposes the implied claim by those espousing color blindness they have a natural and morally superior perspective on race. In contrast, Annamma et al. illuminate color-evasiveness as intersectional, purposeful, and willfully ignorant: "To avoid talking about race is a way to willfully ignore the experiences of people of color, and makes the goal of erasure more fully discernible" (p. 156). Applied to the example of principal Jack Maddon at the beginning of this chapter, race-evasiveness is clearly ethically problematic.

Evading race is widespread in U.S. schools (Schofield, 2010): it can be found in urban schools (Beachum et al., 2008; Brooks & Jean-Marie, 2007; Khalifa et al., 2014; Theoharis & Haddix, 2011), suburban schools (Lewis, 2001; Welton et al., 2015), and rural schools (Tarca, 2005). Research studies of school leaders also reveal how color-evasive thoughts and actions impede leaders' abilities to dismantle the challenges encountered by students of color attending those leaders' schools (Aveling, 2007; DeMatthews et al., 2021; Ryan, 2003; Solomon, 2002). Recent attacks against critical race theory and diversity, equity, and inclusion initiatives are the latest aggressive uses of race-evasive ideology. Emergent research addresses how political discourse attacking critical race theory makes it more difficult to address the injustices experienced by students of color (Applebaum, 2023).

Additional research describes race-evasiveness and identifies the practices of strong, race-conscious leaders. In their study of race in suburban schools, Anjalé Welton and her colleagues (2015) found school leaders who continue to apply race-evasive practices even while recognizing their increasingly diverse student body. Such practices by school leaders result in their direct categorization of racial inequities as deficits among students and families of color rather than as systemic inequities (Welton et al., 2015). DeMatthews et al. (2021) have distinguished between equity leaders who are improvement-focused and those who are what they refer to as "intersectional-focused"; the latter category of leaders differs in that they pay attention to the intersection of identities such as race and disability and refuse to accept the status quo assumption of students of color disproportionately assigned to special education. Intersectional-focused leaders are far more critical and cognizant of their students' and their families' unique cultural needs and strive to remake their schools into communities holistically capable of serving students' needs (DeMatthews et al., 2021).

RACE CONSCIOUSNESS

As we mentioned in Chapter 1, race-conscious leaders identify and acknowledge the significance of race as a social construct having cultural significance, historical importance, and material effects on the lives of real persons. Furthermore, such leaders recognize race as a component of individual and group identity and a source of strength, resistance, and moral value.

Cultural Significance

A first sub-component of race consciousness is acknowledgment of the cultural significance of race. As Toni Morrison (1992) argued, racial difference—especially the contrast between whiteness and blackness—holds a key place in the American cultural imagination. In her touchstone work, *Playing in the Dark: Whiteness and the Literary Imagination,* Morrison recounted the role of race in canonical American literature in the construction of self, agency, and goodness. In colonial-period literature, the construction of "American Africanism" names and personifies (in the bodies of Black people of African descent) the anxieties and fears of an emerging nation, rationalizing the enacted violence and exploitation by colonists in the name of building a unique national identity.

As she explained, "The image of a reined-in, bound, suppressed, and repressed darkness became objectified in American literature as an Africanist persona" (pp. 38–39). Morrison showed how authors contrast the Africanist persona with a white, male identity characterized by autonomy, authority, newness, and absolute power. She argued that the presence of Black persons as racialized others contributes to the continual construction of the American identity. Black persons are present, they are imagined as others, and so American authors generate an Africanist identity directly in contrast to those "desirable" traits that count as American traits. As she writes, "It was this Africanism, deployed as rawness and savagery, that provided the staging ground and arena for the elaboration of the quintessential American identity" (p. 44).

This juxtaposition of themes persists in the construction of whiteness and blackness in 20th-century American literature (Morrison, 1992). Morrison argued that the work of American authors is thereby based upon an "imaginative and historical terrain" (p. 46) of American culture, notable because the presence of racialized others always made up a shared understanding of American identity. Throughout her literary examples, whether through the work of Herman Melville, Edgar Allan Poe, Ernest Hemingway, or Willa Cather, the Africanist presence is dehumanized—Africanized characters serve as forces to be dominated by white characters, whether physically, emotionally, or morally, in service to the white, American characteristics of autonomy, authority, newness, or absolute power. As evident in Morrison's analysis of Cather's novel *Sapphira and the Slave Girl,* authors often lack the imaginative capacity to recognize the dehumanization they enact to construct their characters. Authors, in essence, claim to evade race while employing it. As Morrison argues, the insistence that race is not important (or no longer important) is another part of the racialized culture's strategy:

> Statements to the contrary, insisting on the meaninglessness of race to the American identity, are themselves full of meaning. The world does not become raceless or will not become unracialized by assertion. The act of enforcing racelessness in literary discourse is in itself a racial act. (p. 46)

This literary strategy is evident throughout culture, whether employed by authors to heroize their white main characters or by Supreme Court justices to announce the end of the legality of race-conscious college admissions. Powerful evidence of the significance of race should not be ignored by any professional in a position to serve the needs of students growing up in the midst of this contentious culture. It is vital school leaders know that race has cultural significance; race-conscious school leaders should develop and maintain a learning orientation toward race, racial experience, and racism. If their experience is limited, it will show in how teachers, students, and families perceive leaders' beliefs and values (DeMatthews et al., 2021). Acknowledgment of the cultural significance of race may operate as a corrective to color-evasive cultural tropes that pervade the beliefs and practices of so many school leaders. As in all U.S. schooling contexts, acquiring historical perspective on race in Pittsburgh and neighboring communities is an essential component of race consciousness.

Historical Importance

The second subcomponent of race consciousness is the historical importance of race and racism. Echoing Morrison's (1992) treatment of how canonical American literature, race, and racism figure prominently in the development of the American cultural imagination, U.S. history and the histories of individual school communities are of foundational importance to race consciousness. Muhammad Khalifa (2018) recommends that school leaders understand how their leadership practices fit within the historical experience of the communities in which they work. Parents and other members of school communities ascribe meaning to schooling and their children's experiences within a long-term frame of their overall life experience. As Khalifa advised, schooling practices are best understood within a context of historical marginalization. In the case of an urban school in a historically Black community that district officials sought to close, Khalifa recounted how the superintendent chose to ignore both issues of racialized history and charges of racism against him. As Khalifa theorized, race-neutral approaches to leadership attempt to erase the history of marginalization and contemporary meanings ascribed to a community's experiences.

Becoming race-conscious requires leaders to learn and respect the cultural and historical role of race and racism not only in the larger culture but in their particular communities. Race is important not only for students, but also for their parents and families, and leaders need to understand how race affects the lives of students and families in their communities. The development of race consciousness is especially important for leaders whose identities align with dominant culture and who may not have experienced the cultural, historical, and material effects of race and racism on their own lives. Parents, families, and other members of the school community who have experienced racialization, minoritization, and marginalization carry those experiences into their engagement with school. As Khalifa (2018) argued, "Racially oppressive issues like redlining, disinvestment of manufacturing jobs in minoritized areas, and economic disinvestment in the Black community—all issues that are not ostensibly related to education—actually all became major factors in how parents viewed schooling" (p. 43).

In the context of this book, the history of race and racism in the Pittsburgh region has led to disparities in wealth, health, and educational access and to the maintenance of racialized housing borders and school district boundaries (Trotter & Day, 2010). Pittsburgh was home to the world's largest steel industry in the early 20th century, drawing workers from rural and urban U.S. areas and large numbers of immigrants from Eastern and Southern Europe. During the first Great Migration after World War I, Pittsburgh drew Black people from the South and from other urban centers as its manufacturing economy boomed (Trotter & Day, 2010).

Patterns of redlining and other race-motivated practices in Pittsburgh's history have led to a legacy of residential segregation by race (Rutan & Glass, 2017). With its large waves of migration during its rapid industrialization and its geography of many rivers, creeks, and hills, Pittsburgh and its greater metropolitan area developed as a patchwork of racial and ethnic enclaves (Trotter & Day, 2010). By 1930, Black residents were concentrated in three neighborhoods within Pittsburgh's city limits (Rutan & Glass, 2017), with similar enclaves established in the other, smaller industrial municipalities in the region. By the 2020 U.S. census, these early-20th-century residential patterns were still largely in place (Trotter & Day, 2010). As evident in U.S. census data, residential integration finally began to budge in the Pittsburgh area during the last 20 years, as surrounding communities have become more racially diverse. This movement has occurred along with gentrification. Economic expansion within the city during the last 20 years has driven some city residents with lower incomes to surrounding communities, altering the demographic makeup of some former industrial areas that had been predominantly white (Center for Race and Social Problems, 2015; Rutan & Glass, 2017; Trotter & Day, 2010). This evolution has resulted in a patchwork of school districts in Pittsburgh and Allegheny County with representation from multiple racial and cultural identities and socioeconomic statuses. Such change is emblematic of demographic change throughout the United States, with differential composition of neighboring school districts in metropolitan areas and segregation within larger, unified districts resulting in differential access to high-capacity schools (Reardon et al., 2012; Welsh, 2019).

Critical to race consciousness is that school leaders understand how their school settings fit into the larger social fabric of their communities. School districts are parts of larger communities, and while accountability policy encourages competition between neighboring school districts, school leaders have a responsibility to *all* their students and their larger communities. Learning the cultural and historical significance of race and racism in a community should be part of the work of being a school leader, and it should be an important part of the work of educating school leaders in graduate programs.

Material Effects

Another feature of race consciousness is knowledge about the material effects of racism in multiple contexts so a leader may come to understand the effects of racism in their community and how it affects their district and schools. As documented throughout history, racism causes both immeasurable and measurable economic and health disparities as it minoritizes and marginalizes particular groups of people (Hank et al., 2018; Mercado et al., 2024). Material effects are demonstrable differences in life outcomes and access to resources and systematically different experiences with social institutions such as the legal and criminal justice system, education, social services, and health care. For instance, the long history of structural racism reduces life chances and life expectancy for minoritized persons in the United States; the COVID-19 pandemic both exacerbated this difference and made it more evident (Yearby et al., 2022).

As has happened throughout the United States, a continual history of exclusionary policies and social practices of subjugation have led to measurable disparities in wealth, educational access, housing, and health outcomes in the Pittsburgh area (Trotter & Day, 2010). Pittsburgh began an economic decline after World War II, and as with every other economic downturn since industrialization, the city's decline disparately affected Black residents (Trotter

& Day, 2010). Continual decline of the local steel industry and subsequent emergence of Pittsburgh as a reimagined economy around higher education and health care has affected Black and white Pittsburgh residents differently. The region's more recent economic activity has disproportionately benefited white and wealthy residents, grown the suburbs, and gentrified the urban core. Continuing effects of racism were documented in the 2010 U.S. census, which documents racial disparity in economic wealth, education, and overall health (Center for Race and Social Problems, 2015).

Gaps in educational opportunity are reflected in preschool, public school, and private school enrollments. For instance, the Pittsburgh metropolitan area has a higher percentage of enrollment in private schools than the national average. In 2006 to 2010, 68.4% of white students attended public schools in the city, while 31.6% attended private schools (see Table 2.1). For Black students, 92.4% attended public schools, while 7.7% attended private schools. Within the city, 31.6% of white students, 7.6% of Black students, 22.6% of Asian students, and 16.1% of Hispanic students enrolled in private schools, while corresponding public-school percentages were 38.6% white, 50.8% Black, 1.8% Asian, and 2.6% Hispanic (CRSP, 2015; the CRSP report used the Census term "Hispanic"). Racial disparities in enrollment are echoed in graduation rates, educational attainment, and standardized proficiency measures in reading and math.

Economic disparities appear in poverty rates, unemployment, and median household income; in Pittsburgh, Black families report half the median income of white families (Center for Race and Social Problems, 2015). Residential disparities include the devaluation of housing in historically

Table 2.1. School Enrollment in Pittsburgh and Allegheny County, 2006–2010

K–12 Enrollment	White	Black	Asian	Hispanic/Latinx
Pittsburgh	38.6%	50.8%	1.8%	2.6%
Allegheny County	71.1%	20.1%	2.5%	1.9%
United States	53.5%	15.5%	4.1%	22.4%
Public School Enrollment	**White**	**Black**	**Asian**	**Hispanic/Latinx**
Pittsburgh	68.4%	92.4%	77.4%	83.9%
Allegheny County	84.0%	92.3%	87.0%	84.3%
United States	86.4%	93.7%	89.3%	94.6%
Private School Enrollment	**White**	**Black**	**Asian**	**Hispanic/Latinx**
Pittsburgh	31.6%	7.6%	22.6%	16.1%
Allegheny County	16.0%	7.7%	13.0%	15.7%
United States	13.6%	6.3%	10.7%	5.4%

Source: Center for Race and Social Problems (2015), using data from 2010 U.S. Census.

Black neighborhoods, differential access to automobile ownership, and differential reliance on public transportation (Trotter & Day, 2010).

The material effects of racism are also evident in the experiences that minoritized persons have with social institutions. The institutions and the persons they employ have inherited implicit biases through generations of subjugation, leading to socially motivated misperceptions, cognitive biases, and aggregated racialized behavior among social actors contributing to racial social experience (Banaji et al., 2021). Leaders in these social institutions, such as school leaders, are in a position to challenge this material state of affairs, but this opportunity for transformation is made more challenging because of the systemic nature of racism: "The challenge in controlling racist habits is that they are the cultural default" (Banaji et al., 2021, p. 15).

Strength, Resistance, and Moral Value

Throughout the history of racial subjugation, identification as a member of a minoritized racial group has also been a demonstrated source of strength, resistance, and moral value (Baldwin, 1963/1998; Carter, 2009; Love, 2019; Quigley & Mitchell, 2019; Rivas-Drake et al., 2014; Tatum, 2017; Walker & Snarey, 2004; White & Young, 2016; Yosso, 2005). These overlapping aspects of racial identity are important sources for work against racism and toward more equitable educational opportunities for children. Historical movements such as the Black Panthers, the Black Power movement, and Freedom Schools have built upon racial identity as a strength. In other parts of the United States, the Chicano movement is another important resource. Lesser-known exercises of professional responsibility, such as the network of Black teacher associations that sustained segregated schools (Walker, 2018), are sources of historical strength.

The strength of racial identity is evident in research on racial identity development. In her work, Dorinda Carter (2008) explained the direct benefit of a positive racial identity for Black students, who face structural constraints on their opportunities for educational attainment and social and economic mobility. Key is developing a critical awareness of how racism operates to perpetuate inequalities and building a strong identification with their own racial group affiliation. Building upon extant research about the value of positive racial identity, Aisha White and Colleen Young (2016) reported on racial identity development in the Pittsburgh area. White and Young found widespread awareness among young children about race and racial identity and widespread interest among parents and early childhood educators in resources and strategies for cultivating positive racial identity. They found limited systematic resources to support that work, so while the efficacy of positive racial identity is supported by research, its recognition and cultivation as a resource in educational institutions is lacking.

Resistance to racial subjugation has been critical to the survival and sustenance of communities of color as they have worked to obtain and sustain educational opportunities for their children. As historians such as James Anderson (1988) and Vanessa Siddle Walker (1996, 2018) have documented, Black communities across the American South resisted laws that forbade their education and labored intensively through decades of Reconstruction subjugation, Jim Crow–era enforced segregation, and inequitable desegregation to build schools. Similar resistance occurred throughout the United States for Black and Brown communities resisting racism, subjugation, and double taxation for the construction and maintenance of schools. In Pittsburgh, Black civic, religious, and social organizations flourished throughout the 20th century (Trotter & Day, 2010). Sometimes ebbing, sometimes flowing, political action was enacted through the NAACP, the Universal Negro Improvement Association, the March on Washington Movement, and the Communist Party. Black citizens' political mobilization created sustained efforts for justice, first through the Republican Party and, by the 1930s, via a shift to Democratic Party politics. Organizations led by people of color maintain a strong presence in the Pittsburgh area.

The moral value associated with race consciousness derives from these traditions of strength and resistance and the stories of working for justice (e.g., Bass, 2009; Walker & Snarey, 2004). As we explore in greater detail in Chapter 3, racial identity can be a profound source for moral grounding of educational practice, drawing from the commitments of educators who base their practice in generational commitments to struggles for freedom and human dignity. Caring for individuals as well as communities under conditions of subjugation makes humane and just action vital. The often abstract ethical theories come into clearer view through the narratives of individual lives, when individuals enact their moral commitments in their lives to work for justice.

These ideas intersect with the concept of *positionality*, which encapsulates the individual histories and identities of individuals in relation to race, ethnicity, social class, and all relevant aspects of experience (Alcoff, 1988). We prefer the concept of positionality to alternatives such as subjectivity, identity, or bias, because positionality highlights the relations of power between differentially situated individuals. Power is shifting and shiftable, and one's positionality can be expected to shift in relation to others and their positionality. As Linda Martin Alcoff (1988) and Richard Milner (2007) have argued in relation to social science research, those in positions of power must recognize how their positionalities relate to all those they encounter. For a school leader, we contend that positionality determines capacity to demonstrate strength, resist the hegemony of white supremacy, and demonstrate a moral compass that bends the arc toward racial justice for students.

RACE CONSCIOUSNESS IN EDUCATIONAL LEADERSHIP

Research exploring aspects of race and racism in school leadership emerged in the 1990s and has expanded our understanding of leadership for social justice (Oplatka, 2014). As educational administration scholar Izhar Oplatka noted, social justice has a relatively recent presence in school leadership research, and he argued that much work remained to be done to articulate how attention to race and racism contributes to social justice leadership. Significant developments have come from wider discourse about educational inequities, including arguments for advocacy leadership (Anderson, 2009), justice-oriented practice (Ladson-Billings, 2006, 2013), and culturally sustaining pedagogy (Paris, 2012).

Recent research on culturally responsive school leadership is clear on the significance of race, racial difference, and antiracism in a school leader's areas of expertise and concern. Making use of concepts and conceptual frameworks including Black feminism, critical race theory, social justice leadership, and antiracism, school leadership researchers provide evidence for the significance of race consciousness in leadership practice (Briscoe & Khalifa, 2015; Brooks & Arnold, 2013; Dillard, 1995; Gooden, 2012; Khalifa et al., 2013; Theoharis & Haddix, 2011). Moreover, allusions to ethical practices pervade this research, and ethical foundations are often implied in the commitments of race-conscious leaders to families, children, and communities of color (Theoharis & Haddix, 2011). Khalifa and his colleagues (2013) noted the cultural relevance and historical significance of community engagement in communities of color:

> The value of collective wisdom and community-based pedagogical spaces . . . is not a novel concept for people of color—a people who have consistently drawn on extended kin constructs and community-orientated learning environments to buttress the miseducation and alienation from mainstream schools. (p. 507)

Prior research on the preparation of school leaders showed that color-evasive practice has pervaded graduate courses in the 2000s (Gerstl-Pepin et al., 2006; Shields, 2004), the 2010s (Diem & Carpenter, 2012; Johnson & Campbell-Stephens, 2014), and the 2020s (Chang-Bacon, 2022). Even where social justice enters a curriculum, color-evasive perspectives have dominated (Gerstl-Pepin et al., 2006). More than a decade ago, Sara Diem and Bradley Carpenter argued that graduate programs need to make sure future school leaders are "familiar with and refute the theoretical constructs of color-evasive ideologies that infiltrate the educational system" and equip them with "a pragmatic guide on how to confront issues informed by color-evasive ideology" (Diem & Carpenter, 2012, p. 103).

FROM COLOR-EVASIVE TO RACE-CONSCIOUS

Generating leadership practice that acknowledges and promotes race consciousness requires understanding how leaders understand race and racism. In the remainder of this chapter, we call upon the words of school leaders who participated in our interview study. We offer these study results as a tool for thinking about how school leaders can move from color-evasiveness to race consciousness. We organize our findings into three sections or bands—holding to color-evasiveness, recognition with minimal capacity, and cultivating race consciousness. Each is displayed in Figure 2.2 as a band. Within each band is a series of rings emanating from the center—the normative view of color-evasiveness. The ordering of

Figure 2.2. Race-Evasive Caring

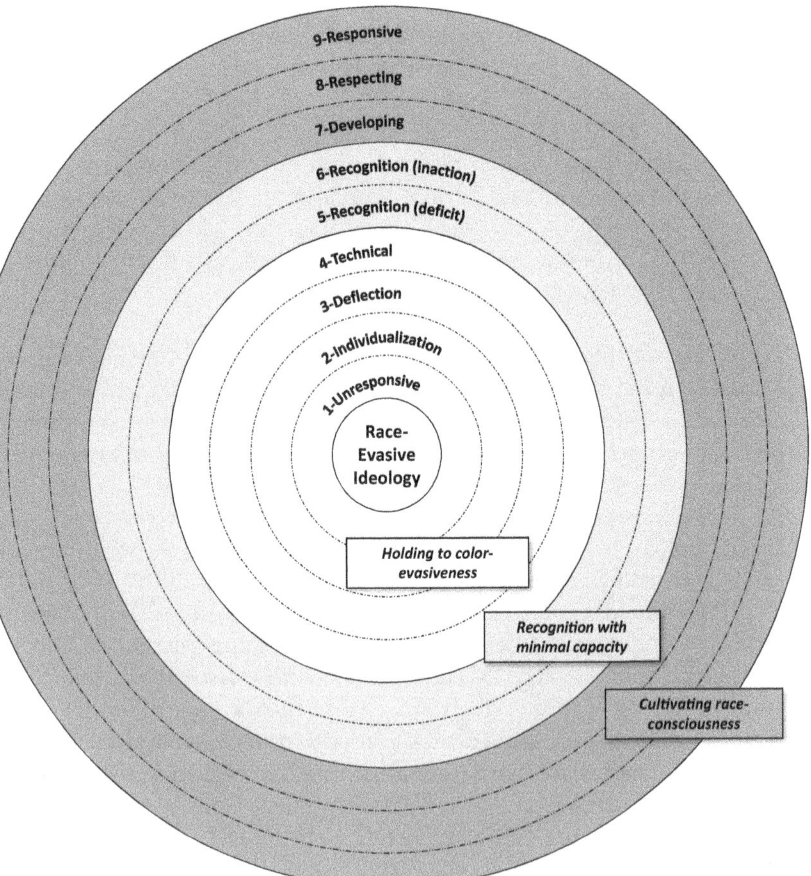

the rings within the bands is meant to suggest relative distance from the center (representing relative distance from color-evasive ideology) rather than necessarily to suggest a progression through stages. Since some perspectives across the three bands and nine rings were represented by small numbers of respondents, we suspect a larger sample would yield additional rings of race-evasiveness and additional rings to describe the process of coming to race consciousness.

Color-evasiveness is further split into four rings, each representing a theme found in one or more of the nine color-evasive school leaders: (1) unresponsiveness, (2) individualization, (3) deflection, and (4) technical recognition. The second band, recognition with minimal capacity, corresponds to three school leaders in two intermediate rings in Figure 2.2: (5) recognition with deficit, and (6) recognition with inaction. In this section, respondents recognize race, but that recognition does not correspond to identifiable race-conscious practices. The third band—cultivating race consciousness—is home to the perspectives of 10 school leaders in our sample across three rings: (7) developing, (8) respecting, and (9) responsive. Leaders in this band provide examples of race consciousness or show clear progress and nearness to that perspective (see Table 2.2).

Holding to Color-Evasiveness: The First Band

School leaders whose perspectives occupy the first band of color-evasiveness use multiple strategies of minimization, which Bonilla-Silva (2014) describes as a common strategy, mostly by whites, for disputing the salience of race "as a factor explaining blacks' collective standing" (p. 91). Blacks consider race and racism much more salient. We found minimization in two types of school settings. Quite frequently, color-evasive leaders in predominantly white settings ignore race and racism until challenged by parents or until an explicitly racist incident draws public attention. We also found minimization in the high-poverty settings we studied that also had nearly equal percentages of Black and white students. Color-evasive leaders in these settings minimized the significance of race, racism, and racial identity, touting how well their students get along; they instead attributed significance to students' living in poverty.

Unresponsiveness. We describe as *unresponsive* those leaders who most clearly meet the definition of color-evasive ideology. When leaders described the value of Black and Latina/o students, they limited it to the value these students brought to the predominantly white student population. Leaders ascribed the presence of these students as providing other students with a "real-world" experience and contributing to "acceptance." Kevin Labby is one example. In his school, less than 5% of students are of color, and less than 10% qualify for free or reduced-price lunch. Labby stated his student population is "pretty much white overall, so any diversity that we have, I

Table 2.2. School Leaders and Their Color-Evasive and Race-Conscious Perspectives

Participant	Gender	Race	Position	Type of District	% students of color[1]	% free/reduced lunch[1]
Unresponsive						
Kevin Labby	Male	White	Principal	Upper Middle-Class Suburban	<5	5–10
Michael Labette	Male	White	Principal	Suburban	10–25	60–65
Individualization						
Laura Foster	Female	White	Principal	Upper Middle-Class Suburban	<5	10–15
Paul Eaby	Male	White	Principal	Upper Middle-Class Suburban	<5	<5
Dan Gibson	Male	White	Principal	Suburban	5–10	25–30
John Hall[2]	Male	White	Principal	Suburban	5–10	15–20
Deflection						
Jack Maddon	Male	White	Principal	Upper Middle-Class Suburban	10–25	45–50
Scott Aboud	Male	White	Principal	Urban	26–50	60–65
Technical rational						
Logan Sanders	Male	Black/White Biracial	Principal	Upper Middle-Class Suburban	<5	<5
Recognition deficit						
Emma Badell	Female	White	Principal	Urban	26–50	70–75
Dennis Gable	Male	White	Principal	Urban	26–50	55–60
Recognition inaction						
Bill Roberts	Male	White	School Leader	Urban Charter	51–75[3]	65–70[3]

Developing						
Peter Ingram[2]	Male	White	Principal	Suburban	<5	10–15
Respecting						
James Smith	Male	White	Principal	Urban Charter	76–100[3]	80–85[3]
Ella Klein	Female	White	District Leader	Urban	51–75[4]	65–70[4]
Elizabeth Ida	Female	White	Principal	Upper Middle-Class Suburban	<5	5–10
Andrew Baker[2]	Male	White	Principal	Upper Middle-Class Suburban	<5	<5
Responsive						
Scarlett Johnson	Female	Black	Principal	Urban	76–100	90–95
Ethan Knight	Male	White	District Leader	Urban	51–75[4]	65–70[4]
Maya Gaffney	Female	Black	Principal	Urban	26–50	80–85
Arthur Lawrence	Male	Black	Principal	Urban	26–50	60–65
Allison Edwards	Female	Black	Principal	Upper Middle Class Suburban	<5	10–15

Note: Pseudonyms are used and percentage of students of color and of students on free and reduced-price lunch have been given in ranges to protect the identities of participants.

1. School data collected from the U.S. Department of Education Institute of Education Sciences, National Center for Education Statistics, Common Core of Data for the 2013–2014 school year.
2. These participants held perspectives within other rings: (Hall, *respecting*), (Ingram, *individualization*), and (Baker, *technical*).
3. The state's profile data is used for these two charter schools.
4. The high school data is used to represent the district.

think it just helps to bring richness to our program. You know it allows the students [to] interact a little bit more with how the real world is."

In Labby's mind, the presence of students of color adds "richness" to the school community and provides white students with a sense of the "real world" (Lewis, 2004). In essence, Labby views the presence of students of color as instrumental to the education of white students, rather than being responsive to the needs and interests of his Black and Latina/o students. As evidenced elsewhere in his interview, the education of students of color is not a specific consideration for this unresponsive leader; indeed, leaders in the first band could not readily say how many students of color were enrolled in their schools. This suggests to us that these leaders don't often think about their students of color and don't think of the racial demographics of their schools as significant for their leadership practice.

Another suburban white male principal, Michael Labette, leads a junior-senior high school with 10–25% of its population identifying as students of color and 60–65% qualifying for free or reduced-price lunch. Despite larger populations than in Labby's school, Labette expresses no plans to identify disparities in attainment among his school's students of color. While discussing the race-conscious use of data, Labette admits, "I don't know if we look at it that much. . . . I don't think we even break that down."

Both Labby and Labette illustrate leaders' lack of race consciousness when interpreting data. For example, when asked how he uses data to support his students, Labby flatly shared, "There is no specific plan for that, you know. If we see a group isn't performing like other groups we use that information to take action." Teachers at Labby's school have had no professional development about how better to serve students of color, and he believes they draw from their teacher preparation programs for the expertise to work with students of color. Since the research literature suggests that teacher preparation programs are largely color-evasive in their approach (Chang-Bacon, 2022), their preparation is not likely substantial. Unresponsive leaders typically reveal they offer no specific teacher training about race and culture and no use of race or culture in data-based interventions. Arguably, the relatively small percentage of students of color enrolled in these two school settings is used to provide leaders with a rationale or cover for their lack of race consciousness. Unresponsive leaders fail to convey particular knowledge of those students of color who attend their schools. Indeed, such leaders appear oblivious to their students of color or only acknowledge their presence as value added to white students' educational experiences.

Individualization. Characteristic of the next ring, *individualization*, is that leaders downplay the significance of race and instead rely upon a claim that they see all children as unique individuals. This perspective was the most common of the color-evasive themes. Although a focus on individuality seems fair, and these participants tended to express care for their students, the color-evasiveness embedded in this ring became evident when leaders were specifically questioned about how they meet the needs of their Black and Latina/o students. Laura Foster, a white female principal at a suburban elementary school, exemplifies the ideological moves school principals in this category make. Foster described her school as being a "fairly homogenous group of students, but I would say we do have some racial diversity. I'd say maybe our African American population for a suburban area might be a little larger than some other schools around this area." Made up of 10–15% students who qualify for free or reduced-price lunch and less than 5% children of color, her school nevertheless has a greater proportion of Black students than neighboring suburban elementary schools.

Foster recognized the cultural diversity that Black and Latina/o students bring to her school, and she also felt it is "difficult for me to say, because I don't, I often just don't really see. I guess I see kids as individuals, so I feel like they all bring value to the school." A color-evasive perspective such as Foster's becomes problematic, as research studies show; educators who give impressions of caring, but whose caring is amalgamated with color-evasiveness, disadvantage students of color by perpetuating inequalities (Gerstl-Pepin et al., 2006; Patterson et al., 2008). Foster's color-evasiveness limits her ability to use data to make decisions that can meet the needs of her students of color. She stated, "I think we use [data] the way we would with any of the students. . . . in the same way. I think we really look at kids as individuals, so however it would affect them individually, I think it would be the same way as for any other groups."

Although she readily highlighted the number of students of color in her school as higher than in other, nearby suburban schools, Foster revealed that her school lacks both emphasis on and teacher training for cultural competency. As suggested by her language use (and reinforced by our work with educational leadership graduate students), the close proximity of individualization to color-evasiveness limits leadership considerations beyond the boundaries of their own background knowledge and training. An individualization perspective paradoxically allows leaders to treat students of color as if their racial identities and experiences of racism do not matter. Rather than treating people as individuals in their fullness, as they claim to do, leaders consider each person as disconnected from their histories and cultures.

A white male principal of a suburban elementary school with less than 5% students of color, Dan Gibson is a school leader whose color-evasive perspective sustains and reinforces his lack of capacity to respond to the unique needs of students of color. His articulation of the identifiable characteristics of his school reveals his lack of experience in working with students of color. When asked to describe his school, Gibson provides details about the percentage of low-SES (27%), special education (8%), and gifted students (3%) enrolled in his school, yet he does not mention the number or percentage of students of color. Moreover, a major focus for Gibson is the "response to intervention" (RTI) system for students, implemented without consideration for students' race or other background characteristics or needs (DeMatthews et al., 2021).

Gibson demonstrates his lack of language for thinking and talking about race and about race-conscious practices. Gibson expresses his belief that "every single individual kid brings value . . . , a unique perspective, they bring their own home life culture." By approaching leadership from a color-evasive perspective, Gibson minimizes students' identities and deflects understanding the unique experiences of students of color in the larger school context (Lewis, 2003). For example, Gibson does not use data-based decision-making to justify support of and resources for his students of color. As he explains, "We don't have a hugely diverse population anyway, so I think my answer to that would be similar. You know, they're in those [RTI] tier groups that we're trying to identify and support." As this interview excerpt illustrates, a lack of "huge" diversity in Gibson's school encourages and justifies his color-evasiveness. As a result, he does not think about racial difference in his school and has no race-conscious practices to implement.

As our data suggest, individualization confirms a leader's ideological commitment to color-evasiveness. Under the rubric of treating each student as an individual, students' *social* identities never come into play. Without the competency to understand how racial identity and racism contribute to students' individual experiences, leaders therefore ignore a significant aspect of students' individuality. Choosing to enact an individualized approach to students of color perpetuates the multiple lacks in leadership capacity that come together to shape a leader's beliefs, practices, and values.

Deflection. Deflection, the third color-evasive ring, occurs when leaders wave away complaints of inequitable school practices, instead positioning the complaints as excuses or untruthful (Bonilla-Silva & Forman, 2000; Bonilla-Silva et al., 2003). Deflectors ignore whatever structural constraints that contribute to inequity and show no interest in changing curriculum, policies, or practices. Jack Maddon, the suburban elementary principal described at the opening of this chapter, practices deflection. Provided the opportunity to engage parents who find his school's treatment of them racist, Maddon deflects the core insight of the significance of race. This example leads to projecting—suggesting those who critique racist policies are the ones being racist.

Another leader in this category, Scott Abbott, is the white male principal of an urban high school. Abbott emphasizes his students' deficits associated with poverty, reflected in the experiences of both white and Black students at his school. About one-third of the student population is Black, and about two-thirds of students qualify for free or reduced-price lunch. The school struggles to meet state accountability benchmarks across the board.

While Abbott recognizes differences between his Black and white students' experiences, he sees their differences as limited:

> I get that there is a difference, there definitely is. But, there is also a lot of similarities, and . . . one of the things that I have found with the Black and the white kids in this school is that they are very attentive of each other. Like the Black kids—they understand their culture, you know, they understand what their community is like, and the white kids are the same way. . . . They understand that each group does things differently.

The differences Abbott acknowledges, however, do not translate into his own leadership practice. Deflection appears in the following excerpt from his interview:

> I once had a teacher . . . tell me that the one thing she wanted to be better at is teaching Black males how to read. And I don't know of any teacher who *(trails off)*—that is a group that is a subgroup of kids who are notorious for struggling in school. Find that answer, you won't be teaching here, right, you are making millions of dollars. . . . There are things that [my teachers] could do better, sure, but I think for the most part . . . they do a pretty good job dealing with diverse groups of kids.

The teacher Abbott speaks of went on to ask for resources to improve her capacity. However, Abbott interpreted the request as impossible to fulfill, despite the availability of literature, resources, and professional development in his county that could directly respond to the teacher's stated interest and demonstrated need. He has no sense of urgency, no acknowledgment of lack of capacity, nor an intervention plan to better support his Black students, although he knows the Black males and Black students in general at his school continue to perform poorly on standardized tests.

Abbott also emphasizes that white and Black students seem to get along well at his school. The absence of fights between white and Black students suggests to him that students are getting along well:

> Knock on wood, we have not had a racial issue in this building in the 6 years I've been principal. When kids fight, typically they are the same race; we don't have a whole lot of issues of kids . . . being in conflict with each other because of cultural differences. And I don't know what the reason for that is, but here it is a strength more than a weakness for us.

Abbott implies that since white and Black students do not seem to be fighting each other, he has no "racial issues" to deal with. Knocking on wood, Abbott suggests it may only be luck that something has not occurred. "Racial incidents"—typically acts of overt racism that come to light publicly—routinely occur in schools, and as conveyed by the news accounts discussed at the beginning of Chapter 1, students of color often come forward to indicate that racial incidents fit with their regular, ongoing experiences of race and racism in schools.

The mechanism of deflection marks color-evasiveness as an action-based process. Deflection occurs in settings where there is clear evidence of the significance of race, racial difference, and/or racism in the school, but the school leader downplays its significance or ignores it altogether. The ideology of color-evasiveness is particularly influential in limiting any race-conscious actions or practices, short of a racial incident that may cause a leader to react. As evident later in this chapter, responding to a racial incident may force a leader to stop deflecting, but it does not necessarily challenge that leader's color-evasiveness.

Technical Recognition. The last of the four color-evasive perspectives is "technical recognition." In this ring, race is recognized as a concern but remains a superficial one (Lewis, 2004); there is no evidence that this recognition affects leadership practice. Our one example, Logan Sanders, identifies himself as Black/white biracial and leads an elementary school in a wealthy community. The racial diversity in his school comes from the large number of Asian American and Asian immigrant families, many of them recent immigrants. While the school appears diverse, there is little socioeconomic diversity and a very small number of Black and Latina/o students.

When asked to share an example of his efforts to support his Black or Latina/o students, Sanders pointed to his intervention efforts with one Latina student who had poor attendance. Along with other staff members, he participated in a home visit intervention: "Mom was not very well involved. I don't know if it was a language barrier, but we tried many opportunities, but her work schedule also threw an obstacle our way because she worked in the evenings." Additionally, he acknowledges, the student sometimes took care of a younger sibling if the younger child was sick and the mother was expected at work. Sanders reveals neither the effectiveness of this home visit nor the specific nature of their school-based interventions for the student and her family, so it is difficult to interpret how the experience reflects his practices. In the broader context of his interview, however, his statements suggest this mother breaks the pattern Sanders expects of parents in his district. Sanders contrasts this one Latina mother's involvement with the level of involvement he has come to expect from parents in his school district; working parents without reliable resources for childcare are the exception in his school.

The interview data from Sanders suggests that it is possible for a school leader to recognize race or ethnicity as significant to student experience and yet not be able to point to any specific practices that enact that recognition. Since Sanders is the only leader who conveys a technical perspective, his situation may be rare. Few schools in our region enroll such high percentages of students of color from relatively high-wealth families. In a largely wealthy district with a limited number of residents who live in poverty there may be a dynamic created wherein race itself is technically recognized by school leaders, but its significance (and the presence of racism) is evaded in favor of the perceived significance of social class.

Recognition With Minimal Capacity: The Second Band

Moving now further from the center of Figure 2.2, some leaders more explicitly identified the value of race for their students (see Table 2.2). These leaders carried with them some lingering color-evasiveness that drifted into deficit thinking and lack of action. Analyzing the perspectives within this band demonstrates the limited value of recognition and the appeal of deficit thinking and inaction. Echoing prior research, we found that recognition of race does not necessarily inform or challenge leaders' biases, their beliefs about people of color, or the assumptions that guide their practice (Horsford & Clark, 2015), such as associating people of color with poor performance (Bonilla-Silva et al., 2003; Forman & Lewis, 2015).

Recognition With a Deficit. Leaders who demonstrate recognition of race may concurrently convey deficit perspectives. While their recognition may make them appear to move away from color-evasiveness, this appearance is misleading, since they do so carrying racialized generalizations about the abilities and interests of their students. As one example, white female principal Emma Badell leads a middle school with approximately equal percentages of Black and white students and a free or reduced-price lunch rate higher than 70%. Informed by her more than 20 years working in the district, Badell's race consciousness conveys a subtext of a deficit mindset toward the school's students of color and students living in poverty.

Badell revealed some asset-based race consciousness when she shared her opinion of the value brought to the middle school by Black and Latina/o students: "The value is their culture and understanding them and where they come from." But when she explained her understanding, she stated: "Sometimes one of the biggest challenges with the Black community is getting them to change their perception that they can't do it. . . . And we need to tell them that they can." In her response, Badell did several things simultaneously and in a contradictory fashion. Despite her acknowledgment of the value of race and culture, she quickly tied it to tired, deficit-heavy tropes about Black children and families, who she described as devaluing education and lacking confidence (Bonilla-Silva et al., 2003). She conveyed a deficit mindset and a "savior" mentality (Love, 2019) toward students and families. Badell also conveyed that in her school the number of Latina/o students is very small, so she effectively ends up reducing any mention of students' race and ethnicity to the categories Black and white.

White male high school principal Dennis Gable similarly conveyed recognition with deficit. Combining a benevolent concern for his students of color and students living in poverty with distinctly deficit-based undertones, Gable described himself as a school leader who builds relationships with his Black students, yet these cultivated relationships have failed to lead to more-focused culturally responsive interventions. His favored position—focused on the poverty of his white and Black students—is consistent with a color-evasive perspective, but Gable does not consider taking race-conscious action to improve his understanding of the school's students and families. He commented that, in his school, African American students struggle as a subgroup in testing:

> I predominantly equate it to poverty. . . . Special education students struggle. . . . Our predominantly white population don't do real well either. . . . They are not achieving quite as high as they should as well.

In identifying subgroups scoring below others on standardized testing, Gable placed Black, special education, and underperforming white students in the same low-achieving category. His response underlines his disregard for the significance of race.

In discussing his connection with students, Gable gave an example of how he incentivizes student effort on standardized tests by rewarding them with pizza. He shares data about standardized tests with them to encourage effort. While he demonstrates recognition of the racial identities of his students, at the same time he shares his deficit-based perspective that Black students at his school lack an emphasis on education at home: "I think that's where our students, our African American students, there is not really an emphasis and importance at home. There is not an emphasis and importance at home for many of our students."

Although Badell and Gable stopped short of adopting a fully color-evasive ideology, quotations from their interviews suggest that the race consciousness they have developed is strongly deficit-based (Valencia, 1997). For example, Badell shared a program she has been a part of that is meant to get more students of color to enroll in honors and AP classes; to her surprise, students and families of color reveal they are indeed interested in improved access to higher-level courses:

> When we talked to the parents, they were like, "Oh, we didn't know that our kids could do this." So it's giving them that information. Here, in our particular building, we started a National Junior Honor Society last year, and trying to instill on our kids the importance of getting good grades . . . we were surprised at the number of students that were truly interested.

Upon being surprised about the interest and turnout, Badell could have easily taken responsibility for not providing this desired information previously.

Within Badell's depiction of her school's new initiatives designed to engage more Black students in advanced courses and starting a Junior Honor Society, she revealed how her deficit-based mindset nevertheless limits her ability to see the value and assets of the school's students of color and their families and her responsibility to know their interests.

For leaders in the "recognition with a deficit" category, negative stereotyping of both families and students constrains their recognition of race, leaving them with limited capacity to act upon their recognition. Approaching race with this limiting frame has broad consequences on a school's culture since leaders who downplay their students' strengths and interests discourage teachers from building their own capacity and imagination, lowering expectations of what is possible and failing to make full use of existing resources in the school and community. Leaders' success with initiatives to engage students and parents should reliably lead to additional opportunities and expanded capacity. Leaders who see only challenges miss opportunities to build upon existing strengths and to provide what students want and need for their own educational goals.

Recognition With Inaction. Unlike recognition with a deficit, the "recognition with inaction" ring includes those who hold an asset-based view but fail to take corresponding action. The white principal of a charter high school, Bill Roberts, noted that the student body at his school "mirrors the city," approximating the nearly even percentage of Black and white students in public schools within the city limits. His school also enrolls more than 70% students who qualify for free or reduced-price lunch. He considers his school a model for research and development and argues student diversity is vital: "What we really want to see is [how] this comprehensive model of culture and education make a difference with all students, and to do that we've got to make sure that we have a heterogeneous, multicultural group to work with." He did not express deficit-based perspectives of families, instead emphasizing the responsibility of a school and teachers to engage students in their interests. It is important to Roberts that all students believe "what they are doing is important and connected to something of value for them."

When asked about teachers' level of capacity to teach in a culturally responsive manner, Roberts pinpointed a need to develop their capacity: "I say 25% to 35% of our faculty needs some additional supports, which we are trying to provide [for them] to understand what it means to teach in a culturally diverse and economically diverse environment." Roberts recognized that some of his staff members need training in working with a diverse student population to improve their pedagogical practice, but while Roberts takes a cultural approach, he is limited in his attention to race in all his leadership practices. Roberts indicated he embraces data usage in his leadership, but when asked how he uses data to support his students of color, Roberts first took a short pause and, after collecting his thoughts, answered, "I don't know if we have ever thought [about] it . . . looking at data that way."

As important as cultural diversity is to him, as much experience as he has with populations of students of color, he revealed a lack of capacity in his leadership practice to implement race-conscious practices with his staff. It is unclear why Roberts holds back in his practice, considering his stated values and perspectives about multicultural diversity. However, we argue that the sheer dominance of color-evasiveness requires more of a leader than simply an expanded perspective about the value of diversity. Effectively resisting color-evasiveness requires that leaders possess and utilize tools to cultivate race consciousness and hold a commitment to actions and practices to change structures and systems that perpetuate racism and inequality.

Cultivating Race Consciousness: The Third Band

In the third band of color-evasive leadership fall those leaders who do embrace race consciousness to some extent within a perspective that remains partly (or at base) race-evasive. We divide them into three rings: developing, respecting, and responsive. School leaders in the third band revealed how the farther away leaders are from a color-evasive perspective, the more specific race-conscious leadership practices they engage in. These leaders conveyed specific value about race and racial identity, and they depicted practices leaders can follow to make a difference in practice. Some of these leaders referred to culturally responsive or culturally relevant instruction, they highlighted their efforts to make their teaching faculty more racially and culturally diverse, and they named practices to counter the lack of representation of students of color in opportunities such as honors and Advanced Placement courses. Further, they rejected deficit-based perspectives about students' families. However, only in the final, outermost ring of this band, characterized by *responsiveness,* do we begin to see evidence of real leadership in race consciousness and adoption of effective individual actions that characterize a race-conscious leader. As we explain later in this chapter and subsequent chapters, those actions include curriculum, instruction, and structures that seek to understand and to fully respond to students' needs and interests and to cultivate meaningful relationships that fully respect students and their families.

Developing Race Consciousness. In the first ring within this outer band we place the leaders capable of the delicate work of developing or shifting from previously held color-evasive perspectives. Peter Ingram is a white male high school principal in a suburban setting; less than 5% of the student body is students of color, and the free or reduced-price lunch rate is 10–15%. Ingram was on the cusp between a color-evasive perspective and developing race consciousness. Rather than minimizing diversity, Ingram highlighted that his school "has a lot of different diversity; we just don't have a large population." His school context, positionality, and perspective play parts in a critical transitional point for him as a leader, specifically since Ingram's school had recently experienced a public incident during which some students used racial slurs. This incident seemed to push Ingram toward a more race-conscious perspective:

> We recently had some training this year around diversity, hearing from our students. We had the Department of Justice come through. . . . So awareness is up a little bit [more] than it's been in the past. . . . And so I've said to minority students that I don't walk in your shoes, I'm not going to say that I do. So, you have to share your thoughts. . . . You have to tell us what you need. . . . So those voices are important. . . . So we have different forums put together.

Having experienced an external intervention for some racial and racist incidents, Ingram conveyed the importance of his "not large" population of students of color being more safe. He also conveyed some vulnerability, since he does not possess all he needs to enact race-conscious practice. At this point we see that he is developing knowledge and skills, and he also relies on students to notice the limitations in adults' capacity and to come forward, so while he is engaging in some action (in contrast to those who demonstrate recognition with inaction), his move toward race-conscious leadership continues to develop.

Nevertheless, unlike those leaders who demonstrate color-evasive perspectives of unresponsiveness and deflection, Ingram highlighted several measures he has explicitly taken to improve his school's racial climate. He sought the advice of his school nurse, a Black woman, on what could be done for professional training, and at the time of the interview was excited about a newly hired Black teacher, who at the time would become the only Black teacher in the school: "we don't have very much diversity on our staff. . . . So we understand that it's important to add diversity to staff. . . . adding a quality teacher with a diverse background." Here Ingram demonstrated his intention for positive change.

While facilitated training can be helpful to begin this process, reliance on small numbers of persons of color to come forward in predominantly white spaces reveals a significant limitation to his responsiveness, as it implies that students are themselves responsible for pointing out limitations in adults' capacity. As we argue in Chapter 1, many schools systematically ignore students' and families of color's perspectives until racialized incidents are made public or when students engage in activism to make their voices heard.

Respecting. On the next level, we place school leaders who demonstrated the perspective that they *respect* racial difference. School leaders with a respecting perspective demonstrated both recognition and valuing of cultural differences, along with some limited implementation of race-conscious strategies. For example, James Smith, a white male, has led his K–8 charter school that is predominantly Black (98%) for more than

10 years. He previously worked in a wealthy suburban district but feels less of an outsider working in a school with a greater percentage of students of color. Reflecting on his leadership experience, Smith said of white educators' cultural backgrounds, when compared to their students':

> I think that it comes down to the person as an individual. How do you relate to different people? How do you relate to different cultures? And if you can do it, then I think it's not a problem in teaching [to] a different culture. . . . I always said that I never tried to fit in wherever I was, I tried to be myself, but just *respect* wherever I was. (emphasis added)

Here, Smith adapted the language of individuality, expressing his respect for racialized experience, but includes color-evasive perspectives. Smith maintained any educator can educate students from different backgrounds, but that it is essential that an educator's perspective be centered in respecting different cultures.

Although he believes all educators can teach children of color, he nevertheless expressed an awareness of the importance of students being taught by educators that look like them. In reflecting on his own racial and gender positionalities, Smith stated: "I am a white male running a, basically a Black organization. But it has always been about trying. . . . you know being who you are and respecting where you are." As we explore in greater detail in Chapter 5, Smith's quest to understand racial identity has influenced his practice in a nearly all-Black school. Smith purposely hires people of color to serve on the school's teaching and administrative staff because he wants the school to be "a place where [a Black student] is seeing adults that look like that child succeeding and being their mentors." In addition, Smith conveyed this perspective without falling into deficit-based perspectives.

Genuinely respecting diversity means a leader has to have a positive perspective about diversity. In her high-wealth district, white female principal Elizabeth Ida embraces the diversity of her school's student population. She leads a middle school with less than 5% students of color and 5–10% of students qualifying for free or reduced-price lunch. The small percentage of students of color, Ida indicated, is about equally split between Black and Asian American students. Echoing some other principals in this band who see value in diversity, she said:

> We need to bring diversity in. . . . It brings the real world into our bubble here many times that can be created. . . . Part of our job, I feel, is to let them know that there is life outside this bubble, so we embrace diversity without making a child ever feel like . . . they have to talk about their cultural differences or share any of their experiences, but [what] we hope is that they're proud of it and that they will [share their experiences] because when students are learning from their peers, that's amazing.

In contrast to unresponsive school leaders, Ida exhibited a more balanced concept of the value of difference. Diversity is not just a value that benefits privileged students. Ida described how engagement with difference is important developmentally for middle school students:

> We need diversity. We need students to understand and, especially at this age, when they're adolescents, everyone's very egocentric. They're very concerned about themselves, and exposing them to other students of different cultures, different races, different religions is even more challenging at this age because it's all about themselves.

Leaders with respecting orientations recognize the importance of teachers' abilities to work with students of color. While she is not very specific here, Ida believes her teachers are capable of working with students from many cultures:

> I would say the skillset . . . to reach diverse learners is good, meaning . . . if we have students who are African American in a class, I think [teachers] have the knowledge to know how to engage students, to make students feel included, and how to help expose students to everyone's perspectives and points of view.

While Ida expressed confidence in her teachers' abilities, she neither named the specific knowledge and skills she believes her teachers have, nor did she mention to what extent she provides professional development to build teachers' capacity, so it is possible her ideas on respecting difference remain mostly abstract.

In a different school context, Ella Klein expressed similar concerns that students and teachers respect each other's differences. Klein is an administrator in a district with more than 50% students of color and about two-thirds of its student body qualifying for free or reduced-price lunch. In her district, Klein noted the differences between a largely white, female, and middle-class teaching force and an increasingly racially and ethnically diverse student population, reflecting a national trend:

> Teachers need to realize that they come from different backgrounds. If they can appreciate where the kids come from and then let the kids appreciate where they came from, then we can find a common ground. So it's about *respecting* each other's cultures. (emphasis added)

In contrast to Ida's confidence in her teachers' abilities, Klein mentioned teachers' "fear factor": She is aware that teachers in her district do not all have the perspective needed to build relationships across cultural differences:

> This country right now, race is blowing up. I mean, it's blowing up, it is in your face, it is what it is. And we have to deal with it. But sometimes I think people don't know how to deal with it.

Speaking in 2015, Klein recognized that teachers need to be talking about race and implied that leaders cannot avoid providing space and time for building their staff's capacity around race and difference.

We want to acknowledge that Ida's and Klein's assessments of teachers' abilities arise from the leader's perceptions, which brings up a limitation of this category. Leaders with a respecting orientation speak directly to the presence and value of racial difference, identifying aspects of students' racialized experience that point to inequities. Leaders in this category may arguably engage in some practices that can be considered responsive to the needs and interests of students of color. Nevertheless, besides Smith, these leaders neither discussed examples of practices or actions evident in the next category (responsive), nor did they provide examples of how they use their position of power to disrupt structural inequities.

Responsive. Finally, in the perspective at the outermost ring of our color-evasive model, school leaders with a *responsive* perspective more clearly translate a race-conscious leadership perspective into action. These leaders disclose and recognize their advocacy for students of color via well-developed, well-articulated race-conscious leadership. In this outer ring one finds specific features of race-conscious leadership: culture, history, material effects, and strengths. Responsive leaders counterbalance the leadership practices of school leaders found at the two, inner-band, color-evasive perspectives. Significantly, these responsive leaders also demonstrate capacities for changing educational structures. School leaders with this perspective are distinctively situated to meet the call for serving diverse students, families, and communities.

Scarlett Johnson, a Black female principal in a predominantly Black urban elementary school, was in her second year as principal at the time of data collection. Although she was a recent addition in this leadership role, she had previous experience as a teacher, principal, and central office administrator. While speaking on her perspectives about student learning, she explained that "our curriculum is one that is changing to make sure that we have things that are culturally relevant for our students." She provided multiple examples of responsive curriculum, to the point of her receiving permission from the school district office to vary, at times, the standardized, scripted curriculum used by most schools in the district.

Furthermore, Johnson is well aware of the particular diversity her student population represents. Her responses contrast starkly with those provided by color-evasive school leaders unaware even of the demographics of their school's students. In identifying racial subgroups within her school, Johnson indicated her students are predominantly Black; she also shared how two students from Polynesia had recently enrolled. Johnson discussed her actions to ensure the Polynesian students were integrated into the school culture:

> I reached out to our ESL director, 'cause they are getting ready to go on an extended vacation. I said, "I want to have a celebration and I don't know much about [their Polynesian nation]; help me to put together a celebration." So, we are going to have an ocean-theme celebration to send my babies off. And [I'm] just wanting . . . teachers to be more receptive of them as well. Although there is only two of them, they too are important people in our world. We want to make sure that they see their culture [and] their heritage represented here at the school as well. So, we can do better.

The significance of Johnson's thinking and actions are threefold. First, she recognized the specialized need to support her students from Polynesia. Second, she recognized her limitations toward her cultural understanding of these two students. Third, she reached out to others in order to meet the needs of her students and to implement what she learned. Unlike race-evasive leaders such as Ingram and Maddon, Johnson was compelled to action by her lack of knowledge—to obtain the knowledge she needed to better serve her students, to recognize them, and to welcome them into the school community. Johnson's example challenges the narrative presented by those school leaders with color-evasive perspectives whose school's context—having a low number of students of color—influences those leaders' decisions to remain unresponsive to specific needs of students of color.

Another responsive leader, Arthur Lawrence, a Black male urban secondary principal, revealed how he incorporates culturally relevant practices and discusses race and how race relates to student achievement. He explained how recent work in his school has been influenced by his engagement with *Courageous Conversations About Race* (Singleton, 2015), a resource which has helped him extend work he was already doing: "We always have to keep that open eye towards practices that may not be equitable and how are we addressing those things within the school." Lawrence explained the various race-conscious practices he works to implement in his school to support students of color. For example, Lawrence demonstrated how he commits to race-conscious practice by ensuring "that students see people that look like them whether they are teachers, whether that is through bringing mentors into the building. . . . we try to ensure that minority presence within the school in other ways." Here, Lawrence revealed how he enacts his responsive perspective to support the needs of students of color. He goes beyond respecting difference to the development of a clear sense of how the presence of mentors of color matters, as well as specific additional ways to bring what he calls "minority presence" into the school. Lawrence personally takes on this responsibility, extending what the district is doing.

When responsive leaders face significant obstacles to enacting race consciousness in their school settings, they not only name those obstacles—all school leaders face them—they also commit to action to persevere. In addition to the challenges of fitting responsive practices into district structures, Johnson has found her work with her faculty to be a continual focus of her attention. For instance, her commitment and clarity of responsiveness guides interventions when some teachers may show a lack of respect for students and families of color. This leads her to engage teachers in difficult conversations at times, work that requires a strong frame. Meanwhile, Lawrence struggles to get all his teachers on board, yet persists with his race-conscious efforts. Likewise, Allison Edwards encounters teacher resistance. As a Black female elementary principal in a high-wealth and predominantly white suburban school, Edwards works against the actions of some of her teachers who exhibit deficit-based perspectives about students of color and children living in poverty. As we describe more fully in Chapter 4, Edwards challenges her teachers to acknowledge when their teaching methods exclude and marginalize students.

Common among responsive school leaders is an asset-based perspective on families. School leaders in this third ring navigate their relationships with families of color without holding onto deficit-based ideologies, and they push others away from such views. Maya Gaffney, a Black female principal of an urban middle school, explained:

> If I have a parent who physically does not come to the school, I don't look at that this student is lacking a third of their support system. Because some parents just can't come. . . . I can't hold that against the child.

A responsive school leader turns their leadership practices away from ideologies that can lead to deficit mindsets. In contrast to leaders who might find themselves surprised when parents are interested in opportunities for their children (as evidenced by the "recognition with deficit thinking" perspective), responsive school leaders not only assume parents have high expectations and support their children's education, but they also want to understand specifically what those expectations and supports may be so that educators can reinforce those areas within the school setting. These leaders don't simply fill in what they don't know about families with assumptions of deficit. As Gaffney illustrates, making assumptions about what amounts to appropriate parental involvement is unnecessary and counterproductive to fostering mutually reinforcing relationships. As a result, leading a school is far less about compensating for outside-school limitations in students' lives and far more about building upon children's and families' needs and interests and providing opportunities that inequitable educational systems systematically deny children through marginalization and subjugation.

MULTIPLE LACKS

To compare the perspectives of race-conscious leaders to those of their less capacious peers, we can identify several lacks. For some leaders, there are multiple lacks. The lacks span belief, value, experiences, and practices:

(1) lack of language for thinking and talking about race,
(2) lack of asset-based perspectives,
(3) lack of experience living and working with racially diverse populations,
(4) lack of thinking about race-conscious practice, and
(5) lack of ideas about how to implement race-conscious practice.

The five lacks we theorize cross the bands of color-evasiveness, and they are a danger because they stop school leaders from overcoming color-evasiveness and evolving to embrace race-conscious leadership. These lacks are critical to identify in a leader's practice, because they point to areas that require attention, development, and action in leadership preparation, leader selection, and professional development.

Multiple lacks can manifest in leaders for various reasons, a common reason (mostly among white leaders) being a lack of personal experience with persons different from themselves and communities different from their own predominantly white and middle-class communities. The five lacks are present in all school settings, but they tend to be more pronounced (and perpetuated) in predominantly white and middle- or upper-middle-class school settings where leaders tend to ignore both relatively small numbers of students of color and those children living in poverty. Witness the number of leaders described in our data who were unsure even of the presence of children of color in their buildings or who overlooked opportunities to focus upon race-conscious practices. In some school settings, leaders were more likely to recognize the number of children living in poverty but, in some cases, leaders point to these children's small numbers and leaders' responsibility for attending to their needs were thought to be modest in the context of the overall wealth and success of their schools.

Our listing of multiple lacks in beliefs, practices, values, and experiences draws not only from the words of leaders whose perspectives fall within the first, most color-evasive band of our model; lacks are also evident in second-band color-evasiveness—or recognition with minimal capacity—wherein lacks in experience and perspective limit the capacity of leaders to engage in more responsive practices. Our analysis also relates to the capacities of school leaders operating in an outer ring—specifically the contrast between a respecting and a responsive perspective. Recall that the chief difference between these two perspectives is that responsive leaders address specific knowledge and practices that serve their students of color. Although we identify only four participants who hold what we term a responsive perspective, the variety of beliefs, practices, values, and experiences among these four individuals suggests that responsive race-conscious school leadership is possible for many leaders of various backgrounds. Further, we believe a responsive perspective is necessary before a leader can make any real claim to addressing gaps in achievement and opportunity. We suspect that leaders who demonstrate a respecting perspective are the leaders most likely to become responsive leaders. To identify what respecting leaders are lacking in order to become truly responsive, they can start by looking for the five lacks listed above.

As we explain in more detail in Chapter 7, professional development and leadership preparation are two areas where implications for this work are fairly clear. More work needs to be done by school districts on their administrators' own multiple lacks. School leaders need help in recognizing the gaps that reflect their lacks in capacity (Marx & Larson, 2011; Taylor, 2006) and in opportunity for self-reflection (Bonilla-Silva & Forman, 2000; Theoharis & Haddix, 2011). Leaders who aspire to become race-conscious can also learn from leaders who already are more race-conscious, including those who are responsive in various demographic situations in schools. Race-conscious leaders are findable, which gives hope that we can find, and build, more. An absolute precondition for furthering this goal is frank and open dialogue that faces race and racism. We assert that open dialogue about race and racial issues needs to occur critically and openly because to advance equity in education, we must recognize the vast ramifications of race and what it means to provide equitable opportunities.

Extensive literature on color-evasive perspectives comes out of the work of teachers and focuses on teachers (Johnson & Campbell-Stephens, 2014), yet, as we understand, more research is needed that examines the effects and influences, long-term and longitudinal, of leaders who enact a color-evasive perspective (Bonilla-Silva, 2014; Gallagher, 2003; Lewis, 2001). Consideration of data relevant to the four inner-band perspectives—unresponsiveness, individualization, deflection, and technical recognition—suggests that color-evasiveness is school leaders' prevalent perspective. For these school leaders, who are mostly in predominantly white schools (or in schools with students of color and white students living in poverty in about equal numbers), race and race consciousness appear to be insignificant features of leadership practice (Welton et al., 2015). The two second-band perspectives—recognition with deficit and recognition with inaction—demonstrate the lingering hold of color-evasive ideology on leadership practices, even when school leaders recognize race and racial difference. There are limits to such awareness, leading either to attribution of deficits to children, families, and cultures or to inaction—not strategies for changing practice or leading a school in a new, more equitable direction.

Another aspect we want to recognize is the fluidity of the multi-ring perspectives we present. Three of our participants—John Hall, Andrew Baker, and Peter Ingram—conveyed perspectives containing elements from multiple rings. For example, Hall talked about seeing students as individuals, but he also revealed a more race-conscious perspective compared to other respondents in the individualization ring. Meanwhile, Baker shared strong language from his previous experience as an urban principal focusing on narrowing so-called achievement gaps, conveying similar perspectives to respondents we describe as "respecting." Yet, as a principal of an upper-middle-class suburban school, he also shared the technical/rational perspectives of his more race-evasive colleagues. For example, Baker said that a racial gap in test scores "does not mean that race leads to the achievement or that poverty leads to achievement or affluence leads to achievement . . . but there is definitely a connection between the two." Locating himself in distinctly different contexts during his career makes Baker an interesting case. It reinforces the notion that experiences living and working with diverse populations can help develop race-conscious perspectives and practices. It also raises the question about what happens to leaders' perspectives and practices when they move into settings with relatively few students of color.

Lastly, Ingram, whom we place within the developing ring, also hinted in his interview at a previous color-evasive perspective when asked about how he uses data to support his students of color: "Well, once again, if you're looking at students as individuals, I don't think we're looking at it more or less from a color perspective, more from an individual student perspective." This statement only makes sense if Ingram believes that race is not a part of what it means to be an individual. Although Ingram revealed a third-band perspective of "developing" into a responsive race-conscious school leader, it appears he previously held a color-evasive perspective and without continued effort he could easily slip back to those color-evasive perspectives.

The fluidity of color-evasive perspectives suggests that leaders who exhibit multiple lacks have work to do to become responsive. For each lack that a leader has, deeper experiential engagement seems essential. Changing perspectives without having such experiences is undoubtedly a challenge for leaders, graduate faculty members, and professional development providers. As we continue to explore other aspects of race-conscious leadership ethics in subsequent chapters, additional opportunities to address these multiple lacks come into finer focus.

CONCLUSION

As we explain in this chapter, race-conscious leadership means being attuned to multiple aspects of race and racism and their influence on the experiences of children in schools. We suggest that leaders who exemplify race consciousness in their leadership demonstrate it within four aspects: culture, history, material effects, and strengths. As we argue and support with evidence in subsequent chapters, race consciousness is only the beginning of race-conscious caring for school leaders, but it proves a profound foundation, because without an open and strengths-based view on race and racism, leaders will falter in their ability to relate to children and communities of color. Race-evasiveness also makes it difficult, if not impossible, for school leaders to lead teachers in developing their own race consciousness, and lacking a race-conscious perspective can forestall teachers' own efforts to serve every student well and equitably. Without a race-conscious perspective, school leaders make negative assumptions and employ deficit-based perspectives when considering the lives of children and their families. Their beliefs then inform practices that further perpetuate deficit-based perspectives and needlessly curtail local and long-term opportunities for children of color. As we next show, race-evasive perspectives undermine the widely expressed principle that leaders should care for all children in their schools.

CHAPTER 3

Critical Caring

Figure 3.1. Critical Caring

Laura Foster is a white female elementary principal in a small suburban district. The school serves more than 500 students, with less than 5% students of color and just under 15% low-SES student population, and is located in one of the most affluent communities in the county. While the school draws from a diverse socioeconomic population, it has a lower percentage of low-SES students than the county average, and it lacks the racial and ethnic diversity of other urban communities in the area. It is known for its innovative educational programs, and teaching and administrative positions in the district are highly sought after.

When Foster talked about the children who attend her school, it is clear that caring is essential to her educational philosophy. She described their needs as the most critical consideration in leadership decision-making. She shared, "My approach to leadership and to working with people, in general, is just about building relationships . . . So, I think the students know that I care about them and that I want what's best for them." Foster positioned herself as student-centered in her leadership style. She wants all children to know that she has their best interests at heart, that she cares for them, and that when she administers discipline, she is fair to them and their peers.

Foster takes her leadership responsibility for student learning seriously. She stated, "I think first off, I'm responsible for student learning by ensuring that the teachers are prepared through professional development, that they're exposed to and encouraged to pursue new research-based, maybe new approaches to teaching." Foster sees herself as an instructional leader responsible for creating structures and a learning culture for her teaching staff. Alongside her instructional leadership she embeds the idea of caring. She stated, "I think that many parents comment on how the teachers are really caring, how they're professional, how they just take an interest in the individual needs of the students." She is confident that her caring perspective and that of her teachers, based at the individual level, are key to her effectiveness as a school leader.

However, our discussion with Foster reveals some unfulfilled commitments to caring in her leadership practices, particularly in the area of race and ethnicity. Foster acknowledged the need for culturally responsive training as part of her professional development with staff. She also recognized the importance of understanding the cultural background of her teachers in relation to her students. When asked about the skill level of her teachers in working with diverse students, she commented:

> I don't know that they have any special training in that area . . . I would say there isn't really any special training. I mean, every now and then, we'll have maybe some professional development about just diversity in general . . . I can't really think of anything recently.

In our work with school leaders and graduate students preparing to become school leaders, we often encounter a reluctance to accept or admit the existence of racial differences and the effects of racism on the educational opportunities of students. Many leaders combine this color-evasiveness with the abstract notions of caring for all children that Foster exemplifies. In this chapter, we refer to this approach to caring as a kind of impersonal caring (Code, 1995)—a particular approach to caring that falls short of more genuine and critical caring. We found the impersonal caring Foster demonstrates especially among leaders from white and middle-class backgrounds. Impersonal caring reproduces racist power relations and reinforces standardized and competitive notions of educating children. Many of the same school leaders maintain the color-evasive ideology discussed in the previous chapter. As we focus on the visions of caring of Foster and our other interviewees, we show how standpoints of caring accompanied by color-evasiveness limit a leader's ability to think about and implement practices that can better support students of color.

THE NEED FOR A NEW SCHOOL LEADERSHIP ETHICS

As this chapter reveals, we contend that school leaders need to take a *critical caring* approach grounded in relational caring, narrative ethics, and collective responsibility (see Figure 3.1). Through theory and empirical studies, researchers have extensively examined the role moral perspectives can play in leadership practices and the importance of caring leadership is widely held (Beck, 1994; Shapiro & Stefkovich, 2011; Starratt, 2004; Stefkovich & Begley, 2007; Strike, 2006). At the same time, the emergence and growth of school accountability policy and its focus on equitable educational opportunities have led researchers to advocate that school leadership practices should both promote better outcomes for all students and be grounded fundamentally in caring moral perspectives (Shapiro & Gross, 2013; Starratt, 2014; Stefkovich & Begley, 2007).

Building on such work, some school leaders in our study have shifted toward a different vision for educational praxis in the current educational climate—a vision characterized by communal rather than individualized responsibility (Freire, 1990/1970; Hargreaves & O'Connor, 2018). These school leaders believe that all leaders and teachers must pair a deep sense of caring for the students and communities they serve with a race-conscious awareness. In this chapter, we point to examples from school leaders who significantly depart from the near consensus about the significance of caring when race and class enter the conversation. As we demonstrate, differential views of caring and responsibility appear in conversations with the principals, and there are variations in perspectives on racial diversity. Examples of caring relations in school leadership could include regular communication with students and their families, providing support for students' emotional and social needs, and fostering a sense of belonging and inclusion in the school community. We find that the genuine care needed for students of color and students living in poverty is often lacking among principals who evidence minimal or no culturally responsive care.

We believe it is critical for school leaders today to consider what it means to accept educational responsibility at a time when efforts to effect change have been hampered in the sociopolitical arena. To succeed as critical caring, the quality of caring relations is of utmost importance, and as a growing body of literature affirms, leaders with the knowledge, experience, and dispositions to engage students in respectful and culturally responsive relations are vital. Despite the challenges, there is a potential for change, and this should give us hope and optimism (Khalifa et al., 2016; Louis et al., 2016).

Relational Caring

Caring theory has been widely prominent in education, and education scholars have greatly expanded its initial formulations from Carol Gilligan's (1979, 1982) and Nel Noddings's (1984) early work. A glance through Google Scholar shows that in the 40 years since Gilligan's theory on caring was published it has been cited more than 65,000 times, while Noddings's theory of caring has been cited more than 17,000 times. Gilligan articulated a psychological theory of moral development based on women's experience, and Noddings developed a philosophical ethics of caring based on the experience of women parents but explicitly available and applicable to ethical actors of any gender.

Briefly, Noddings (1984) offers an ethics based on the quality of the relation between the *one-caring* and the *cared-for*. In Noddings's theory, the one-caring exhibits *motivational displacement*—placing the needs of the cared-for ahead of other motivations of ethical behavior—and *engrossment*—learning the cared-for's needs, interests, and projects. This theory works in contrast to dominant Western ethical theory (Frankena, 1973), which embeds patriarchal norms, typically in the form of abstract and universal moral principles (deontological ethics in the manner of Immanuel Kant), the relative value of competing moral outcomes (utilitarian ethics in the manner of John Stuart Mill), or the cultivation of morally desirable character traits (virtue ethics in the form of Aristotle) (see Frankena, 1973; Marino, 2010). In contrast to these Western traditions, Noddings favors attention to caring for others' needs and interest ahead of abstract rules, principles, character development, or universalizable outcomes.

In education, Gilligan and Noddings opened up new approaches to professional ethics for teachers and leaders. While these authors' theories of caring have been lauded for their critique of patriarchal norms in theorizing, much more still needs to be done to make the core insights of caring applicable in work against racism (Beauboeuf-Lafontant, 2002; Green, 2004; Thompson, 1998; Walker & Snarey, 2004; Watson, 2018). For instance, educators have identified a need to link educators' experience of race and ethnicity and their experience of caring (Louis et al., 2016). The critical caring we suggest cannot be completed unless the motivations of the cared-for are known, honored, and supported. Educators urgently need to develop their knowledge about the history of racism in the United States and the longstanding resistance to racism. Without a strong relationship backed by considerable knowledge, the cared-for cannot receive care, and the relationship between the educator and student is compromised.

The combination of abstract notions of caring for all children and race-evasiveness leads educators to uncritical assumptions of sameness (Thompson, 1998; Walker & Snarey, 2004) and misplaced empathy (Todd, 2004). Educators who consider racial differences insignificant to their history may make deficit assumptions about children of color. In addition to limiting caring to an individual act of responsibility, evading race projects one's own experience on others, and when enacting empathetic feelings, one projects one's own emotions onto others. In school buildings with largely minoritized populations of students and predominantly white teaching staff, this disconnection could lead to systematic and pervasive misapplication of empathy—color-evasive educators with similar backgrounds could encourage each other to project their assumptions onto an entire student body. This is problematic considering that in the 2017–2018 school year, 78% of public school principals were white, 11% Black, 9% Hispanic, and 1% Asian (NCES, 2019).

The same misplaced empathy can occur in schools with small populations of nonwhite students. Unable to become engrossed in relation due to the evasion of race and its significance in the lives of children, specifically the experience of racism and its collective resistance, impersonal carers are unable to think and act past their own presuppositions about how students feel, how to care about them, and how students should respond to caring.

What is more, the acceptance of relational ethics, a concept that emphasizes the importance of ethical relationships and interactions, as of great significance to school leadership practices becomes evident with a brief examination of U.S.-based educational leadership standards. For example, the concepts "care" and "caring" appear numerous times in the National Policy Board for Educational Administration (NPBEA; 2015) leadership standards. Specifically, Standard 5 calls for "Community of Care and Support for Students," with a relevant substandard stating:

> [Effective leaders] [c]reate and sustain a school environment in which each student is known, accepted and valued, trusted and respected, cared for, and encouraged to be an active and responsible member of the school community. (p. 13)

The choice of "cared for" appears intentional as a particular approach to leadership ethics evident in school leadership theory.

At the same time, race-conscious school leadership research suggests that knowing how to care for all children is not systematically evident in school leaders (Bass, 2020). Recently, calls for culturally responsive school leaders have been grounded in equitable leadership (Diem & Carpenter, 2012; Gooden & O'Doherty, 2014; Touré & Thompson Dorsey, 2018). The literature on culturally responsive school leadership underscores the significance of race, racial difference, and antiracism as areas of expertise and concern for a school leader. These are not just issues to be aware of; they are crucial areas that a school leader must be well versed in. Allusions to ethical practices pervade this research, and ethical foundations are often implied in the commitments of race-conscious leaders to families, children, and communities of color (Theoharis & Haddix, 2011). History also provides substantive examples of schooling and leadership practices that sustained Black schools that organized themselves around principles of caring and justice through decades of professional struggle for equitable opportunities and resources for children attending segregated schools (Walker & Snarey, 2004).

Narrative Ethics

As an alternative approach to ethics, *narrative ethics* has a long history, particularly among subjugated persons struggling to survive and assert their humanity in an unjust and inequitable world. Narrative ethics draws universally applicable theories about right action from the lives of individuals and the imagined lives of literary figures. Narrative ethics has a long tradition in activist and civil rights struggles and is well grounded in African American literary and philosophical tradition (Walker & Snarey, 2004).

We are calling for narrative ethics to expand caring in professional leadership ethics to make it more applicable beyond the race and class position in which it materialized. A more typical philosophical approach to expand caring has been to place caring in dialectic tension with justice. We believe caring and justice should not be placed in opposition to each other but instead redefined and grounded in narrative ethics as working simultaneously. In their historical research, Vanessa Siddle Walker and Renata Tompkins (2004) demonstrate that principals and teachers in Southern segregated Black schools served in the roles of counselor, encourager, benefactor, and racial cheerleader, roles essential to creating a caring community. In these roles, caring was always understood as being in service to justice. Following this model, embodied forms of leadership ethics are called for—articulated, enacted ethics that take into account the leader's history, positionality, and reflective ways of being in the world (Blackmore, 2010). A narrative approach to ethics recenters the experiences of those with an embodied understanding of racism. Stories of leaders and teachers working against racism are relevant, vital learning tools for such work. Frames drawn from ethical theory help articulate meaning from narratives, conveying the ethical work in what Andrea Green (2004) calls "different rooms." For instance, readers and hearers of narratives may be placed in the position of witnesses of narratives and may be challenged to reconstruct their ethical stances accordingly.

For our purposes, we are most concerned with leaders enhancing their caring ethics by critically reflecting upon their own experiences and witnessing differential experiences of race. Critical caring in service to race consciousness requires experience, reflection upon that experience, and challenges to one's assumptions about children of color. Assuming that one knows enough about children to care for all of them equally or as individuals is a fallacy. School leaders commonly claim caring as an ethical value; knowing how to care is another thing entirely. We suspect this gap between confidence and competence about caring for students of color is why race-conscious praxis is a challenge for school leaders without backgrounds and experiences engaging racial differences. While school leaders may understand in the abstract the need to care for all children, they fall short if they do not have the racial awareness capacity to enact that caring. Leaders need to understand the needs and interests of racialized and minoritized children and families, act in ways that convey genuine caring to those receiving the caring, and follow through with additional practices that make caring consistent.

Collective Responsibility

Although caring has become a well-accepted concept in education and educational leadership, some scholars have also called attention to limitations arising when the caring relationship lacks the required quality of connection. Lorraine Code (1995) names as "impersonal caring" the approach to caring that works on behalf of others without knowing their issues and concerns. Impersonal caring in education occurs when school leaders and teachers believe they know their students' best interests but lack the relational capacity to understand the needs and interests of their students. Those school leaders who demonstrate impersonal caring hold beliefs embedded in their own limited experience and are not empowered with knowledge about the needs, interests, and lived experiences of those in their care. Leaders taking an impersonal caring approach act in ways that project their interests, concerns, or biases. Impersonal caring is especially notable in the educator who proposes to care for all children equally but evades color. An educator drawing on the scope of experience of caring in their own life may not understand that children's knowledge of caring, particularly across race and ethnicity, could be significantly different from their own (Lopez Kershen, 2018).

We learn another significant idea of collective responsibility from philosopher Gert Biesta (2004), who argued that when accountability policy was taking firm hold of education policy internationally, the concept of responsibility was rhetorically and conceptually co-opted through the implementation of high-stakes accountability policy, and responsibility (for students) became conflated with accountability (for test scores). In the logic of neoliberalism that drives many efforts for systemic reform (Biesta, 2004; Lipman, 2011), economic relations between parent and school and between school and state overshadow the teacher–student relation and guide the actions of school leaders and teachers. Although accountability policy is ostensibly based on democratic ideals—the general uplift of educational quality and more significant equity of access to strong educational experiences—the ideals are compromised when the pedagogical relation is supplanted in importance by this economic relation (Biesta, 2004). For example, this economic relation is marked by school personnel having to protect their school from the threat of being labeled as low-performing, being taken over, or being reconstituted. Educators become more concerned with protecting the school than with enriching their students' educational experience.

Next, we break down what is meant by the concept of *responsibility*. Breaking it into two semantic components—*response* and *ability*—one can begin to conceptualize responsibility as having the ability to respond to the wants and needs of others (Starratt, 2004). Breaking it down in such a way surfaces a couple of suppositions. First, there is something to respond to, a particular want or need that the one responsible understands, appreciates, and can interpret accurately. Second, the one taking responsibility must be capable of responding. These two aspects of responsibility suggest that mere interest in responding to others is insufficient; one must be attuned to needs, recognize them, and know how to respond appropriately.

Responsibility is a significant component of Black feminist theories of knowledge (Collins, 2000; Roseboro & Ross, 2009). For Patricia Hill Collins (2000), the more substantial knowledge claims are those trusted by communities; she argues that African American communities trust those who take full responsibility for their claims and have the experiential and lived knowledge to support those claims. Trusting knowledge without those assurances presents a danger to those made vulnerable in institutions such as schools. Drawing from an experience of continual struggle for liberatory education, Donyell Roseboro and Sabrina Ross (2009) connect responsibility to educational practice. They name teaching as coming from "a permanent state of resistance" (p. 35) that requires collective rather than individual effort:

> This liberatory ethic of care is based on collective work and responsibility, not individual effort, worth, or merit. It is an ethic of care infused with love, humility, passion, and power. But, most of all, it is an ethic of care that must be political, that is rooted in an understanding of the home and the spiritual as politically creative spaces. (p. 36)

Responsibility ultimately is for the uplifting of all students, and so any individual action is done in the larger context of the project of liberation.

Required for a notion of collective responsibility is an appreciation for the larger social context in which individual actions are placed. Leaders need to understand the histories and specific positioning of their work in relation to U.S. history and to have a clear sense of their relation to the communities they serve (Yosso, 2005). Both privilege and marginalization have histories, and leaders must appreciate their places in both. Leaders need to recognize the allure and the easy trap of the evasion of race and racism and—as part of communal efforts to reckon with living history—stand firm in their race consciousness and their opposition to racism. Such an approach applies whether leaders are working in urban, suburban, or rural contexts and regardless of the proportion of children of color in their schools.

FOUR APPROACHES TO CARING

In this next section, we introduce four approaches to caring, which represent variations in how school leaders talked about caring. First is the critical caring we have described so far in the chapter, and the others are approaches to caring that fall short of the components of critical caring: tough love/tough luck caring, color-evasive caring in "fortunate communities," and caring with minimal responsiveness. The distinctions in school leaders' talk about caring leadership was significantly informed around the discussion of racial differences among their students. While these four approaches sometimes overlap, for the most part they are found in isolation in particular individuals, as indicated in Table 3.1.

Critical Caring

As we explain earlier in this chapter, leaders who ground their work in critical caring bring a community-based approach to caring: They examine patterns of oppression and domination, challenge power relations and taken-for-granted practices and processes, and identify steps for corrective action on behalf of *all* the students, families, and communities that the school serves. Relationships are an important consideration for school leaders with a critical caring perspective. In order to enact critical caring, school leaders need to be continuously aware that affirming relationships with students and families is not a given regardless of one's own beliefs, social identities, and status as a school administrator. In the following, we introduce four leaders who provide examples that highlight various dimensions of critical caring.

Scarlett Johnson conveyed a manner of caring for her students cultivated through the development of relationships, which she fostered through her recognition that connections are not easily established. She has to go beyond the assumption that simply being nice will lead to relationships with students and families. For example, she believes, "Parents treat me well because I treat their kids well." At the same time, Johnson has dealt with some encounters during which parents have expressed that they do not trust her and told her that she does not understand their situation. Rather than withdrawing from engagement with parents, she interpreted these encounters through this understanding: "I represent the system. I represent that whiteness, white privilege."

As a Black woman leading a predominantly Black elementary school, Johnson understands the parents' perception of the unequal power dynamic between the community and the school. Part of being an effective leader is recognizing that positive relationships with the community members you serve are not always straightforward and a given. Johnson understands that she has to go beyond assuming all it takes to make a mutual connection is to be amicable with students and families. It is vital for her that students and families understand her commitment to them. She constantly advises her staff to "not look down on children," which is very important. "How do we talk to kids? Why would you say that to that particular child? You got

Table 3.1. School Leader Characteristics Sorted by Theme

Participant	Gender	Race	Position	Type of District	Level of School	% Students of Color[1]	% Free/ Reduced-Price Lunch[1]
Community-based caring							
Scarlett Johnson	Female	Black	Principal	Urban	Elementary	76–100	90–95
James Smith	Male	White	Principal	Urban	Elem/Middle	76–100[2]	80–85[2]
Maya Gaffney	Female	Black	Principal	Urban	Elementary	26–50	80–85
Arthur Lawrence	Male	Black	Principal	Urban	Middle/High	26–50	60–65
Allison Edwards	Female	Black	Principal	Suburban	Elementary	<5	10–15
Tough love/tough luck caring							
Dennis Gable	Male	White	Principal	Urban	High	26–50	55–60
Emma Badell	Female	White	Principal	Urban	Middle	26–50	70–75
Scott Abbott	Male	White	Principal	Urban	Middle/High	26–50	60–65
Michael Labette	Male	White	Principal	Urban	Middle/High	10–25	60–65
Bill Roberts	Male	White	Principal	Urban Charter	High	51–75[2]	65–70[2]
Color-evasive caring in fortunate communities							
Jack Maddon	Male	White	Principal	Suburban	Elementary	10–25	45–50
Dan Gibson	Male	White	Principal	Suburban	Elementary	5–10	25–30

Paul Eaby	Male	White	Principal	Suburban	Elementary	<5	<5
Peter Ingram	Male	White	Principal	Suburban	High	<5	10–15
Laura Foster	Female	White	Principal	Suburban	Elementary	<5	10–15
Logan Sanders	Male	Biracial	Principal	Suburban	Elementary	<5	<5
Kevin Labby	Male	White	Principal	Suburban	High	<5	5–10
Caring with (minimal) responsiveness							
Andrew Baker	Male	White	Principal	Suburban	Elementary	<5	<5
Elizabeth Ida	Female	White	Principal	Suburban	Middle	<5	5–10
John Hall	Male	White	Principal	Suburban	Elementary	5–10	15–20
Ella Klein	Female	White	Director	Urban	District	51–75[3]	65–70[3]
Ethan Knight	Male	White	Superintendent	Urban	District	51–75[3]	65–70[3]

Note: To protect the identities of participants, names listed are pseudonyms, and percentages of students of color and of students on free and reduced-price lunch are indicated as ranges.

1. School data collected from the U.S. Department of Education Institute of Education Sciences, National Center for Education Statistics, Common Core of Data for the 2013–2014 school year.

2. The school's state profile data are used for these two charter schools.

3. The high school data are used to represent the district.

to analyze it and hold each other accountable." For her, education is about "nurturing and caring for each other" and is a "vehicle for giving back."

Her caring also plays out in how she approaches the curriculum. The point of developing literacy, she said, "is to find your voice and to get it heard." To her, students finding their voice requires understanding how and why one's voice has been marginalized in the first place. Thus, she pushes for students to understand their marginalization and sets a foundation for students of color to challenge the social structures that maintain that marginalization, which she demonstrated by her support of her elementary students organizing and participating in a peace march in the school's neighborhood. She advocated for and received a waiver from her district so that her teachers would not need to teach the scripted curriculum provided to other schools in the district. In addition, her school's social studies curriculum ensures that her children learn African American history beyond critical historical facts and figures "so that they might understand the long history of resistance and achievements."

As we explain in greater detail in Chapter 5, Johnson's work with teachers, students, and parents is grounded in an ethics of commitment to children, their community, historical knowledge, and cultural sustainability informed by her race-conscious perspective. She not only cares about the children in her school but also the needs and interests of the community, which inform her practice; she knows how to care for the children in culturally appropriate ways. She understands that for some children, "school is something that is done to them," because that is what she experienced through a good portion of her early education. It was not until a teacher praised and supported her that she believed herself capable. This ethical framing of her practice is born out of struggle.

Another Black woman principal, Maya Gaffney, also revealed how critical caring and race consciousness inform how leaders reframe deficit language and sustain an asset lens. When asked about the demographics in her school, without looking at any data, Gaffney shared, "We are now [a] 30% white, 30% African American, probably 25% Nepal[ese], 15% Hispanic community. And we have a small population of students who are from Somalia. One or two [from] Uzbekistan and Iraq." Gaffney's response demonstrates critical caring by showing she has a finger on the rich diversity in the student and family communities she serves. This attention transfers to recognizing the cultural capital students bring to the school (Yosso, 2005). For example, she described that some of her staff members blame parents for student performance, which is related to deficit-framing of children's families from racial and culturally diverse backgrounds. Gaffney acknowledged the power dynamics: "in terms of parental involvement, what that means is largely based on the perceptions of what parental involvement means to the dominant white culture." She sees and challenges taken-for-granted approaches in school that hinder appreciating the community cultural wealth of students and families of color.

Gaffney demonstrates critical caring in her leadership by enacting the standpoint that any system that impedes student learning needs to be changed. She helps her teachers grow, and she is very willing to provide unsatisfactory evaluations to teachers who do not seek growth:

> I am not doing my job [as] an instructional leader of making observations and giving teachers feedback to grow their practice or, if the practice is not improving, doing what I need to do to make sure they find another profession or exit them out of this one. I have done the students a disservice; that is ultimately my job. And if I feel that there is a teacher who I wouldn't want my child to be in that classroom, then they are not appropriate for the students here, and that is typically my barometer.

In her view, leadership responsibility must center on students. She sees herself as a change agent rather than a component of the system, and she wants to change the system that impedes student learning.

Arthur Lawrence's positionality as a Black man is essential to his leadership approach and invited our consideration of Black masculine caring as a frame for understanding his ethical grounding (Bass, 2016). Lawrence understood the historical significance of his identity within societal views and recognized the significance of being a role model for students of color in his building. He described the importance of presenting himself as a competent, business-like leader to counter pejorative stereotypes of Black males. Lawrence acknowledges achievement disparities between white and Black students and other students of color and commits to a sense of responsibility to remove barriers and provide opportunities for success. He shared the following perspective:

> Our focus is on educating and providing all of our students with the right amount of support needed to be successful . . . No matter where they are from and no matter their previous experience . . . given the right amount of support and the right amount of time, they can certainly achieve at a high level.

Lawrence fosters an asset-based perspective of what can and must be done to improve student learning opportunities. An example of this is further seen in the conversation he had with his instructional committee that includes race consciousness with his critical caring in the examination of data:

> We can look at our Advanced Placement tests and say, "Okay, this is where we were with our African American students. What can we do to get more [African American] students enrolled in these classes and passing these tests?" Those are things that we can do as a result of testing.

In the above response, Lawrence revealed a willingness to engage his leadership team in conversation that examines patterns of inequities and seeks a process to identify possible solutions.

While the critical caring participants described so far work in urban districts, critical caring is also relevant in suburban districts. Allison Edwards had just completed her first year as principal of a suburban elementary school that had recently seen a growth in students eligible for free or reduced-price lunch and a small but growing number of students of color (although both represented less than 5% of the student body). Edwards's ethical stance takes on what the literature has identified as an "other mothering" approach, characterized as social, emotional, and educational nurturing (Case, 1997). Reflecting on the completion of her first year in the district, she highlighted a significant responsibility she had challenging the deficit ideologies some of her teachers and middle school administrator colleagues held. Edwards shared how often in her conversation with her teachers discussing struggling students she would hear replies like, "These kids just don't get it because . . . ," and her counter to such comments would always be, "Okay, they don't. They aren't ready, but we have to do things differently." Such a response points to how Edwards attempts to challenge taken-for-granted deficit thinking (Valencia, 1997) some educators hold, particularly with respect to marginalized students.

Often, when schools allow deficit ideologies to go unchecked, the schools bring about patterns of oppression and power relations that dictate cultural norms. The need to challenge deficit thinking more strongly is especially evident in schools with a lower number of students of color and low-SES. Edwards must address her teachers' line of thinking that places blame on students so she can refocus teachers on meeting the needs of struggling students. According to Edwards, "I have a 5th-grader that is reading at a 1st-grade level and doing math at a 1st-grade level—those are my kids." Note here how she stakes a personalized claim to "my kids" in her efforts toward equity in her school.

The last example of critical caring plays out in a charter school context. James Smith has been the leader of an urban charter school for more than a decade. Smith inherited a culture where educational stakeholders could feel welcome to share their perspectives. He has made sure that community is fully embedded in the institutional norm of the school. It is important to note that the school is situated in a neighborhood that is minoritized and attached to deficit language from external people. Smith shared a story: While standing outside greeting his students (as he always does) after his school had been recognized with a National Blue Ribbon award, a woman community resident who had no children in the school looked at him and commented, "We did it!" Caught off guard, he asked, "What did we do?" The resident replied, "We won the Ribbon." This interaction gave Smith the sense that "the neighborhood felt a part of [the school being recognized for a national award]."

Providing all stakeholders with a voice, including those that might not match his own, he has pushed to develop

> a culture of respect [and] warmth throughout, where everybody feels like they have a part of it [and] I disagree with some parents sometimes and . . . it's being able to disagree . . . listening to their side and not have them leave with them saying, "He didn't listen and there was no point in that meeting." If there is something that needs to be done that we are trying to compromise on a solution, I try to get parents engaged. If a parent calls me and says something is missing or we need to do this or that . . . you know, "What are your ideas for that and how can we do it? Can you be a part of that?"

Engaging parents and families and tapping into all community residents, regardless of whether they have children in the school, captures the spirit that Smith has purposely maintained from previous leadership and illustrated how he has worked to support caring ethics by dismantling the power relations that tend to take the voices and relationships with students and families of color for granted.

We characterize critical caring school leaders as leaders who understand material, historical, and cultural context and understand that responsibility for students' success goes beyond the limitations of their work system. For the Black principals we interviewed, their identity and heritage are vital considerations in their understanding of the communities in which they operate and serve as meaningful rationales for a schoolwide curriculum that goes beyond the standard, limited inclusion of important dates and facts. For white critical caring school leaders, their ability to recognize race, be vulnerable, and be open to sharing power with the community becomes important. Leaders demonstrate critical caring by transgressing the rules and structures laid out for them by the district they work in, whether it is a curriculum that erases the knowledge of people of color, instructional approaches that attempt to normalize student learning, or structures that reserve certain content for students with advanced achievement. For all critical caring school leaders, collective responsibility is historically embedded and fundamentally political, and they speak of their students and community of color and low-SES as sources of knowledge (hooks, 1994).

Tough-Love/Tough-Luck Caring

We present the *tough-love* and *tough-luck* caring perspectives to represent an ideological difference and disconnection between school leaders and children of color. School leaders who express *tough-love* caring demonstrate concern for their students but with a limited range of interest and knowledge about students different from themselves and a limited capacity for action; leaders who express *tough-luck* caring surrender and consent to their inability to uplift the academic and social well-being of students of color and students living in poverty. A significant determination of tough-love and tough-luck caring is that leaders operate from an expectation of how things should be, grounded in meritocratic beliefs. In schools with low-income or mixed-income populations, tough-love and tough-luck leaders demonstrate a savior mentality and impersonal caring, especially when it comes to the experiences of children of color.

To illustrate the perspective of tough-love in action, we spotlight Emma Badell, a seasoned white female middle school principal. She wields tremendous power in her district and is unafraid to demonstrate it and advocate for what she believes is best for her building. She advocates for her students in a community of declining educational resources, fighting for their opportunities and offering programs and services to expand access to children and parents.

Forming relationships is very important to Badell; however, she demonstrated a limitation of her caring, revealing a problem when power dynamics are not interrogated. Badell pointed to how the district recently began serving three meals a day to all students, with afternoon activities built around in-school dinner times. She identified the school as a place of refuge for students; yet the way she conveyed this is framed with a deficit perspective on children and families. For instance, when asked to describe her students, her response was:

> A good word to describe them sometimes would be needy because we are the safe haven for them. As I said, because of families, the community, and a lot of what's going on in the community, we are the stable force in their family, in their lives.

In the above response, her perspective is limited by seeing students, families, and the community as lacking in safety and stability and the school as the only stable element.

In Badell's recognition of social issues impacting her students, there is a gap in her knowledge about student interests and parental concerns for education. For example, when she offered greater access to honors courses and established new after-school programs, the number of students and families of color wishing to take advantage of them surprised her:

> In our particular building, we started a National Junior Honor Society last year and trying to instill in our kids the importance of getting good grades. And that was our kickoff year, but we were surprised at the number of students that were truly interested. So, we're trying to instill in them here the importance of coming to school and getting good grades, and these are the rewards. Afterschool programming helps because the whole academic and tutoring support is such

> an important part of that [for] the kids—we got so many applications for our afterschool program that the kids want to do it.

Badell's tough-love caring demonstrates, on the one hand, a desire to support her students academically by creating opportunities. On the other hand, these actions are restricted or diminished because she lacks recognition of any cultural wealth that her students and community have or offer (Yosso, 2005). Aligned with impersonal caring, she believes the school needs to instill and convince students about the value of education; she doesn't understand what students want and doesn't appreciate it, even when students' values are evident in their high level of interest.

As a veteran leader in the district, Badell shared several examples of negative views about families' opinions of the value of education. She positioned some families as not valuing education and some students as not understanding the importance of the subject matter. Although she maintains regular contact with parents and strives to be responsive to their calls, something is missing in her relationship with parents. While she sometimes had caveats about not wanting to generalize, she tended to paint with a broad, negative brush. Her stories suggest a personal style she characterized as tough and fair in an environment of relative scarcity and challenge, reminiscent of traits glorified by the New Jersey principal Joe Clark of the 1980s and *Lean on Me* fame.

While she lives in the community, Badell seems disconnected from the lives of the students of color in the community, especially those living in poverty. The way she talked about community and her practices show she is undoubtedly concerned for the welfare of her community of students and families, but there is no evidence of race consciousness in her leadership practice. Her caring seems to come up against a racial barrier and does not reflect a sense of collective responsibility for the students of color in the community she serves. Her impersonal caring leads to more of a savior mentality.

Working with a student population similar to Badell's is Dennis Gable, a white male high school principal. Gable talked about his leadership focus on building relationships with his students and pushing his teachers to do the same. He shared, "I feel like the relationships that are built with students impact their learning," and "I feel like my relationship with parents is very positive because I return phone calls immediately, I return emails in the evenings, and I am always accessible, and they know I care about the kids." Gable also discussed how he pushes his staff to be "authentic" with students, and students are aware when educators build a caring relationship with them and when educators do not seem to care. For him, commitment to the school and his relationship with students sits at the core of his tough-love perspective. He stated:

> I think that the commitment to this place helps build relationships with kids. It's being at every event, supporting them, holding them accountable, and being tough on them when it is necessary, but also being there to pick them up whenever they need [to be] picked up.

His response implies that he has internalized that the best leadership style for an environment with economic and social challenges is tough and fair. In the tough-love perspective, leaders determine what is suitable for their students and feel that what they are doing is in the best interest of the students and parents—yet such perspectives come from a predominantly deficit lens. Gable concluded his view on his relationship with students: "It is a tough thing to balance when a lot of times you have to be the bad guy or the disciplinarian to get your point across. It is not something that I hesitate doing."

It is evident that Gable works on building relationships and cares about the school he leads; however, it became apparent that his race consciousness resulted in deficit thinking. His reflection about student performances on state testing was, "I think that's where our students, our African American students, there is not an emphasis and importance at home, there is not an emphasis and importance at home for many of our students." From such a perspective, he generalized a deficit ideology regarding students and families that does not match his stated caring relationship.

In some instances, Gable seems mindful of the importance of race and racial differences. Still, his vision of students and families is more attuned to their socioeconomic challenges than to racial identity or challenges students and families face due to racism. When discussing some white members in the community, he shared, "I think we still have some race things here. I think that leads into, Well, if I send my child to this other school, there [are] more kids that look like them there." His perspective is complex. He recognized some race issues; at the same time, he downplayed race when he commented, "I mean our African American students, they struggle when it comes to looking at subgroups with testing, but I predominantly equate it to poverty." Poverty is the foremost concern for his practice, and he undervalued the significance of race and ethnicity.

Tough-luck caring is similar. Scott Abbott illuminated a starker approach. Abbott, a white male principal of an urban high school, said that 26–50% of his students are children of color, and 60–65% qualify for free or reduced-price lunch. He grew up in a predominantly white context and did not attend schools with many students of color. He seemed to accept low expectations for students while acknowledging the contexts of poverty in which his low-performing students live. He described his school as a combination of "haves and have-nots." Abbott has low expectations of the "Black subgroup" at his school, especially Black males. He applied a social reproduction perspective in being content with the high-achieving students scoring well enough for his school to continually earn "adequate yearly progress" in the state accountability system.

Abbott believes that parents with low educational attainment lack the social capital to know how to get their kids to and through college. Still, he does not see his school, himself, or the teachers as responsible for providing insights or tools. While Abbott talked about personal accountability a great deal, he did not articulate his ethical responsibilities as a leader to serve students from varied backgrounds and hold teachers accountable for increasing life chances for marginalized students. For example, he acknowledged the struggle in his school to support Black males with disabilities better:

> The Black subgroup. . . . the students in that subgroup that are struggling are almost all special education kids, and you know to address them specifically would be . . . I mean, it sounds terrible to say, almost like applying the same response twice. You know, we feel like what we are doing is helpful, and there are only so many hours in the day, you know, to address academic issues, and to me, that subgroup of Black males, there is more than academic issues that cause their academic difficulties *[pause]*, and we don't do anything about it frankly—unfortunately, we don't.

In the above reflection, Abbott revealed no sense of urgency or an intervention plan, although Black males and Black students generally continue to score low on standardized tests. He does not seem to be a culturally fluent leader, nor does he think he needs to be more critically, culturally, or race conscious. More importantly, he resigned himself to the underachievement of Black males. He seems to accept that tough luck cannot be avoided, providing our most drastic example of a tough-luck caring perspective.

Color-Evasive Caring in "Fortunate" Communities

Another popular approach to caring was *color-evasive caring* in what principals described as "fortunate" communities. These principals indicated caring is vital to them and their leadership practice. Still, they demonstrated neither race consciousness nor culturally responsive leadership. For these principals, their caring was color-evasive, and responsibility for students of color was nearly absent. Prior research demonstrates this lack of race consciousness or culturally responsive leadership has a profound impact on students of color, as it perpetuates a system that favors race conflict avoidance in predominantly white school settings (Diamond et al., 2021; Welton et al., 2015). On the one hand, principals who share this perspective take pride in knowing the names of all the students in their buildings, even in large buildings, and advance rigorous methods of instruction and high standards for teacher performance. On the other hand, school leaders with this caring perspective are often caught flat-footed when racial incidents happen and purposely brush off how students and families of color interpret their actions and inaction.

Most white principals who display color-evasive caring in "fortunate" communities lead predominantly white schools in suburban districts and have little to say about racial competence, as in the case of principal Laura Foster, whose story leads off this chapter. The perspective of "fortunate" communities, where the principals credit a good deal of the school's success to the involvement and expectations of the parents who send their children to school there, has a significant impact on students of color. This perspective often leads to a lack of responsibility for students of color, as caring and responsibility are tied to the concept of equality, reflecting a mindset of meritocracy, effort, and personal striving. Moreover, in nearly all cases of this approach to caring, school leaders avoided race talk and did not convey race-conscious approaches to engaging their staff and students, further exacerbating the situation for students of color.

An example is Kevin Labby, a white male who leads a high school that enrolls less than 10% students of color. He revealed a capacity for responsibility for students; for example, he stated, "You want to give them every opportunity. And that is sort of the value, is presenting options and giving kids, you want to be able to give them all regardless of background access to the best." Nevertheless, his practice does not demonstrate this value in action. There was no discussion of race in his school. As shared in Chapter 2, Labby leaves the training or development of culturally responsive teaching to teacher preparation programs and offers no in-service professional development in their current teacher roles. We see that individuals like Labby do not know what they don't know and downplay racial issues as necessary subjects of discussion in their schools.

Meanwhile, meritocracy is an essential value for Peter Ingram, a white high school principal in a predominantly white district with a range of family incomes within the middle class. Evoking some of the spirit of "tough-luck caring" described above, Ingram spoke about "our forefathers and pioneers" who "did the hard work, and no one was there handing it to them." Without the memory of racism and colonialism to contextualize his recollection of U.S. history, he used this rationale to support the value of discovery-based learning. He advocates learning by doing and hard work; students should "roll up their sleeves and do the work."

As mentioned in Chapter 2, a racial incident led Ingram's district to invite an outside organization to conduct interventional meetings with students and staff at his school. Reflecting on the school's response to such incidents, he said that students of color have important voices, and he counts on them "to tell him what they need." Locating responsibility partly in his role but primarily placing it upon the students of color seems consistent with his meritocratic philosophy of education. This approach limits a school leader's capacity for change because the responsibility is on others, not on the leader, to do the hard work. This lack of action and the tendency to blame others for the lack of change is a critical issue that needs to be addressed. While Ingram spoke to more recent self-learning of the "power" of racial training that was part of an external intervention, his other comments conveyed his more long-held beliefs on a level of personal responsibility that would be inconsistent with race-conscious and culturally responsive leadership (Khalifa, 2018).

In our study, most white principals in affluent suburban contexts adhered to color-evasive caring perspectives. Jack Maddon, the principal whose race-evasive views open Chapter 2, recognized the problem of educators' creating and believing certain generalizations, sometimes reinforced by using data to focus on subgroups. While recognizing the flaw in generalizing and being careful to self-correct his statements, he struggled to acknowledge his own generalizations. For example, in revealing his opinion on how the low-SES group of students in his school scores lower on testing, he quickly shifted his language by adding, "Not all of them, of course. I don't want to generalize." He did it again when he shared that parents of low-SES students lack the tools or are skeptical of education because of their own bad experiences. He then self-corrected: "Again, it's like a lot of them want the best for their child, don't get me wrong, I'm not trying to say."

Maddon's lack of perspective about race and culture appeared again when he addressed the unfairness of how his school is judged in the state accountability system: "You're blaming schools for all the ails that may come from their home, or whatever. And they don't want schools to blame variables. . . . I would love it if they could make the parents more accountable as well." Maddon's language seems to convey the conflicting pressures for accountability (for scores) and responsibility (for children) that Biesta (2004) highlights as so problematic. He demonstrated a critical gap in his responsibility: He cares about how others view his school in the district and others in similar districts, which constrains his ability to be more responsive. While Maddon seems to understand the contextual and societal factors that create opportunity gaps and hamper poor students of color concerning academic achievement and performance on tests, he wavered toward blaming parents, suggesting an incomplete commitment to responsibility.

Finally, Maddon demonstrated his responsibility toward students with a framework based on justice. He revealed a challenge for some teachers who need help connecting to some students' perspectives. His recognition, however, does not lead to action. While he may identify a need, something stops him from acting with a caring response. He stated, "Sometimes I want to take the whole group down there and let's visit some houses and visit some kids, 'cause it really brings perspective to it." Despite expressing such sentiment, Maddon shared that he has not implemented any professional development for his staff that would provide them with the opportunities to experience the cultural wealth (Yosso, 2005) of his racialized and marginalized communities. While he critiqued others for their lack of knowledge about students and families, he did some blaming of his own. Leaders who tend to blame others (be it individuals, institutions, groups, or policies) limit their ability to make meaningful changes for marginalized students. For leaders in color-evasive caring in "fortunate" communities, either race is nonexistent, or a strong foundation of meritocracy and generalization with deficit language is the norm.

Caring With (Minimal) Responsiveness

The fourth caring approach is what we call caring with (minimal) responsiveness. We place minimal within parentheses to symbolize the limits to that responsiveness revealed when paired with respondents', other, more limiting comments. Leaders within this frame of reference demonstrate recognition of racial awareness, but it only partially results in such leaders committing to actionable steps; instead, they enact limited opportunities to demonstrate a more robust, responsible caring for students of color and low SES. Caring with (minimal) responsiveness is characterized by school leaders having a fluid shifting between race awareness and color-evasive perspectives, revealing no actionable steps in their leadership toolkit to resolve racial issues in their schools, and worrying about being labeled as a social justice advocate. These principals occupy contradictory spaces because they align with the cultural and systemic school institutions that nurture such responses. Leaders who demonstrate this theme can be found in schools with a mix of students or predominantly white student demographics.

As we discuss in Chapter 2, among the suburban leaders are several with emergent race-conscious perspectives, in contrast to the color-evasive caring evidenced by some of their suburban peers. In some of these settings, student populations have been changing, and principals have been preparing teachers to be more responsive. As this theme suggests, there was capacity among some suburban principals for race-conscious caring. This capacity is significant for schools experiencing changing demographics and for countering the invisibility that isolated students of color may experience in predominantly white schools—and/or the hypervisibility when it comes to discipline issues or the exoticizing of students of color athletically or artistically (Carey, 2019; Ellison, 2013).

John Hall identified building relationships as an essential part of his leadership approach. A white male, he leads an elementary school with 5%–10% students of color and 15%–20% qualifying for free or reduced-price lunch. In contrast to some other school leaders in suburban districts, Hall drew his appreciation and value for diversity in students from his previous experiences working in a more diverse district. According to Hall, students of color "bring a lot to the classroom," and teachers need "to find a way to incorporate those students, their backgrounds, their beliefs, their cultures into what you're doing in the classroom." Hall openly shared his belief that "racism or prejudice . . . still exists a lot today," and he acknowledged his responsibility to challenge teachers' deficit perspectives about students. In his predominantly white school, an increasing number of students were becoming eligible for free or reduced-price lunch, and teachers complained that students were not performing as well as in the past. He attempted to guide teachers to rethink their instructional practices rather than blame students or resort too quickly to special education referrals when other approaches had not been tried.

However, for principals like Hall leading predominantly white schools, it was not always evident that appreciative views about children of color translated to critical caring. At times, these leaders demonstrated a semblance of color-evasiveness. For example, when asked about the skills of his predominantly white teaching staff to work with Black students at his school, Hall responded, "To me, it's common sense, and anybody that's a teacher should have those skills to work with them. They should, but they don't, you know." Informing his perspective about his teachers was his personal belief that to "me personally, color and race and that stuff doesn't matter to me. It's more, what are we going to do for that kid?" Such a response reveals the complexity when leaders hold the dual perspective of being race-conscious while minimizing race's significance.

Meanwhile, Ethan Knight, a white male superintendent of a mixed urban and suburban district, also revealed the contradictions of this caring theme. Knight said his role as a superintendent was to work with the educators in the district and get them to care about their students. He has told teachers during staff meetings, "I want you to care for children in your room. I want you to care for them as individual human beings—with stories and lives, needs and desires and that *you* can help them." It is evident that Knight holds a strong principle of caring ethics, and he revealed a race-conscious perspective at many points. For example, when asked for his understanding of the achievement gap, part of his response was: "The educational system that we have built and put in place is great if you're Caucasian. It's not so good if you're African American or Latino or some other ethnicities."

However, Knight also demonstrated contradictions when discussing the efforts in his district to make the curriculum connect more with the diversity of students in his district, stating it should be "culturally relevant, but again, I really hate that term. But I can't think of another one at the moment." Further, while he also believes that discussion of cultural competency and equitable pedagogical strategies with educators are connected to social justice issues, he made clear, "I am not a social radical." Holding such perspectives raises the question of how authentically Knight can implement transformative and culturally responsive practices when sharing a disdain for such topics and resistance to identifying with social justice principles.

These two examples present the complexity and limitations found in caring with (minimal) responsiveness: Understanding racial differences and systems of oppression does not inevitably imply culturally responsive leadership or success in building capacity for culturally responsive practices among school personnel. As a distinct approach, caring with minimal responsiveness captures a gap between openness to critical caring and practices that enact commitment to collective responsibility.

CONCLUSION

This chapter provides examples of school leaders who exhibit critical caring and those who exhibit impersonal caring, which we characterize as tough-love/tough-luck caring, color-evasive caring in "fortunate communities," and caring with (minimal) responsiveness. Caring in these cases is either not race-conscious or minimally race-conscious, and while leaders routinely embraced caring, the leaders also conveyed deficit and victimization perspectives about children and families. This amounts to impersonal caring. With neither context nor disposition to guide the building of capacity for critical caring, school leaders who demonstrate impersonal caring need to be willing to engage race as a significant area of difference. We attribute the wide variation in ethical perspectives we found in our study to an ethics gap in school leadership practice—a lack of attention in principal preparation, professional development, and practice on how to lead a school community around caring for the needs and interests of a racially, culturally, and socioeconomically diverse population of students.

While our study has found critical caring lacking predominantly among leaders from white and middle-class backgrounds, it should be noted that leaders of color can also exercise the power of impersonal caring in various settings. The clear danger of impersonal caring is the perpetuation of erasure of people of color and their experiences. Educational leaders have a crucial role to play in implementing change. When combined with race consciousness, attention to justice, and ethical praxis, we believe critical caring can lead to profound changes in practices, structures, and systems.

Critical caring is a more appropriate form of caring for school leaders, and it requires relational caring, which is the desire to experience difference voluntarily and to be open to learning beyond one's own limited experience about the wants and needs of children and families in one's care. It requires a disposition akin to Todd's (2004) notion of a *pedagogy of ignorance*, in which the educator operates from the position of not assuming knowledge of others and instead is interested in learning from others. Critical caring is a practice—it is an embodied ethic with continuity between prior experiences and current school context.

As we explore further in Chapter 5, narrative ethics—learning from the moral lives of others and ourselves—can help with developing more critical caring. One practical way to engage with narrative ethics is to seek out networks of school leaders known for their equity commitment and listen to their stories of antiracist work. Another practical way is authentically creating space and time for student voices—particularly students of color—and respecting and listening with intent to learn. With students' voices, educators need to conduct critical introspective reflections that examine issues of power between adults and students to allow students' narratives to be heard to inform praxis. Witnessing provides one potential approach to learning from narratives so that leaders' ethical perspectives can incorporate their understanding and connection to others' lives and experiences (Ritter, 2008). Black, Indigenous, and people of color in educational communities need to be centered rather than their work, experiences, and wisdom appropriated.

Finally, we believe school leaders need to work on creating critical caring collectively, so that the collective responsibility that is so important to critical caring can grow in a school. It is important to cultivate critical caring in teachers as groups of educators, as members of school communities, who can work together and create a collective capacity in their schools to respond to systemic challenges. Pragmatically, we acknowledge the challenge of building critical caring, yet it is an essential ethical approach that leaders should strive for.

CHAPTER 4

Justice Leadership

Working for Justice in the Gaps

Figure 4.1. Justice Leadership

Allison Edwards is a Black female principal of a suburban elementary school in a relatively wealthy district. Her school enrolls less than 5% children of color; 10 to 15% of students qualify for free or reduced-price lunch, and that number at the time of our interview was growing. Edwards was new to the district, and building and valuing relationships with her students has been very important to her. Edwards proclaimed, "I *love* my kids," and believes her relationships with students "can make it easier for them to come to school." Her leadership is built upon ensuring that every student receives an appropriate education, "meaning that they are cared for, they are loved, and that the external factors that affect them—they are acknowledged. But we still are able to carry on with the business during the school day."

Edwards has encountered resistance from some of her teachers to her approach to working with students of color and those of a low socioeconomic status. Edwards observed that some of her staff members used data to determine a student's level of ability and did not do the necessary work to improve the educational experiences of those students they considered to be underperforming. Edwards believes teachers can use test data to guide their instructional practices, yet she sees some teachers blaming students for not learning; after all, their instruction works for the majority of students. Her response to such teachers was that "we no longer have that option to let those—that [bottom] 25 [percent] down here—to just let them go; it's not appropriate." This statement shows Edwards's resolve that students not be ignored.

Edwards set out to create a culture of open and honest dialogue with her staff. These open dialogues sometimes become fierce and sometimes "more than heated, but I feel like if we don't allow each other to say what is on our mind and what we really feel . . . about standardized [testing] and accountability, we wouldn't be a productive school." Edwards said, "I need to change the culture" of teachers using data as an excuse to place students in lower level classes.

Edwards exhibited many of the qualities of justice leadership, which we explore in this chapter as the third aspect of race-conscious leadership ethics. As she identified the challenges she faced pushing for the educational opportunities that every student in her school deserves, she came to realize she would need to lead these teachers to be more successful in addressing equity and to encourage her fellow principals in the district to center equity in their work. Guiding teachers to improve is a key function of school leadership, and guiding teachers with justice leadership means placing equity and justice goals at the center of practice. With her unyielding optimism, Edwards pointed out that challenging deficit ideas "will be difficult, but it will be achievable."

THE COMPONENTS OF JUSTICE LEADERSHIP

We define justice leadership as having three components: (1) an opportunity gap disposition, (2) an asset-based perspective, and (3) principled resistance (see Figure 4.1). In this chapter, we draw from the research literature that supports these three components. Next, we reveal justice leadership in the attitudes and practices of the leaders we interviewed, and we analyze what it looks like when justice leadership is absent or partially evident. In the absence of justice leadership, leaders emphasize achievement gaps, focus on technical and rational concerns with raising cumulative test scores, and demonstrate a limited capacity for addressing gaps in opportunity. As we show, justice leaders address "justice in the gaps" as either opportunity gaps, achievement gaps, or some combination thereof. They see gaps in student success as arising from lack of opportunity and hold a disposition for reducing or eliminating racial disparities with a focus of critical caring responsibility for students.

The Opportunity Gap

Justice leaders recognize that gaps students experience in their schools are fundamentally gaps in *opportunity*, which are perpetuated by structures and conditions, some within leaders' control and some reflecting large social systems (Carter & Welner, 2013; Milner, 2020). In response, justice leaders create structures and conditions within their control that foster opportunities for all children, while also working with other leaders to change their school systems and structures.

The adoption of the No Child Left Behind (NCLB) Act in 2001 and Every Student Succeeds Act (ESSA) in 2015, with their emphasis on standards-based, high-stakes accountability reform, has pressed school leaders to become more aware of educational disparities. A stated intention of both NCLB and ESSA was for accountability systems to challenge public K–12 school institutions to produce improved achievement results for all students (Fusarelli, 2004). One outcome has been the prominent discussion of using data to identify and remediate racial and class gaps in educational success. Districts and schools have greater access now to various forms of data, providing multiple tools for school leaders to identify patterns in student learning and to focus on particular areas to develop interventions and to revise curriculum. As borne out in schools in our study, data emphasize the existence of differential achievement test scores by race, social class, and sometimes a combination of both. Of course, not all schools disaggregate their data by race and class, and even in those that do, methods to use that data effectively are not widely shared.

Advocates of more equitable educational spaces have responded to these ineffective efforts by arguing for a shift in how educational inequities are framed. Multiple education scholars have called for a shift in focus from an achievement gap to an "opportunity gap" (Milner, 2020), an "educational debt" (Ladson-Billings, 2006), or a "receivement gap" (Venzant-Chambers, 2009), to indicate a shift in language and worldview that challenges educators to deepen and broaden analyses of their educational practices. Historically, race has had an influence on how individuals perceive differences in student achievement scores in the United States (Carter & Welner, 2013; Howard, 2010). The gaps in test scores between white students and students of color have predominantly been portrayed by policymakers and many researchers as impartially determined failings of individual students (English, 2002).

Establishing and attending to an opportunity gap disposition is helpful and necessary because public K–12 educational systems were established in the United States within inherently inequitable social structures, and social policies have done little to challenge those structures and conditions. Social structures can either enable or impede any well-intentioned policy (Chu, 2019; da Silva et al., 2007). Under such conditions, identifying gaps in achievement is insufficient; as Boykin and Noguera (2011) argue, "If we are not willing to acknowledge and confront the numerous barriers to the opportunity to learn that many poor and minority children experience, greater progress in reducing racial disparities will be difficult to bring about" (p. 7).

The school leader is a vital agent for this important work of attending to opportunity gaps. As Leithwood et al. (2020) argue, evidence suggests that strong school leadership has a significant effect on the quality of teaching and learning in schools, which in turn has a direct effect on student experience. In our analysis of school leaders in this chapter, we demonstrate the importance of the ways they talk about differentials in opportunity and achievement. We can expect how school leaders engage their practice with the "gaps" will in turn influence students' educational experience. As we show, an opportunity gap orientation leads to more promising practices for educational equity.

Student Assets

The recognition of student assets is the second component of justice leadership. Justice leaders see children and families as possessing strengths and abilities routinely suppressed and ignored by adults in positions of authority, social institutions, and social arrangements. To counter the pervasive deficit perspective that permeates public education and causes educators to blame students, justice leaders draw from a historically and structurally situated critical consciousness of the material realities associated with oppression: the documented and real effects of racism, for instance, and the material struggles of those living in poverty. Justice leaders hold an appreciation of the strengths that communities of color bring to their school experiences despite the myriad gaps in opportunity they experience through marginalization and subjugation.

In previous chapters, we address the importance of treating children and communities as having assets rather than deficits. In Chapter 2, we incorporate an asset-based perspective into the model of race consciousness, and in Chapter 3, we showed that critical caring depends on an asset-based perspective and engrossment in the wants and needs of children. In the context of justice leadership, the emphasis is on the significance of an asset-based perspective for understanding the social conditions and structures that constrain the educational opportunities of children. An asset-based perspective is essential for the kind of critical consciousness school leaders need to operate within the social structures and conditions that seek to constrain their work for justice.

An asset-based perspective arises in response to the highly dominant "deficit perspective." Once one grasps the concept of a deficit perspective, one clearly sees the role this nefarious concept has had in educational practice and educational research. As Richard Valencia (1997) explained in his edited book, *The Evolution of Deficit Thinking,* deficit thinking is the attribution of failure (such as failure to meet an established benchmark) to characteristics of individuals who then need to be fixed or remediated. In some cases, deficits get attributed to deficiencies associated with racialization and marginalization. The language of deficit and disadvantage positions children living in poverty and children of color as outsiders requiring protection to save them from their circumstances (or perhaps from parents deemed as neglectful or as unaware of the best interests of their children). Educators, even those who understand themselves as desiring to serve disadvantaged children, fail when they position themselves as benevolent interventionists to fill gaps they blame on children and their families.

Educators perpetuate deficit perspectives when they do not know the real lives of the children and families in their school communities. Breaking down the deficit perspectives of practicing school leaders in our graduate classes through critical questions, it is often clear that educators hear stories of apparent neglect and then attribute those across entire groups. Doing the work of racism and classism, leaders regularly tell sad stories about their students and attribute the sad part of the story to a vaguely cultural cause, forming twisted notions of what families of color and/or families living in poverty value or don't value and contrasting such unfounded views to their own values. These perspectives negate for entire groups of children and families the agency they possess to live creative and fulfilling lives.

To counter such negative thinking, critical scholar Tara Yosso (2005) developed the important concept of *community cultural wealth* as an alternative to the popular notion that children who do not achieve as well in school lack cultural capital. Instead, Yosso emphasizes the breadth of knowledges that children and families bring to every encounter, even or especially when those knowledges are systematically underappreciated by institutions grounded in dominant culture. Community cultural wealth is a source of strength and transformation; understanding this has led to new approaches to educational leadership practice (Khalifa et al., 2016). Enacting an asset-based perspective requires developing a different kind of disposition toward school communities. As a disposition open to learning *from* and *with* school communities and not *for* them it leads to questioning standardized measures of achievement imposed through inherently inequitable educational research and policy.

Principled Resistance

The third component of justice leadership is principled resistance. To work against constraining structures, conditions, and practices, leaders need principled resistance to the pressures that would harm or hinder the educational experiences of children. Principled resistance is action based on core principles (of justice, fairness, and ideals of the good) taken to resist the harmful exercises of power that external forces pressure school leaders to perform. In their positions of power, school leaders need to ascertain when they are put in a position to exercise power unjustly and draw from their principles—both professional and personal—to act justly. These pressures come from all directions—above, below, and beside the level of the school leader. Principled resistance requires clarity of purpose and intent in educating children of color and children living in poverty, developing curricula that are culturally sustaining and enriching, and guiding teachers' own capacity building for race-conscious caring practice.

Alternatives to the achievement gap and deficit thinking require resisting social pressures that would have those in powerful positions perpetuate inequities. As Ruth Johnson (2002) has argued, any push for higher expectations for all students will encounter resistance. School leaders facing external demands for accountability to test scores have been pressured to make educational decisions that foreground test score performance rather than the educational experiences of all children. Those schools labeled low-performing and threatened with takeover feel the pressure acutely (Carnoy et al., 2003). Leaders facing such external pressures are regularly tempted to convert the external pressure they feel into internal pressure for test score improvement (Gunzenhauser, 2012). Resistance to the normalization that accompanies powerful examinations requires clarity of purpose. For example, leaders need to know when to resist curriculum materials that sacrifice rich content and cultural responsiveness for test readiness, how to prepare teachers to engage these materials critically, and what battles to fight to insist on high-quality instruction for all children, not just those who test into high categories.

Leaders need to recognize the role they play in helping teachers become stronger educators in the face of pressures for test score performance and the role they play in fostering equity-conscious school cultures. The differential effects of accountability policy on schools already positioned to do well on standardized tests and schools that are targeted for improvement (Carnoy et al., 2003) should be a clear indication that current structures and conditions are biased against schools that enroll the most children of color and children living in poverty. As we show, these differential effects also play out in schools with small percentages of children of color and children living in poverty. The temptation is to minoritize children and ignore the responsibility schools have to provide students with educational opportunities. Pulling students with lower test scores from arts instruction for additional test preparation is an example of educational practices that limit opportunities for children. As educational leadership researchers Shoho, Merchant, and Lugg (2011) argue, to address issues of fairness and equity, school leaders "must be prepared to adapt, change, and most important, challenge existing educational policies and practices, whether they originate at the building, state, or national level" (p. 46).

Principled resistance is an essential and challenging task for a school leader as an exercise of power against the normalization of the examination, described in Gunzenhauser's previous book, *The Active/Ethical Professional: A Framework for Responsible Educators* (2012). In summary,

Gunzenhauser demonstrates how accountability policy distorts educators' practice; he urges educators to actively resist the normalizing power relations of accountability policy and act from an ethics of social responsibility for all children. The book follows the social philosophy of Michel Foucault (1995/1975, 2005/2001) in his analysis of how modern institutions discipline individuals and try to make them docile bodies. The institution of the school, like the institution of the prison, fosters self-discipline in individuals, who willingly act in ways that curtail the possibilities for action (in current parlance, they obey in advance [Snyder, 2017]). Through "technologies of power," institutions become sites where persons exercise power in relation to others, in ways they may or may not intend (and for Foucault [1995/1975], a technology can be any social process that has embedded rules and structures).

Related to school context, examples of technologies that leaders need to address with principled resistance include dress codes, student organization rules, and examinations, whether they are chapter tests, state assessments, or SATs. To the extent that educators understand the rules of the technologies as social process and treat them as meaningful, those processes can be rather powerful. Those that don't measure up to what is termed normal by the process are then subject to being named as deviant; they qualify for remediation, lose access to privileges, and are made miserable or pushed out. For instance, a dress code can help establish what counts as an acceptable body, policies that student organizations must follow can discourage the creation of a Black student affinity group, or an SAT score can be treated as a definition of an appropriately prepared college student. Through such social processes, schools establish what it means to be normal. However, schools don't do this work by themselves. Colleges participate in exercises of power that make the SAT more or less powerful, for instance; note that the most selective colleges were the first institutions to make the SAT optional for their applicants, a calculated exercise of power that does not lessen selective colleges' positions of power. As less-selective colleges eliminate the SAT requirement and fewer students take the test or submit their scores, it becomes less powerful.

The reason to explain these exercises of power is to surface how slippery and diffusively power operates when we understand power from a Foucaultian standpoint. All of these technologies of power require the acceptance of individuals in micropolitical exercises of power. A similar process is what sociologists refer to as reification—the treatment of social constructions as real. Standardized tests are social constructions, in other words, and they are real (and powerful) to the extent that we treat them as real (and powerful). Standardized testing is only one kind of technology existing as a powerful social process in schools. Any policy, however well-intended, can become a powerful social process. Policies certainly reflect the intentions of their authors, but when it comes to controlling people, their effects as they are enacted are what matter most, particularly to students who are in any way minoritized and especially to those minoritized by race and socioeconomic status.

When school leaders act, they are part of networks of power that exist prior to them. Institutional racism precedes any school leader action. Symbolic words and actions draw on social power to further minoritize students; for example, imagine a high school parent orientation meeting where the director of student activities shows a slide of popular clubs to give parents a sense of which clubs students could join. She tells parents that not all clubs are listed; in fact, two particular popular clubs—the Gay-Straight Alliance and the Black Student Organization—are not listed. Their symbolic absence, whether intended or not, is consonant with social pressure to invisibilize LGBTQ and Black students. To carry the point through, here the school leaders have missed a simple opportunity to resist the social and political pressure to make nondominant persons unspeakable. The leaders could have exercised principled resistance; they missed an opportunity to demonstrate justice leadership (as well as care and race consciousness) by listing the clubs and indicating that they are popular and active.

Incorporating principled resistance into justice leadership requires a leader to have a clear sense of how power operates, to identify how their actions affect others, especially those minoritized, and to create conditions where the effects of power are made clear so that they can be changed and replaced. A leader needs some clarity about how and why they are acting—that's the principled portion. They also need to resist the exercises of power that lead them to minoritize persons, to evade race, and to place them outside of the realm of caring. As is the focus of this particular chapter, they need to resist curtailing students' educational opportunities.

JUSTICE LEADERSHIP IN ACTION

Educational leaders' dispositions toward achievement and opportunity shape how they perceive and enact justice in the gaps. While almost all our interview participants attested to being advocates for educational equity, school and district contexts undoubtedly shape leaders' dispositions toward justice leadership. Our data suggest that some school leaders who enroll a critical mass of students of color will see gaps in opportunity and then build conditions and structures to create more opportunity that builds upon students' strengths and interests.

While we found some efforts by school leaders to adjust their dispositions toward language accentuating opportunity gaps, many school leaders continue to perceive the achievement gap in an abstract and technical manner. For instance, only two participants specifically used the term "opportunity" to describe the gaps they experience in their schools. Two others in this category conveyed the concept without the term. Of the other 18, some used language that suggested a developing opportunity gap framework (perhaps without knowing about or recalling the concept). Some kept their language abstract and technical, and others seemed to ignore gaps entirely. We also heard some leaders point to a gap in their students' efforts.

Based on study of these variations in perspectives on the idea of educational gaps, we argue that a school leader's disposition toward gaps seems to influence whether and to what extent they take action to address justice in the gaps. School leaders are certainly influenced by both personal experience and school context (Hallinger et al., 1996). Table 4.1 sorts the respondents into four categories based on their dispositions toward justice leadership—those who hold an opportunity gap disposition, those who demonstrate an achievement gap disposition, and two subgroups of leaders who straddle those two dispositions. In what follows, we explain each with examples from the interviews.

The Opportunity Gap Disposition

For the participants who are mindful of the gap as a gap in *opportunity*, the disposition toward their students is asset-based, grounded in the value of community, and expressed as a commitment to them and their communities that they intend their students to see and understand. These leaders exercise justice leadership by resisting attempts by their districts, teachers,

Table 4.1. Dispositions of Participating School Leaders

Achievement Gap (Abstract/Technical)	Indeterminate Straddlers*	Evolving Straddlers**	Justice Leadership
Kevin Labby	Bill Roberts	Arthur Lawrence	Scarlett Johnson
Paul Eaby	Ethan Knight	James Smith	Peter Ingram
Logan Sanders	Dennis Gable	Jack Maddon	Maya Gaffney
Laura Foster		Andrew Baker	Allison Edwards
Scott Abbott		Elizabeth Ida	
Emma Badell		John Hall	
Ella Klein			
Dan Gibson			
Michael Labette			

* School leaders whose disposition has elements of both achievement and opportunity gap, but not clearly determined to be asset-based.

**These school leaders expressed the gap in a technical and/or abstract manner, yet their approach is asset-based with discussions focused on issues of equity and some tenets of opportunity gap.

and society at large to blame and marginalize children and families. Further, these leaders' dispositions are connected to their positionalities—their individual histories and identities in relation to race, ethnicity, social class, and experience (Alcoff, 1988; Milner, 2007; Shapiro & Gross, 2013).

Among the school leaders in the study, Scarlett Johnson responded with the firmest critique of the concept of the achievement gap:

> So, that is something that I hate, that terminology, so I don't use it. I don't like the word, the terminology achievement gap, because that puts it on the child. It kind of blames the child . . . because it is their achievement, it's a gap in your achievement versus a white child's achievement.

With some resentment, Johnson described her antipathy toward the language of the achievement gap because it places a judgment on the student. She replaced it with a clear understanding of what the literature calls the opportunity gap: "What I like to call it is an opportunity gap. Our students have not had the same opportunities. . . . But, as soon as we give them those opportunities, they can achieve at or above the level of white students."

Johnson's disposition toward the opportunity gap is further explained by the value she ascribed to the diverse population of students in her school and neighborhood:

> *Flores:* What value do Black and Latino students bring to your school?
> *Johnson:* Tremendous value, tremendous. That's the foundation of our school . . . I love diversity, pass that flavor, [it] teaches us so much, that we can teach each other. . . . Our students . . . they bring the richness of their cultural experiences . . . They bring us certain strengths and resiliency to them. That regardless of what we don't have, regardless of what people think about us, regardless of what our community doesn't have, we still are strong, we are still proud, we still care, we still choose to be here, and that strength, that's what keeps us going.

In a lighthearted tone, Johnson indicated her belief that diversity is mutually enriching. Furthermore, she declared the community she serves influences her dispositions. In the passage above, when she talked about the community, she shifted from "they" and "them" to "we" and "us," communicating a positionality connected with her students, a positionality distinct from most other school leaders in the sample. Johnson named her school as a community and identifies with the community in which she works. She merged herself with the students and demonstrated immersion in the community in ways other leaders did not.

As evident elsewhere in the interview, Johnson's disposition toward her students reflects a personal and professional commitment. Students' perseverance drives her; she said she could not be an educator "without our kids saying 'I am still here, I am still in it, I still want to be here.' And they show up every day with the same attitude—'I am here'—and that is powerful." She recognized resilience as a particularly important asset. For Johnson, leadership means providing her students with the same opportunities as those who are more affluent or who attend more affluent schools.

Two other leaders presented similar sense-making about an opportunity gap but without using that specific language. Both are Black women, Maya Gaffney and Allison Edwards. Gaffney had just finished her first year as principal of an urban middle school after serving as an assistant principal for several years at another school. Her language about the achievement gap incorporated concern for equity:

> Our situation is to look at things from an equity standpoint. Equity does not mean equal, but right now I think the achievement gap is largely attributed to giving everybody the same thing, because . . . we don't look at how people learn things differently, we don't look at cultural competency. . . . [When teachers tell me] "I treat all of my students the same" . . . well, to do that is a disservice, because they are different.

In this statement, Gaffney demonstrated the distinction between equity and equality and further conveyed the importance of educators acknowledging cultural differences among students.

Something of Gaffney's disposition can be understood in how she prioritizes relationships with her students:

> I try to get to know them, know where they live, know their parents, understand their circumstances . . . We have kids that come to our school, they have lots of baggage they come with. And so I try to make sure I have relationships with kids so that if there is something going on with them that I need to know that is impacting their ability to learn, I can figure out what I can do, so that obstacle is not in the way. While they are here, for the time that they are here, it's to make things as smooth as possible, so they can focus on learning.

This statement shows something of the resolve of Gaffney's concern for appreciating students coming with assets; regardless of the circumstances that her students face, her responsibility as a school leader is to make sure students have the opportunity to learn.

Gaffney identified two forms of opportunity gaps relevant in her context—her school district's gifted and talented model and access to highly effective teachers—that, according to her, perpetuate racial achievement gaps. Herein she shared her interrogation of inequities in the system of schooling:

> [Students in the gifted program] are in separate classes, they have separate education, sometimes they have better teachers, and so that [contributes] to it too. The other part of that I think sometimes also is . . . when we think about teachers and quality of the teachers, our students who are the most neediest weren't getting the most highly qualified teachers, so they were behind even more.

Here, Gaffney presented two practices that researchers have widely documented and presented as a common cause of the opportunity gap: assigning the most qualified teachers to gifted programs and advanced courses and assigning the newest and least qualified teachers to the students who would most benefit from strong and experienced teachers (e.g., Miranda et al., 2014; Oakes, 2008).

Like Gaffney, Allison Edwards had just completed her first year as principal of her elementary school, after being an assistant principal in another district. Edwards situated the achievement gap as based on students' race and SES. Edwards said that the value and meaning of education "is to give everyone *hopefully* an equal opportunity, a fair chance at being successful. And not just money successful, but being a productive citizen." Moreover, she made the following remark about what education would be like if she were in charge:

> It would be ensuring that every child is getting an appropriate education . . . meaning that they were cared for, that they were loved, that their external factors that affect them, they are acknowledged. But, you know, still be able to carry on with the business during the school day.

As the above response illustrates, Edwards named a major argument made by opportunity gap scholars—acknowledging the external factors to engage effective in-school practices. She named her responsibility to educate all students, regardless of external factors, maintaining a strengths-based perspective. It's her responsibility, in other words, to bridge the opportunity gap. For Johnson, Gaffney, and Edwards, their positionalities as Black women contribute to their dispositions toward their students (Alcoff, 1988), and their ethical frames of reference are informed by their personal histories (Walker & Snarey, 2004). Leaders with white or male positionalities also drew from their background experiences, identities, and ideologies to talk about gaps in achievement and opportunity, including Peter Ingram, a white male leader introduced in Chapter 2. While Ingram used the language of opportunity gap (and is the fourth of four leaders in this category), its incorporation into his other beliefs suggests a distinctly different view of his role as principal.

When he first talked about gaps in achievement, Ingram immediately talked about opportunity: "The achievement gap to me is opportunity. . . . We're with students seven and a half hours a day, 180 days a year—that's an opportunity." Variation in opportunity comes from outside the school, what Ingram referred to as "outside baggage." As a school leader, his approach is "to minimize the baggage and to put them in the educational environment where they can find something that they can embrace." Further, he commented that "our job is to find that little spark that each and every student can embrace. And I think you do that with proper coaching, and differentiating your lesson, so that every kid feels welcome."

Ingram's perspective on opportunity needs to be coupled with his perspective on meritocracy, as discussed in Chapter 3, in which Ingram referenced the hard work of "our forefathers and the pioneers." Ingram had this to say about the relation between education and opportunity:

> Education provides the threshold for opportunity. Some people think the world is full of opportunity. I believe that you make your own opportunity. And through education, that once again opens the doors so that a person will enable themself to have multiple opportunities and not be one-dimensional.

Similarly meritocratic in this passage, Ingram conveyed the importance of "making your own opportunity." Ingram went on to clarify the role of education in providing opportunities. A variety of opportunities are necessary for all students to provide "a service back to the community." For Ingram, it is the responsibility of the school to provide opportunities and the responsibility of students to take advantage of those opportunities. In comparison to the other leaders in this category, it is not clear how far Ingram is willing to go to create opportunities that all of his students would recognize and embrace. Recall from Chapter 2 that Ingram does not express race consciousness. It is clear that while having a perspective about differential opportunity is important for race-conscious leadership ethics, it is insufficient for addressing the structural inequities that have led to differential opportunity. So we see the need to have both the opportunity gap disposition and race consciousness.

Abstract/Technical Leadership

In contrast to justice leadership, we found a more prevalent set of dispositions in our school leader participants—an abstract/technical leadership that combined an abstract disposition toward equity with a technical concern for gaps in achievement test scores. This orientation spanned many types of schools and districts. School leaders in schools with a small percentage of students of color revealed a lack of direct strategies to reduce the gaps. For example, Kevin Labby, a white male in his 4th year as principal of a suburban high school with less than 10% students of color, does not use data to support his students of color. As Labby said: "There is no specific plan for that, you know. If we see a group isn't performing like other groups we use that information to take action." This statement is consistent with his further remarks about his school context and his lack of a stated disposition toward supporting students of color. His claim is abstract ("If we see a group . . . we take action"), but his leadership practice does not take gaps into account.

In the last two chapters, we mention another leader in this category, Scott Abbott. A white male, he was in his 5th year as principal of an urban high school in an old steel town. His student population—high poverty and nearly equal percentages of white and Black students—could provide a context to spark a justice orientation. Yet we found that was not the case. Recall his conversation in Chapter 2 with a teacher who wanted to know more about teaching Black male students how to read. Recall he rebuffed the teacher's interest. He repeated that sentiment when he explained how the school uses data to support students. Asked how he uses data to support the diverse population of students in his school, he started with a laugh and followed with a pause: "We don't do it in general . . . Everybody knows that you should be using it . . . but it is so time consuming and we have so many kids who need support that we don't, we just don't do it." On the one hand, Abbott recognizes the abstract need for attending to gaps. On the other hand, he lacks a framework for making it happen. As in interviews with other principals of schools with a combination of both white and nonwhite low-SES students, Abbott had no language or rationale for cultivating a specifically race-conscious strategy, and he saw time as an obstacle. While the gaps in achievement are evident and acknowledged, there is neither the capacity to respond nor the conditions in place to develop the capacity. When confronted with resistance or restrictions, Abbott's disposition commits him to inaction.

Another principal with an abstract/technical disposition is Dan Gibson, a suburban elementary principal described in Chapter 2 as having a race-evasive perspective. Gibson described the achievement gap in his school between the general student body and the approximately one-fourth of the student population qualifying for free or reduced-price lunch:

> Whether it's socioeconomic issues they may be having, home life issues they may be having, it's those identified students that typically don't achieve as well in school because of those factors. So because of those factors, they achieve lower than the students that have those things in place at home, maybe have the experiences, the socioeconomic status. They're more exposed and better prepared for school so they achieve at a higher, faster rate than those without.

In this passage Gibson conveyed the kind of deficit thinking that is so common among educators describing individual students and student groups, such as students testing below the norm, students of color, and students living in low socioeconomic conditions. Gibson used the word "opportunity" to describe the students' background experiences. About students who have lower achievement scores, he said, "It's those students that I guess have right off the bat, maybe less opportunity." He emphasized, "It is truly where they begin and that they begin with less opportunity, I guess." While he used the word opportunity, Gibson used it in a different way, to describe the deficits ascribed to their families and what they have provided them, rather than the opportunities that schools have provided them to meet their needs.

As mentioned in Chapter 2, Gibson's interventions are built around correcting for supposed home-based deficits:

> It kind of goes back to how would I change the world of education, and is there a way, a better way to meet the needs of those kids that may just tread water in math and reading all the time in the regular ed setting, because they don't have some of the support at home, let's say.

Gibson used qualifications around the description of the interpretation of home-based deficits. He said, "those kids . . . *may* just tread water" (emphasis added but not necessarily implied in his speaking) and conjectured as an example ("let's say") that "they don't have some of the support at home." Despite the qualifications, once he has ascribed deficits, there is no accounting for or expectations of strengths or assets. This is evident in the opening of the quotation: While interventions he would like to try—such as tutoring and afterschool opportunities—may be effective and welcome, it seems the efforts he would make to serve the students would require that he "change the world of education."

This passage provides an example of a missed opportunity to exercise principled resistance. Gibson can be seen as accepting the received pressures to raise achievement scores and whatever conditions exist that he depicted as the "world of education." Exercising his power through abstract/technical leadership, his goal is raising achievement test scores, and his rationales are built upon assumed deficits in students' home lives. Further, limiting the language of "opportunity" to mean his perception of their support at home, Gibson is left without language to describe opportunities that schools have not provided these students—opportunities that would enhance their learning rather than merely enabling them to "just tread water."

Straddlers

Recognizing the complexity under which school leaders are situated, not all school leaders fit neatly into the two categories of justice leadership and abstract/technical leadership. We found several leaders in our sample who straddle these two orientations. These school leaders initially defined the achievement gap using the technical language. At the same time, these leaders also demonstrated a semblance of an alternative and shifting interpretation on the gap. Nine of the 22 school leaders were straddlers—five in urban settings, one in an inner-ring suburban setting, and three in outer-ring suburban settings. Each of these school leaders was influenced by their dispositions, beliefs, educational experiences, and work experience. We have grouped the nine straddlers into two subcategories: six "evolving straddlers," who appeared to be growing toward justice leadership, and three "indeterminate straddlers," whose views were difficult to categorize.

Evolving Straddlers. The six evolving straddlers appeared not only to be straddling the two previous categories of justice leadership and abstract/technical leadership, but also to be shifting or growing in their thinking more toward justice leadership. In how they talked about their practice, there seemed to be clear possible trajectories of development.

Arthur Lawrence, a Black male in his first year as principal of an urban magnet school that combined middle and high school grades, defined the so-called gap as the difference between how his school educates Black and other minoritized students in comparison to white students. In sharing his disposition, Lawrence revealed something of an abstract Black–white binary definition that aligns with the abstract/technical leadership ideology, stating, "How are we educating our African American students, our minority students, how do we ensure that they are just as successful as white students on our standardized achievement test as well as in the classroom?" Yet, unlike the abstract/technical school leaders who hold an achievement gap disposition, Lawrence also revealed a disposition that actively and purposely engages with issues of race in his school.

Lawrence emphasized his approach to engage in culturally responsive and culturally relevant pedagogy conversations with his teachers:

> *Flores:* What would you say to a teacher that says, but [culturally relevant practice] doesn't influence test scores?
>
> *Lawrence:* It would influence test scores if you learn how to incorporate pedagogy that is *culturally relevant*. The disconnect is the approach that we take as educators. The conversations that we have, the fact that we don't create scaffolds and put in place instructional practices that tap into our students' interest. So it is not the students that [are] the issue, it's the educator that is the issue.

The interaction reveals the complexity of supporting an abstract/technical disposition about test scores and an opportunity gap disposition toward the value of culturally responsive teaching. For Lawrence, culturally responsive teaching can lead to closing gaps in achievement, and so he attributed continuing achievement gaps (at least in part) to the inaction of educators to apply culturally responsive practices.

Two white male principals working in suburban districts also indicated a straddler disposition. Andrew Baker said that race and class do not predict achievement, "but there is definitely a connection between the two," thus suggesting they may rely on causal relationships for some of their practices. A principal at a school with fewer than 5% students of color and fewer than 5% students eligible for free or reduced-price lunch, Baker also described his experience leading an urban school in another state, which he described as enrolling the "most diverse student population" in the area, with students coming both from public housing and multimillion-dollar homes. He described this experience as both "dynamic" and "beautiful," taking over for a visionary principal who developed a culture of expecting excellence. "We just kept growing the school from there, and it was *[pause]*, professionally it was so exhilarating *[pause]*, but it was also exhausting." Although he no longer works in a school district with the diversity he experienced in his first leadership position, Baker's previous experience in working to narrow the achievement gap—and, by his indication, succeeding—continues to have influence on his disposition on the gap.

Another straddler is Jack Maddon, familiar now to readers for the color-evasive caring described in Chapters 2 and 3. Maddon described how his school has the largest population of Black students (about 10%) and low-SES (50%) students in his district, an otherwise upper-middle-class suburban district. In his 8th year as leader of his elementary school, Maddon identified issues related to preschool experience, nutrition, educational exposure at home, and prenatal care as influencing achievement gaps. Furthermore, Maddon described how the school is directed toward closing the gap.

Maddon stated: "So closing the gap is one of those things that we try. *[Pause.]* We pride ourselves on, we put everything in place. If one intervention doesn't work, then we try another one." As shown from excerpts, Maddon spoke of both asset-based and deficit-based perspectives at the same time, and he engaged in talk mostly about achievement gaps. Although Maddon holds many principles of the opportunity gap disposition, as discussed in Chapter 2, he did not convey race consciousness when describing his leadership practice. In his practice, diversity primarily equates to socioeconomic diversity: "I mean diverse students are the kids that you know . . . we would say the low-SES or the children in the high-SES."

Indeterminate straddlers. Beyond those evolving straddlers are three school leaders whose dispositions about the achievement gap seemed so different and particular to their school contexts that we placed them in their own category. We initially identified them as "other straddlers" and in this chapter we refer to them more precisely as "indeterminate straddlers" (see Table 4.1). These school leaders referred to the gap as an "effort gap," a "cultural construct," or "culture." These school leaders' dispositions also straddle; however, based on the data we collected in their interviews, we cannot interpret with clarity if they convey an asset-based approach. While their views are distinct, as displayed in Table 4.1, their dispositions in relation to the gap mainly hold to the abstract/technical perspective. We explain these indeterminate straddler perspectives to reinforce that school leaders express multiple and at times conflicting views about what it means to address (or to ignore) equity in their schools. While some of the leaders provided some interesting critique from their experience and discussed some important practices (such as building stronger relationships with students), the disparate views and the ways in which they talked about their practices suggest limited ability to exercise the kind of justice leadership that we find in some other school leaders.

Effort gap. Describing his educational practices at his charter high school, director Bill Roberts emphasized high expectations and strong effort on the part of students and teachers. When asked about the achievement gap, he extended that view into a definition:

> My understanding of the achievement gap and a way conceptually to be able to address the gaps that are known in achievement between groups is to view it as a gap of effort—of best effort on the part of a whole bunch of different groups: students, families, teachers, administrators, and school boards . . . and state and federal legislation as well that create policy and funding environments.

The emphasis on "effort" seems to convey a focus on multiple sources of responsibility for student success, including students and families themselves. In our analysis, it was unclear if Roberts took opportunity gaps into consideration or how they might relate to individual or collective effort.

Cultural construct. Superintendent Ethan Knight pointed out the socially constructed nature of testing when asked how he defines the achievement gap. The achievement gap itself is a construct, he said, and he attributed Black and Latino students' systematically lower performance on tests to the structure of schooling, which makes schooling easier to master if a student is from the white, dominant culture:

> In the real world, to be honest with you, I think to a certain level the achievement gap is a construct. It's not a real thing. Because one day they just, somebody just said well, let's look at this data, I mean prior to the—maybe the 70s—I don't know really when, going back into the sixties and fifties, we didn't really know, we didn't really know. Everybody just went to school.

It was unclear in the context of the rest of Knight's interview how this insight influenced his efforts to address gaps in either achievement or opportunity, the former gap strongly evident in the school district profile. Knight mentioned his district's efforts to prepare his largely white teaching force to develop better relationships with students.

Culture. High school principal Dennis Gable attributed his beliefs about gaps in achievement to his personal experiences in urban education:

> Others may argue that [the achievement gap is] exclusively assigned to different groups and subgroups, and I would argue that it really is more pertaining to a cultural environment. Some of the things that are happening around young people and kind of the development of—are you doing homework at home? Are you getting the opportunities that are there for you and taking advantage of those?

In this passage, Gable grounded a deficit perspective in his personal experience. At other times, he spoke to providing multiple opportunities for his students across the board. He described low achievement as a school-wide issue because of the great proportion of students who struggle in his school to perform proficiently on standardized testing.

FROM DISPOSITIONS TO PRACTICES

With the varying class and racial compositions among the school districts in Allegheny County, conditions that support the capacity for race-conscious, opportunity gap leadership varies greatly. Figure 4.2 maps school leaders' dispositions, the external constraints to implementing justice leadership, and the leadership practices that arise from these dispositions. The leadership practices are the plans of action that leaders described to us. Some caveats are important to repeat here: The interpretations are not evaluative of these individuals but a mapping of what they told us. The dispositions, constraints, and practices are based on our interpretations of their interviews. As such, they provide a landscape of possible approaches to justice leadership, and Figure 4.2 captures some recurrent patterns.

In Figure 4.2, the dispositional categories we identified are arranged on the left, indicating the achievement gap and opportunity gap dispositions, an overlapping area for straddlers, and a tangential space for the indeterminate straddlers. As noted in the figure, some leaders with an abstract/technical disposition have no recognizable plan of action for justice leadership, noted in Figure 4.2 as "Inaction." As implied in the figure, inaction faces no resistance or restriction because these leaders maintain the status quo of their system.

The middle section of the figure points to resistance or restrictions that can come from within the district, within the school, or from communities. These challenges may overlap and may occur individually or simultaneously. Resistance from within the district includes lack of resources, competition with other priorities the district deems more important, district initiatives that are inconsistent with justice leadership practices, and the lack of support from district leaders to address justice in the gaps. Within the school, resistance and restrictions can be associated with lack of fiscal and personnel resources, such as limited funds for field trips or the lack

Figure 4.2. Justice in the Gaps

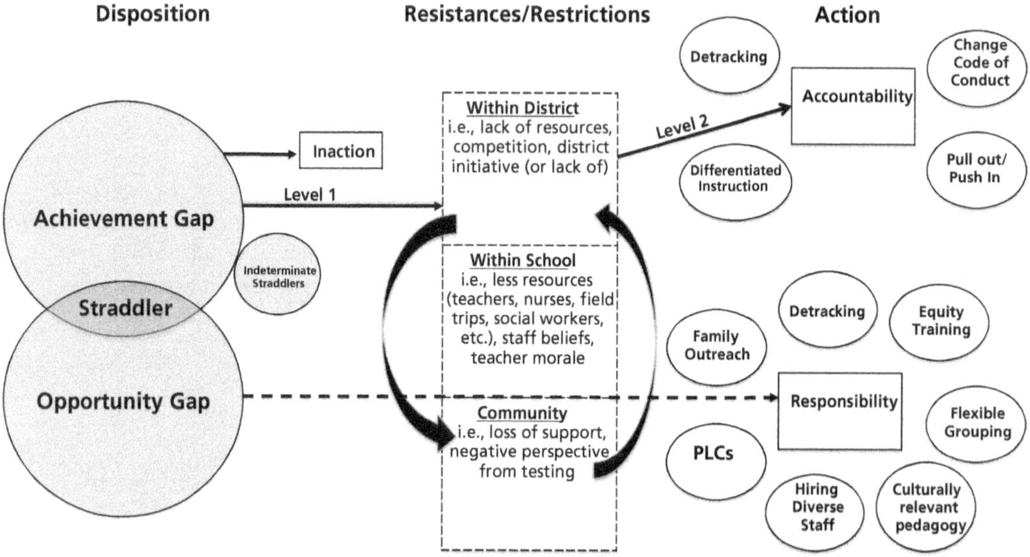

of support personnel such as school nurses and social workers. Staff beliefs about justice work and teacher morale in general can also be sources of resistance. Community resistance can come from lack of support from parents, taxpayers, or school board members about justice work, or from concerns associated with the relative importance of standardized test scores. Some communities respond negatively to the stigma associated with schools being labeled as low performing, while some other communities are wary of any initiatives that detract from the perceived dominance of the school in test score rankings.

On the right side of the figure are the actions participants shared. For leaders with an abstract/technical disposition who decide to take action, we make a distinction between first-level and second-level actions. We characterize first-level plans of action as the ideas that leaders expressed that they have tried or would like to try, but these plans remain first-level plans because leaders have not successfully implemented them, whether through lack of initiative, lack of resources, or lack of support. These ideas would include plans not attempted or plans that met resistance and were dismissed or discontinued.

Beyond the first-level plans of action are the more substantive second-level plans of action discussed by leaders with the abstract/technical disposition. These are practices school leaders said they implement when they are able to break through resistance or restrictions. These second-level plans of action are primarily focused on achievement measured by test scores. Our research suggests that leaders with abstract/technical dispositions (and indeterminate straddlers) typically take on actions for the sake of accountability. These leaders lack race consciousness, and their initiatives are guided by accountability scores.

In contrast, justice leaders have an opportunity gap disposition that facilitates them to firmly and strategically traverse resistance or restriction and commit to plans of action characterized by responsibility for students' educational opportunities, using practices that provide opportunities and respond to student and family needs and interests. Recalling Lisa Delpit's (2006) argument about the serious responsibility to educate other people's children, there is a distinct difference between school leaders who confront issues that can be detrimental to student success and school leaders who evade or avoid issues. Our research identified multiple strategies that school leaders use to address justice in the gaps, enacting the opportunity gap disposition and focusing on responsibility for students' educational opportunities. Family-based initiatives include family outreach and discussions of the data with students and families. Faculty-based initiatives include challenging teacher biases, hiring more faculty and staff of color, creating professional learning communities, and providing professional development on equity practices and culturally relevant or culturally sustaining pedagogy. School-based initiatives include detracking and flexible grouping.

CONCLUSION

School leaders expressed widely varied perspectives on gaps in educational opportunities and achievement in their schools. Only four demonstrated what we are describing as the three features of justice leadership. Despite the currency among scholars of the concept of an opportunity gap, the concept was largely absent from the school leaders' talk. Just one of the participants used the term in a manner found in the research literature, and some used the term as part of a deficit perspective. Others conveyed the general meaning of the concept, but without using the language. School leaders conveying the justice leadership disposition identified gaps in opportunity and spoke about a clearer notion of responsibility for student learning. Justice leadership also signals stronger, more responsible plans of action for addressing "justice in the gaps." Most of these school leaders were the same ones expressing race-conscious and critical caring, suggesting alignment between and among race consciousness, critical caring, and addressing justice in the gaps.

More frequently, school leaders expressed abstract/technical dispositions toward gaps in achievement and suggested their practice was largely guided by accountability to improve test scores. Most, but not all, of these school leaders were the same ones who in previous chapters appeared in color-evasive and impersonal caring categories. Evading race—in the context of this chapter, ignoring patterns of differential opportunities and attainment for students of color—paradoxically leads to attributing differential achievement to racial background, rather than a systematic consideration of practices and conditions that provide differential opportunities (Noguera, 2001). As we suggest in later chapters, these findings should be helpful to practicing leaders, to district leaders selecting school leaders, and to university faculty preparing the next generation of school leaders. We all need to seek and promote leaders with dispositions consistent with the model. We invite leaders who demonstrate impersonal caring, color-evasiveness, and achievement-gap dispositions to accept our challenge to reflect upon their experience and evolve into more race-conscious, genuinely caring, and just leaders.

We recognize that taking responsibility for justice in the gaps requires school leaders to possess both courage and resilience, because not only are these leaders focused on transforming adults (teachers, staff, and other school leaders), but they are also challenging historical beliefs and cultural norms. The strategies justice leaders use, such as challenging teacher biases, require leaders to develop their principled resistance. We believe that school leader dispositions need to be strengthened if their goal is to attend to justice in the gaps. In our respondents, these dispositions were cultivated through personal experience; racial, ethnic, and gendered positionality; and experience working with diverse populations of students. In addition, those dispositions were developed partly through reading about social justice practices. While we cannot claim to know fully about how these school leaders developed these dispositions, among those with an opportunity gap disposition their awareness of their own positionality seemed to make a difference. None of the school leaders with an abstract/technical disposition volunteered that their own positionality might be important, which suggests that cultivating appreciation for their positionality could be a promising practice for current school leaders and for curricular intervention to cultivate justice leadership among school leader candidates.

CHAPTER 5

Ethical Praxis

Figure 5.1. Ethical Praxis

From the beginning of the book, we have referred to race-conscious caring as an ethical praxis. Up to now, we have explored the components of race-conscious caring that can be found under the categories of race consciousness, critical caring, and justice leadership. Along the way we have pulled examples from the school leaders we studied for each of these components and the key ideas for each. In this chapter, we explore in a holistic manner what it looks like to combine these components into a comprehensive ethical praxis (see Figure 5.1). We first explain the meaning and value of moral narratives in deeper detail. We then delve more deeply into the stories from Scarlett Johnson and James Smith, who participated in multiple interviews in which they talked at length about their educational histories and went into greater detail about their leadership practices.

Each conveys their narrative of becoming a leader and sets their unique ethical praxis in the context of their personal history, positionality, and professional experience. We present the two narratives after extending our earlier explanation about the value of narrative ethics and explaining what we mean by the power of witnessing. As coherent stories, these narratives show that ethical praxis is not a theoretical exercise but a practice embodied in particular leaders, a practice that may look different for school leaders with distinct histories and in different contexts. As you read, think about how the histories, beliefs, and practices of others can encourage school leaders to narrate their own stories and to reflect on how they enact leadership in their school settings.

MORAL NARRATIVES

We advocate for an embodied form of leadership ethics in education—an enacted ethics that takes into account a school leader's personal history, social identities, and fundamental moral commitments (Blackmore, 2010). As Robert Nash and Jennifer Jang (2016) explain, "moral meaning-making narratives" bring together all aspects of experience that people use "as they struggle to resolve the inevitable ethical dilemmas they will encounter each and every day in the real world" (p. 4). A narrative takes account of one's core beliefs, their expression in professional life, and how concern for self and others fits into decision making. A narrative can also convey how one responds to the unethical conduct of others or morally troubling structures and social conditions.

Narratives of our inner lives are fairly consistent over time, reflecting our moral selves as developed and expressed through our actions. According to psychologist Robert Coles (1989), narratives describe what it means to "act in character"—what those closest to us come to know as our character traits or virtues, mostly drawn from our life histories as members of moral communities of various sizes and influences, such as families, cultural groups, social communities, and larger, interconnected communities. Narratives draw from what Nash and Jang (2016) refer to as four "moral languages," which are distinct ways of thinking about ethical experience that map onto various "moral spaces" in our lives: "a private moral space, a small-community moral space, an organizational moral space, and a cosmopolitan moral space" (p. 29).

All of these spaces are important, but they regularly come into conflict. Navigating life in these multiple moral spaces challenges us continually, with competing interests and expectations coming into play when people are confronted with situations that threaten their personal moral perspectives. For instance, a public school principal has to take into account the moral perspectives of the school as a secular, pluralist institution, while drawing from their private moral views and balancing the sometimes competing moral views of others in their school communities. Nash and Jang (2016) argue that leaders need to be able to articulate their moral decisions in the language(s) that are appropriate for their settings. Leaders cannot defend their moral decisions solely using the terms of their personal background beliefs, but they need to speak in a more public language of rules, principles, and commitments that promote common agreement.

The Office of Civil Rights investigation at the Norwin School District described in Chapter 1 provides an example for how the moral languages come into play (Haviland, 2024). The OCR exposed school district officials' lack of attention to their legal and moral responsibility to address a racially hostile environment. Based on the administrators' description of the incidents, we could interpret them as relying upon their own background beliefs, which enabled them to minimize and isolate the Confederate flag shirts as dress code violations. This group of administrators made up a small-community space reflecting the character of the dominant culture of the Norwin community that reinforced the minimizing disciplinary actions. Their minimizing actions, in other words, fit into the expectations of the dominant community. The OCR insisted upon a public language that considered the moral perspectives in operation in the community, explained those views as principled, and instituted just remedies. The remedies reflect commitments the district should now make to create a more just community. The district could aspire to engage the cosmopolitan moral space that Nash and Jang (2016) articulate, with much work ahead to acknowledge and understand their important role in effecting change.

How school leaders respond to challenges builds the story of who they are as moral persons. For a school leader with a public role and many relationships to consider, all four of these spaces—private, small-community, organizational, and cosmopolitan—are relevant to their moral narratives. With guidance, school leaders can construct moral narratives that incorporate all of these influences, and at the end of this chapter, we adapt the Nash and Jang (2016) framework specifically for the practice of race-conscious caring. The exercise provides guiding questions so that leaders can articulate their moral commitments and their origins. Each moral narrative should be unique to the school leader. In enacting their notions of race-conscious caring in their roles as leaders, how each leader deals with these multiple spaces and multiple conflicts creates their singular ethical praxis.

Counternarratives and Witnessing

Made more apparent in this turn to narrative ethics are the stories that subjugated persons tell of their experience enacting commitments to justice in inequitable, contested spaces. A narrative approach further invites deeper consideration of the experiences of those with embodied understanding of racism, both in their own experience in the world and in their work with minoritized and racialized students and families. Stories of teachers and leaders working against racism are relevant and vital learning tools for such work. They are often "counternarratives" to dominant narratives about the inequitable spaces in which we work.

As Richard Miller and colleagues (2020) recount, the idea of a counternarrative emerged from similar methodological ideas in social work and Latina/o studies and was adopted first in education for studies of critical pedagogy. Counternarratives are grounded in critical race theory (CRT) and CRT scholars' recognition of educators' stories of confronting various forms of subjugation in educational spaces (Ladson-Billings & Tate, 1995; Solorzano & Bernal, 2001; Solorzano & Yosso, 2001, 2002). Solorzano and

Yosso (2002) present five constructive uses of counternarratives or counter stories. They argue that using counternarratives:

1. creates a community among those at the margins of society;
2. challenges the ideological thinking of center-wing members;
3. discloses the existence of other possibilities and unites communities with the same goals;
4. constructs another world that is richer; and
5. provides the framework to deconstruct established belief systems. (p. 156)

In short, counternarratives challenge the dominant language used to misrepresent people of color and continue their subjugation. Notions of truth provided by counternarratives told by people of color can combat the subjugation of stories that don't fit into the dominant culture. The value or authenticity of the counternarrative or counterstory derives from the experience of the individuals who tell their narrative (Stovall, 2004). Stories of white allies fighting subjugation are also valuable for countering dominant experience and exposing pathways for transformation.

Readers and listeners of stories are in a dual position as witnesses to ethical praxis and as invitees to narrate their own ethical praxis—to critically consider their own stories in relation to their leadership practice. As Martha Ritter (2008) argues, witnessing means acknowledging that one hears an account, recognizes the author, and responds with what philosopher Iris Marion Young refers to as "moral humility." With moral humility, the task of the witness is to understand the experience and be open to experiences that might challenge the experience of the witness.

For our purposes, we are most concerned with how readers witness differential experiences of race and racism and their impact upon ethical praxis. More genuine caring in service to race consciousness requires growth in the ability to care, and that comes from experience, reflection upon that experience, and challenges to one's suppositions. As we discuss at length in Chapter 3, suppositions that one cares for all students equally are faulty; while caring is a popular ethical stance for school leaders, knowing how to care is another thing entirely. Reading various ways that race-conscious caring school leaders have gone about their ethical praxis may inspire readers to seek additional, perhaps local narratives of the praxis of colleagues who are recognized for their equity work and whose backgrounds and experiences are different from their own.

Two Moral Narratives

Scarlett Johnson and James Smith appear in previous chapters, so readers may have already begun to develop appreciation for their remarkable qualities as leaders and practitioners of race-conscious caring. In this chapter, we expand their stories to show how each moral narrative counters dominant narratives about color-evasiveness, impersonal caring, and achievement gaps. These leaders ground their practice in narratives that address the multiple moral spaces they have incorporated into their lives and the ways in which those lives contribute to their leadership. Johnson's narrative further conveys the intersectional identities (Crenshaw, 1991) she draws upon, as a Black woman living in Pittsburgh, to make meaning of her experience.

Elsewhere, one of the present authors explored how the intersectionality of the three Black women leaders who participated in this study contributes to their equity leadership practice (Flores, 2018). He explored their perspectives as counterstories essential to their practices for working intently against structures that subjugate children of color. In this chapter we provide a fuller narrative from Johnson to show how her life story contributes to her ethical praxis. Similarly, Smith's moral narrative also makes use of his social identities and conveys his extended involvement as a leader of a predominantly Black school as part of a Black organization and located in a predominantly Black community. As readers will see, his moral narrative conveys a different kind of counternarrative.

We chose these two narratives intentionally because each provided a full accounting of the leader's background, their reasons for choosing teaching as a career, their trajectories toward school leadership, and full articulation of the components of the race-conscious caring model. While Johnson models all of the most ideal features of the model, Smith does not. Portions of his explanation of his leadership do not rise to the highest levels in our model, which provides some helpful contrast and a reminder that race-conscious caring is an ongoing, lifelong project. Further, our analysis is limited to our conversations with these school leaders. We are certain these leaders have perspectives and engage in many practices they did not talk about in our interviews, and within the interviews, many of the respondents conveyed contradictory perspectives.

Like the ethical theory we are writing about, the following two narratives are relational in nature. Each story was told in a relational context with Osly J. Flores in his role as interviewer, a Latino male, a former teacher, and at the time a doctoral student. The interviews were encounters between a school leader and an educator studying to be a school leader and researcher. These narratives emerged from transcripts from particular encounters marked in history, context, and power relations. The reader is now actively (or passively, depending on your attention) generating meaning about the narrative presented. We are concerned that readers not confuse their narrative encounter with knowing this person. Readers are encouraged to let the narrative be an invitation to understand how the school leader makes moral meaning about their experience within the context of their encounter with the interviewer, to imagine how race-conscious caring has found a home in their experience, and to consider how the reader might narrate their own moral meaning around race-conscious caring. As explained in more detail in the methodological appendix, the interview transcripts used in this chapter are edited for clarity. We retain the instances of informal and nonconventional grammar but delete repetitions and filler words, such as "like," "you know," and "kind of," which we retained in prior chapters when we presented shorter excerpts. We note in brackets when respondents laugh or sigh or when their sentence drifts off.

SCARLETT JOHNSON

> *"Those babies are me. I look in their eyes and I see their potential."*

At the time of her interview, Scarlett Johnson was the principal of an urban elementary school. As mentioned in earlier chapters, during that school year, the school enrolled about 265 students; more than 90% of students were Black, and more than 90% of students were eligible for free or reduced-price lunch; the school is located in the neighborhood where Johnson lived as a child and where her mother still lived at the time.

Johnson's Journey From Student to Teacher

Coming into this principal position, Johnson had several decades of experience as a teacher, principal, and district administrator. She came to education after an educational experience that was at times supportive and at other times hostile to her growth as a student. Johnson remembers as a kindergarten student being referred for a hearing test because the teacher misread Johnson's interest in the activity centers the teacher created in the classroom (made available only at designated times during the school day) over the lessons designed by the teacher:

> My first exposure to school was kindergarten, and I hated . . . I didn't do well because I wanted to play. . . . Coming from a low-income family, there were centers, the toys. I wanted to iron and play with the refrigerator and I didn't have that stuff at home. And the teacher was always trying to bring us over to play with the blocks and do patterns and write stuff, and I wasn't into her, so I'd ignore her. She thought I was deaf. So, I had a hearing test and everything. They come to find out ain't nothing wrong with me. I just really ain't feeling you.

Johnson's educational experience improved by the time she was in the 4th grade, when she first experienced an engaging classroom. She describes this experience as the first time she saw herself as successful in school:

> I didn't start liking school until the 4th grade. We had an amazing teacher. She could play the piano, we actually had a piano in our classroom, we had a hamster, we had plants. It was so lively. . . . She just made school so we did things, we grew things. She would show us pictures—"This is Switzerland," and I wanted to go to Switzerland, and she just was so engaging to us. And that was the first year that I made honor roll. I never paid attention to grades. I really didn't understand what they meant, and from that point on I realized that I had an academic bent. I was good at school. I could do school. So I learned how to navigate it. I think she was my best teacher for a while.

That final comment about her teacher contrasts how she experienced teachers after that point. She moved form a racially integrated setting to a more racially segregated setting for upper elementary school, and it wasn't until she returned to a racially integrated setting for middle school that she found her fit in school again:

> I had some really bad fifth and sixth grade experiences. And some of my worst teachers were Black teachers. It was really difficult, too, Black female teachers. It was hard as a young female then to interact with them. . . . First through 4th grade, I went to integrated schools with white children. But I went to an all Black school, it was horrible. I hated it, I hated it. . . . I found the classes to be unruly. The kids were out of control, and that's not what I was used to. . . . I found it very hard to fit in because I didn't . . . connect with a lot of folks in how they did things.
>
> We went to middle school that had integration around 1980-something. . . . Now I am back in the setting with white children again and I started again achieving really high being with them.

Looking back Johnson attributed her negative experience to the all-Black schools being poorly resourced and poorly staffed. Teachers did not engage her or the other students. Returning to an all-Black setting for high school, she had a somewhat different experience from her upper elementary school, because in high school she was in classes with other students labeled as gifted. While she recalls one specifically strong class, overall she found the experience lacking:

> I went to [high school] and I think the saving at [the high school] was that I wasn't in class with a lot of the nonsense. . . . I was in classes with gifted students, and so we're able to focus on learning, and that is how I was able to achieve there. But I hated being in an all-Black setting. . . . I am not going to say that it didn't—I had some good—now I had great African American history. Mr. Adams, he was awesome. And he really engaged us, Socratically . . . and we didn't have that before, where we wanted to read the books and be able to talk about slavery. But it was something we were interested in. And so, school made

> me compliant. . . . I was compliant, and I knew to get ahead in the school cycle you had to be a compliant person.

In this school, low expectations for Black students was the norm, with her African American history being one exception. The experience taught her that the school most valued her compliance.

While learning what the institution of school desired from her, Johnson modeled what her grandmother had taught her and the faith instilled in her by her parents. She describes her grandmother as her greatest influence and strongest supporter throughout her life:

> My grandmother, she was kind. She extended herself, she gave of herself 100 percent. Physically she worked. My grandmother worked till she was 74. And she saved her money, so that we could go to college, and she wanted us to know that she wanted us to have the opportunity she didn't have. And that was important to her. My grandma spent time with me. My grandmother, I could go to her house after school, and she would have dinner ready. . . . What she taught me was the exchange was: "I am going to cook your dinner, but you going to wash the dishes, and you'll mop my floor, and you will dust around." And she would give me *[laughs]*—and this is the 80s—she would give me like 35 cents *[laughs]*. She'd give you this change, like I could get some Now-and-Later or something. You get in to high school, it's like "Ohh, I am just going to leave this on the coffee table." But she would do huge things, like if [you] needed clothes to go to school shopping, most people are going to K-Mart and stuff like that. Man, my grandma didn't play. She is going to take you down to Gimbels. "You going to Gimbels. You going to go to Kaufmann's. . . . You going to go somewhere big, and I am going to make sure you look good." That was important to her.

While attributing her success in school up through high school to the support from her family and saying that learning and being willing to "play the game" in school helped her achieve in high school, Johnson did not feel prepared to succeed in college, especially in comparison to her college classmates. She attended a small Christian college, which she described as an all-white school that was a "culture shock" and a "horrible transition":

> When I first went to [college], one of the things that I learned was—and I kind of think I always knew—that the education that I got wasn't the same as maybe some of my white friends [who hadn't] gone to an all-Black high school. I took the placement test and found out that I needed remedial reading. . . . I had the lowest English that there was, plus remedial reading my freshman year of college. And it was devastating. . . . My first semester I had a 1.6, and the second one I had a 1.5, and I was crushed. I never had grades like that in my life, [I was] crushed, crushed. My whole family was like *whaaattttt*!!!

While she was continually supported in her education by her church and her family despite her first-year grade point averages, especially her grandmother, finding support from her college instructors was more difficult. She found math particularly challenging, since Algebra II was the most advanced math she had taken in high school. In college, her Pre-Calculus instructor refused to help her:

> I didn't know how to be successful, and when I asked the dude for help, when I asked, Dr. Peters, could you help me? He don't give that kind of help, you need to get in a study group with my friends. . . . When I talked to him, it was like how dare you even invade my sp . . . *[voice trails off]*. He made me feel like chewing gum on the bottom of his shoe.

Lack of guidance and her first-generation status meant that Johnson was taking too heavy a workload starting out compared to what she had taken before:

> My major at the time was chemistry. I was trying to do it, but you need all this math to be able to be good at chemistry. And I was good, but nobody told me in high school . . . I had only organic chemistry my first semester of college. But nobody said, "Hey baby, ease your way in and take some classes to give you the idea." No, I got organic, pre-calc, and I am in remedial reading and English 100.
>
> I never had experienced organic chemistry and I would be in a lab, and our lab was supposed to be from like 3 to 6. And I am leaving the lab at 9, 10 o'clock at night. I finally figured it out *[laughs]*. Everybody been gone. My fingers brown, blue, and yellow. You know it was a struggle. It was really a struggle.

In the predominantly white college setting, Johnson experienced the racial tension of the school and how she was treated:

> I remember telling a white woman who befriended me. We were friends, but I don't know why she befriended me and why she liked me. But, I was telling her how my advisor made me feel—as I was the dumb Black girl. And I noticed her face. And she actually was very offended, and she went to the department chair. And the department chair made my advisor meet with me, and this man is crying and he is apologizing. He never meant to make me feel that way. But that's how I felt. I just felt unsupported, like when I was struggling, he would just . . . like, what was he going to do?

The dedication her grandmother showed her throughout her K–12 school experience continued in college:

> My whole college education, everything that the grants did not pick up, my grandma paid that. She bought every book that I needed for college. And she was so proud when I graduated and I became a teacher. So I wouldn't be sitting here today if it wasn't for her, I wouldn't be here.

Likewise, Johnson's home church community supported her educational journey. She indicated her church was equally important in instilling her ethical ideals. Their support was especially important when she struggled in college:

> My church was so kind that I didn't do well at school. . . . When I went to my first freshman year of college, they sat me in front of the church and put an offering basket they gave me. They taught . . . me what it was to be a good, to live a Christ-like life, be pure, be upstanding, be the good person, help others.

Johnson discovered a career in education in college after the director of the tutoring program asked her to be a substitute tutor:

> So I got into education because the lady who did my remedial reading class needed me to cover. I was walking a friend who wasn't an education major to class and she said, "You know what? They are doing some"—this is my second year—she said "they are doing tutoring" . . . . She asked me to be this little boy's tutor for the day. And I said, "Just one day?" She said, "One day." And I'd been like, okay, I can commit to a night. I tutored this boy and I didn't think anything remarkable came out of it. It was maybe 2 weeks after that, she is yelling and running across the campus towards me and I am like, oh my God, I loved Ms. Smith because she was my away from home mom. And she told me, "You got to come back." And I am like, "Come back to where?" She said, "You got to come back to tutoring. That little boy is not coming back if you don't come back. He loves you." I end up being his babysitter and everything. But she said, "Did you ever think of teaching? I really think you have the gift for it." And that's how I went into education. I changed to general science education so I could be a general science teacher.

Like many educators who get into the field of education, mentors encouraged Johnson at key points in her educational career. She began teaching in a suburban religious school:

> I went to a white Christian school in the suburbs, and it was the horriblest experience that I had because they wanted to control my whole life. And I made \$10,000, like \$1,000 a month—what is that? \$500 a check? When taxes came, I made like \$333 *[laughing]*; it was a joke. But that wasn't what made it bad. I was this creative teacher and wanted to do these great things with the kids. And it was a Christian school, so one of the, I had an astronomy class, and so I had

> the kids put some constellations together, and we hung them across the ceiling in the hallway in a little band, and they were like, "Is this the horoscope?" I am like, "Oh my God! The horoscope. For real y'all?" . . . . And then they had a book, the book was old as Jesus, and it was falling apart, and it was talking about there is no evolution and . . . you know it was just real crazy. Y'all setting up the kids to fail right away. . . . At the Christian school, they didn't like that the kids were attached to me. . . . It was like a deficit for them. And I was one of three Black teachers on a staff of about 65.

She left the school after one year and was unable to find another position. After devoting time to raising her first two children, she returned to teaching in the urban district where she had been a student:

> That's when my world blossomed, because they accepted my creativity, and the way that I could interact with kids was respected. . . . I started as a general science teacher for 6th and 7th grade, and it was phenomenal. Our whole team was new. But it was the best team in the school. We were some dynamite teachers. We rocked. We rocked. So, that was a middle school team, with a literacy and math and social studies, science teacher. We killed it. We killed it.

Growing as a teacher led to new opportunities. Eventually, she was forced to move to a high school position because of seniority rules, and initially, it did not go well.

> I got sent to a high school. And on my list, my period right after lunch, there were 48 kids on the list. And if you ever worked in the school, that don't mean you will get 48 kids. They just put that on there. I am like, that's not going to happen. So the first day of school I had like 12 kids show up 'cause it was only freshmen. I am like, "Oh, that's so nice. I think I am going to like high school. It's going to be great." The next day 48 kids showed up. I didn't have enough seats. I wasn't prepared. They were sitting on the heaters, they were sitting on top of the tables. This was the worst class I ever had in my life. Now, I'd been teaching for five years at this point. This young girl said to me, "Bitch didn't you know we was coming! Why don't you got no damn chairs up in this room?" I am like *whaaattttt*! I have never been through anything like that in my life. They left that room, I went into the back room closet and cried. I am like, "I don't want to be in this high school." I came out that next day and the next day and the next day. With the class of 48 kids. We did labs. I had them until January. The union grieved and they broke the class out of 40. . . . I learned how to win them over, and they worked.

A question arose about her certification to teach biology since she had been certified to teach general science. She assumed she would be reassigned to general science in another middle school, but her principal insisted she stay at the high school:

> My principal looked me in my eyes. She said, "You try to leave this school, I will block it. You're a great teacher, you're going to stay right here. I am not letting you go nowhere." And I end up staying there. She made me go back to school and by then I had my fourth baby. I didn't want to go back to school ever again. . . . But it was her investment in me. . . . I knew that I was a good teacher, but . . . I had never had an administrator cultivate that. . . . But I stayed there for 12 years and I was able to build a reputation with the students. . . . The kids wanted to take me. And I would get assigned the harder kids because I could get them through. I even taught night school and night school kids said that "If I had you the first I would've never failed!" You know it's, being able to engage and I engaged the kids like I felt when I was in . . . that pre-calculus class. I never wanted anybody to feel like I felt with that man. And so I tried my darndest to break down concepts to kids in a way that they would be able to understand it. That was so important to me. That they have an understanding and access and I would tell them things, like, "Honey, this biology is not difficult. These words are like another foreign language to you. When you learn the foreign language you already know what it is linked to. You going to be able to talk the language, you can do this. It is real simple." And take the stigma, "You can be a scientist, why not?" And I talked to them about real life. I remember one little girl coming in saying . . . we were so family oriented and they would ask me for advice about their boyfriends and they were, if they were pregnant they would tell me.

Remembering her experience with her college pre-calculus teacher and the effect it had on her, Johnson was determined to not perpetuate that kind of pedagogical relation with her students.

From Teacher to Principal

Johnson's work with students led colleagues to encourage her to pursue leadership. Having seen poor leadership, she was determined to put herself in a position to become a leader:

> I had one administrator who was horrible and very condescending. Talk to you like a dog, but I was doing a lot of her work. When she needed her work done, she would come to me. . . . One of my colleagues, she was driving me home from work and I was telling her how I hated the way that they treated me, I couldn't believe, and I said I am doing all their work and I just said flippantly, "I should go to school and become a principal for myself. And do what they do. I should be getting paid if I am going to do their work." She said, "You know what, Scarlett, you should. You really should, you have a talent for this." And so I went to school based on that.

Two years after earning her principal certification, she was assigned an assistant principal position at a newly combined middle/high school. The organization of the new school was part of a controversial school closing and reorganization plan implemented throughout the system. Johnson recalled the condition of the school when she arrived:

> They had one [school] up here that was off the chain. It was like something you would see in Philly. They was pulling the fire alarm every 15 minutes, they were setting garbage cans on fire. . . . The worst teachers. I've never seen jokers like this in my life. It was like, Lord! They said, We need you to go clean that up. I went over there. That's how I got into the principalship.

The school's principal chose her for the assignment because of her reputation of being able to work effectively with students. This principal had once observed her keep her composure when a student challenged her during a classroom observation. It was the first of many different assignments in the district.

> I was at that school for a year. I really think the thing that got me kicked out of that school was, it was in a Black neighborhood and I really was cleaning it up. And there were, no exaggeration, there were 22 providers—after-school and mental health and all these different people that were in the school. And I could not get a handle on who is that? What provider is this? Who are these people? I felt as if they were making money off of the chaos—of the Black children. And I put them all in a room and I went through my life with them, what I went through, the traumas I've faced. I got very personal with them. And I told them that my purpose is to serve the children and make sure that children who experienced what I had experienced have every opportunity to be successful: "My school is still in turmoil . . . without your help, 'cause you're here and I can't tell what you're doing. And so I need a list of every child you say you help. And I am going to see if you're helping them, and if you're not, I don't see your impact, we are going to invite you to leave." And once I had said that, a week or two later I was reassigned in another school. All the way across town.

Johnson did not let the reassignment—essentially a disciplinary action—diminish her commitments. Johnson had several subsequent assignments at elementary and middle schools and worked for a period of time in the school district office. At the time of the interview, she had been principal of the elementary school in her home district for one year after leaving the district office.

Johnson's Purpose for Education

Drawing from her experience as a student, a teacher, and a school leader, Johnson described what she believes to be the purpose of education:

> I just believe that education is a civil right and the purpose of it is, we instruct our children that come behind us, so they can find their space within the greater society at large. Whatever that is, we have to direct kids in the way they should go. Their "bent towards" is what I call it, what I was raised as calling it. What's their bent? Yeah, so, all of us have our own natural talents and abilities, and I believe that education is to help students find those natural talents and abilities . . . so they can find their space in the larger society. Not be someone else but to find what their place is. It is all about giving back, paying it forward constantly, to nurture and care for each other.

Johnson contrasted her view to the popular belief that education is about conveying knowledge to students:

> We just can't dump into their little heads what we think they should know. We got to guide them in that path. That is why I said we got to teach them towards their "bent." Now I don't think we do a good job of that as a school. We kind of say you need to know this, this, this, and this, and that's what would get you forward. Instead of saying, really from nurturing, from very early on, what . . . you are really interested in, what would you like to do? And because we have pigeonholed students into these spaces, school has become irrelevant and they don't see it as being important.

Her orientation toward students reflects a service orientation grounded in her experience in her church:

> We did things for other people as a church. We would volunteer in the community. We would make sure people have food. If somebody had an issue, we would bring clothes for them. . . . I was given opportunities to show goodness to other people. And was valued for being able to be good for other people. Service was the key. We served. . . . The pastor, he would say, "The servants serve and the master rewards." And that was our goal. Our goal was to serve. It wasn't to get, we were just taught to be servants.

As she described it, service is not servitude to those in power but service to others in need. Johnson further explained how her experience in her church and as a Christian informs her practice as a person and as a leader:

> I am a Christian, I, and not just that I go to church, but I espouse the principles of Christianity and try to live my life like Christ would live it. I am trying to grow more each day to be like he would be. And so that's the frame I roll out of it. That's what keeps me from coming here and being a bully and cussing people out saying, "Y'all going to do it like this 'cause I said." You know, that's not the type of leader that I want to be. That's not the type of leader that causes change. It's not the kind of person anybody wants to live within their home. That's not

> the kind of parent I want to be. . . . That's not the daughter I want to be to my mother and father. Or the sister I want to be. . . . That's not the person I want to be in a community. I want to leave . . . this world better than what it was before I came. I want to make an impact. And that's part of Christian principles. So, ethically I don't have time to be selfish. Ethically I don't have time to be rude. I don't have time to be fake. I don't have time to be false.

All of her experiences combine into how she approaches her ethical responsibility to her students:

> Those babies are me. I look in their eyes and I see their potential. If somebody didn't take time with me I wouldn't be sitting where I am, so I have seized the greatness in every seat in this classroom. So that's what guides me, that we going to do everything we can for these babies 'cause we don't know what's getting ready to grow. We got to—a whole harvest of amazing people . . . are in front of us. And you might not even know it. I don't think that I was one of them kids where somebody would say, "Yup, she is going to be the one on top." I'd be the last one you would have picked. You'd never know which one it is. You never know which one it is. And so that's what guides my work. Don't sleep on none of them. Don't sleep on one of these babies in this school. They all have tremendous potential.

Johnson translated that vision of not "sleeping on" any of her students into the approach she takes with teachers. The key consideration is not maintaining a pleasant relationship with her teachers, but considering what real effects her actions toward teachers have on her students, her babies:

> So my moral actions, what I have to consider first and foremost, I think the only thing that is important is the impact that it's going to have on the kids. That's how and why [I] approach teachers the way I do. . . . What kind of impact would I have on a child? Because I can't go to a teacher, I know I am from the hood, here, I can get with you, but me getting with you is going to cause you do what to one of my babies? Me allowing you to just do anything because I want to keep us on a good relationship . . . is going to do what to that baby? So I got to push . . . because if I don't push you, you are going to screw over that child. If I continue to let you be stupid you're going to hurt that baby. That's where my influence is—on the kids.

Johnson's Race-Conscious Caring Leadership

As evident from Johnson's narrative so far, she demonstrates race-conscious caring in ways unique to her personal history and her approach to educational practice. It's important to note that our model of race-conscious caring leadership draws heavily from Johnson's interview, along with the small number of other leaders who displayed the features of the model. Among those, Johnson's interview is one of three that contain the most fully realized concepts across all the dimensions of the model. This speaks not only to her capacity as a race-conscious caring leader, but also the thoroughness of her engagement with the interview questions. In this section we summarize how Johnson combines the elements of the model into her unique ethical praxis.

Race Consciousness. In Chapter 2, we explain race consciousness as composed of culture, history, material effects, and strengths. When asked what value Black and Latino/a students bring, Johnson responded, "They bring the richness of their cultural capital." Culture is evident in the story conveyed in Chapter 2 about Johnson celebrating the two students who emigrated from Polynesia. She acknowledged that she did not know specifically about Polynesian culture before, but sought information to make public acknowledgment of the students' culture and heritage.

Johnson's appreciation of communities of color's history of resistance and the material effects of racism are evident in her personal history of having grown up in her school's neighborhood. Yet we also learn there is no free pass here, because racism continues to have its effect; the continued historical permanence of race and racism has inculcated distrust by some members of the Black community. As principal, she has also recognized that she represents the dominant culture and power position of the school district. She pointed out that "even though this is the neighborhood I grew up in" and she had "lived just as poor" as some of the parents, some parents saw her as having "had some type of advantage and so some people are leery of that." When Flores asked her how she has come to perceive that some parents see her as an outsider, she replied, "When I am interacting with them and some of the conflict that we may have had, they've told me . . . you don't understand. . . . You don't know what it is about."

Johnson wants students to find their bent and teachers to cultivate that bent. But where it makes its strongest impact is in her insistence that teachers appreciate the students' strengths. This is especially evident in her insistence in how teachers talk with students:

> Don't talk to my kids crazy. I don't tolerate that. It's not tolerated under me. I pull folks aside 'cause I try not to embarrass you in front of children. But you continue to do it, you're going to get embarrassed in front of the kids, 'cause I've asked you nicely—on several occasions—don't talk to my babies like that. And I had [one] teacher quit—I mean straight walked out. Put the keys on my desk and left because I don't allow it. I don't allow it.

Johnson acknowledged that the work to enact race consciousness is difficult. In her school, the former principal had hired a strong staff that was predominantly Black, and for the most part, the teachers got along well together and were responsive to Johnson's race-conscious approach. For Johnson, race consciousness is vital to her leadership. It provides justification for her curricular decisions, it helps build trust with parents, it is non-negotiable for her teachers, and it is central to her respectful and affirming relationships with her students.

Critical Caring. In Chapter 3, the components of critical caring are relational caring, narrative ethics, and collective responsibility. Johnson is fundamentally a relational ethical actor. Like a caring ethicist, supporting the quality of the relations she builds with students is foundational to her professional ethics. They are "her babies"—her cared-fors in the language of caring ethics. She is fundamentally concerned with their life projects and their life aims, above any and all district aims or teacher goals. She answered this when asked what it means to be a good person:

> I feel that it means being able to be good to other people, having others on your mind. How you can help others reach their goals and be successful and make into the next level. Be able to celebrate their successes, more than you harp on their failures.

Johnson said that caring should be visible in the school. She said this when asked what students would see when they attend her school:

> If you were a student at my school, you would see me. I am the first person you are going to see in the morning when you come in the cafeteria. You're going to get a hug, and I am going to ask you, "How you doing? Where was you at? I missed you." 'Cause like you can't go home, and I be like, "But you didn't miss me did you?" And so, you'll see me in the cafeteria wiping off the tables and throwing away breakfast and making sure we treating each other nicely and being fair and all that stuff in the morning. You would see some teachers who are just as invested as I am. And you would see some that aren't. You would see some that really need to get going, but that's a few. The majority really do care. You would see a lot of caring adults here.

The importance of narrative ethics is abundantly clear—Johnson places her commitments to students within the context of her personal history. Those who read her narrated story can trace the influences from her family, her church, her experience as a student and beginning teacher, and her experience as a Black woman in a society and educational system that has continually placed obstacles in her path.

Collective responsibility is evident in how Johnson prioritizes relationships with the community: "I have a close relationship to this church here, the one down the street. . . . it's important to have the community involved. . . . We can't. . . . do this work by ourselves." Johnson understands that her commitment toward improving the educational opportunities for her students requires establishing a school-community partnership mind-set. At the time of the interview, Johnson was planning to build a computer lab where parents could participate in GED classes. She hoped that these efforts would establish a stronger relationship between the school and families.

Justice Leadership. As Chapter 4 explains, justice leadership is built around an opportunity gap orientation, an asset-based perspective, and principled resistance. As we explain in that chapter, among our respondents, Johnson had the clearest critique of the language of an achievement gap, calling out how it places blame on children who have not had the same opportunities as some of their peers. Johnson spoke about the importance of strong teaching to provide opportunities for students who don't come to kindergarten as prepared as others:

> I have babies who come to us in kindergarten who are not able to recognize a letter, let alone put a sound to that letter, let alone know the colors and their numbers. They don't even know what the number one—couldn't count one, two, three, four, five, six, seven. That's not their fault. There are some things that need to happen prior to them coming to school that they should be prepared for that, and . . . my kindergarten teachers take them. I have kids—I can show you the data—that almost all of them know their letters right now, because the teachers are as skilled in doing their work.

Johnson has extensive knowledge about the strengths and assets of her students. She provided numerous examples and highlighted the importance of naming and building on those strengths:

> Our students, they bring the richness of their cultural experiences, so much different from even mine. . . . They bring us certain strengths and resiliency to them, that regardless of what we don't have, regardless of what people think about us, regardless of what our community doesn't have, we still are strong, we are still proud, we still care, we still choose to be here and that strength—that's what keeps us going. We wouldn't be able to do this work without our kids saying "I am still here, I am still in it, I still want to be here." And they show up everyday with that same attitude—"I am here"—and that is powerful.

In this passage, when describing the strengths of her students, Johnson shifts from third person to first person plural, including herself in the community that is strong, proud, caring, and still choosing to be here. She then transitions to a "we" that includes the resilient educators that work alongside resilient kids who persist in their attendance and participation.

Those strengths are not recognized in an educational system that emphasizes standardized testing as the arbiter of success:

> And it's almost as if they don't see the growth in other areas, the other good things about our kids: they are resilient, that they are persistent. They don't see that, and that is why I hate "achievement gap," because that . . . terminology, when you look at the assessment. It blames the child for where they are. If those kids only did this better, if they only did that better, they would score better on that test. There has to be other measures that we could use to see if kids are making growth.

These perspectives call on Johnson to enact principled resistance to the pressures and expectations that the district and the larger education system places on her students. A year before her interview, when Johnson was working in the district office, her moral core and clarity of commitment to her students led her to take a moral stand. She lost her position, which led to a 3-month period of unemployment before she returned to a principal role. The following reflection demonstrates the principled resistance Johnson needed to make that stand:

> The most successful opportunity for my growth as a leader was having that, having those three months out of work. That conflict with my supervisor and really having to take a stand about my own morals and my ethics 'cause I could have allowed anything to go on. I could have complied with what she wanted just to keep my job and my position. But I didn't. And I am so glad that I was true to myself. In spite of fear—I didn't want to come back to [the district]. I didn't want to come back here, but . . . some of the best work that I ever done has been right here. After and through the fear of what they were going to [do], the fear of repercussion. . . . And then coming to the space I am in. I had to stand on my own and not care what anybody does. And that is kind of where I am. I don't care. I could get fired . . . at the end of this year. I can be fired, for real, because my test scores might not be where they want them to be. But I know I put it on the line everyday.

Resistance also appears in the curriculum and cultivating the professionalism of her teachers. Unsatisfied with the largely scripted curriculum the district provides, Johnson has supplemented the curriculum with materials that give teachers greater autonomy and serve students better:

> I've gotten some permissions to use some other curriculum materials. Because I know they didn't work. But what did change was teachers used to have this autonomy, that they could plan and prepare and do what they felt, but this is what standards have done. If I have the Common Core and I have got to teach this,

> then everybody got to teach this. And what our district did is they got down to the script where, "Say this first, then you say that." More or less teachers . . . went out of it. They stop thinking for themselves. They say, "I am just following what they call the pathway," instead of really looking at their kids and seeing what do your kids need, what does this group of kids need, and give them what they need, and so that's what I have gone back to.

Principled resistance extends to what students are taught. Recalling her experience learning African American history as a high school, Johnson explained the importance of Black students knowing their history and the role of resistance against racism throughout African American history:

> Our African American students don't know enough of their history. We usually just look at their history from the perspective of, "we were slaves," and that victimization, instead of teaching them even about the resistance and even prior to that, what are some of the achievements that we had prior to slavery, even during slavery, even after slavery. And we will go from slavery to the Civil Rights Movement. Rosa Parks was on the bus, and we don't go into so many of the other things, and once they have that understanding of who they are, it's like a light goes on. It's where we came from, really. They almost don't believe it, for real.

The Ethical Praxis of Scarlett Johnson

Johnson's ethical praxis is explained through her story. She has clarity about the role that race has played in her life and the lives of her students—the role of racial identity as a source of strength, the role of racism as part of life, and the importance of race in history. Her commitments to her students reflect who she is as an ethical actor—a caring person who strives to understand the needs and interests of others and encourages others to form a collectively responsible community. Her leadership operates from a clear understanding of the gaps in opportunity that her students have faced, the assets they bring to school, and her willingness to take principled stands to resist what systems have put in place to limit her students and the educators working to serve them.

Not every leader has Johnson's personal history, yet every leader can learn from how she talks about her leadership and the importance of making her leadership practice authentic to who she is. As we expand upon more in this section's conclusion, there is also much to learn about the losses that Johnson has endured to enact her ethical praxis. As Johnson's narrative attests, it is important for leaders to understand the perspectives of their students, their parents, and their families and consider the importance that their experiences as students in their schools will play in students' moral lives.

At the same time, we have to ask if the public—those in her school district and the larger community who have entrusted her with the role of principal in this school, at this time, and under these conditions—has asked too much of her. Indeed, there is strong evidence that it has. As explained in Chapter 3, there is always a danger that the one-caring gives so much of themselves in the service to others that they wear themselves out. Johnson explained to us that her work toward making transformational change in her school has resulted in the loss of her personal self:

> I don't know if it is like that in other places, but I don't know if anybody understands what principals in urban settings . . . what they really . . . the amount of pressure that exists.

Johnson found herself questioning whether people comprehend the pressure that principals face in today's high-stakes accountability environment, which she described as a "crazy" time. Just like teachers, school principals are confronted with the pressures of test scores:

> You know, I lost, and it is sad, it's not . . . I [have] lost a lot of my life. I want to say, since I have taken on the principalship, I don't feel like being around people . . . You are so tapped out that I feel as though I have lost a personal life.

She pointed out that love for her students keeps her coming back, because she doesn't "want to leave them right now." Such a response points to the centrality of caring in Johnson's professional practice and perhaps most of all reinforces the importance of collective responsibility, which Johnson fosters in her role. But simply put, Johnson cannot be expected to bear the weight of caring on her own.

The absence of collective responsibility in terms of structures and supports could be the greatest barrier to Johnson's ethical praxis. It is especially important because of the lack of support Johnson has received and the conditions that make her work more difficult: A high percentage of her students are living in poverty, she has no assistant principal, she has a largely scripted curriculum that saps teacher autonomy and fails to take account of student needs, and she has some particularly weak teachers in the arts areas. Leading in this setting is difficult work that goes against the grain, specifically building a growth mindset among her teachers and cultivating relationships with families. Layering on top of that an accountability system that targets high-poverty schools like hers with threats of closure and takeover due to low test scores, the gross inequity in the system makes it clear that race-conscious caring needs to be embedded in the entire system, not just in the practice of individual school leaders.

JAMES SMITH

"It comes down to the person as an individual. How do you relate to different people? How do you relate to different cultures?"

At the time of his interview, James Smith was in his 15th year as head of a charter school that included about 300 students in one elementary building and one middle grade building. Nearly all children in the school were Black, and about 80% qualified for free or reduced-price lunch. The school is located in an inner-city neighborhood bordering commercial, industrial, and civic areas. The school is affiliated with multiple community organizations in the neighborhood that provide numerous opportunities for students. As James described it, there is great economic diversity among his student population. Here he contrasts the students who qualify for reduced-price lunch and those experiencing severe poverty:

> There is a big difference between somebody who is reduced, and then we have some severe poverty, homelessness. You do see those groups a little bit. . . . Even though we have a uniform policy, you can tell the kids who are struggling to be in the right uniform and to be in a clean uniform and to have those things. And it's unfortunate but true.

As mentioned previously, Smith characterized himself as "a white leader of a Black organization," with its affiliation with Black-led community organizations that provide after-school and out-of-school programs. Smith identified strongly with his family's specific European heritage and credits that upbringing with his identity as a leader. The identity is so strong, that like many other children of European immigrants in the Pittsburgh area, Smith made a distinction between his background and the "white community":

> I was always a little different than everybody else. . . . You're accepted, but you weren't quite accepted by the white community. You were always a little different.

When Smith was 17, the father of a woman he picked up for a date asked him how "guys [from his background] treat their women. And I was like, what the heck is this guy talking about?" Smith's actual name conveys his particular European identity, and having a distinctive name, even in a city full of residents with names of various origins, leads to some surprising interactions:

> I can remember being at the science center with the name tag on, and people would say, "Oh where are you from?" [I said], "I am from Milford Borough.

It's five minutes from here. It's where I was born. Where are you from?" You know? "Oh, you have a foreign name."

Smith grew up in a middle-class community outside the city, one of the many small middle-class river communities settled in the early 20th century that used to be connected to Pittsburgh by trolley car lines. Pride in his cultural and religious identity and his family's strong values contributed to what Smith called "life trainings," contributing to who he is as an educator and how he approaches working with people who are different from himself. When asked about how he was prepared by his family to work against racism or in racially diverse settings, he recalled that he has often been asked that question:

> Somebody asked me, "What did your parents say to you?"—that kind of thing. And I always said they didn't teach me anything like that. They just treated everybody equally. I think from seeing that and watching that. I mean, when my dad talked to somebody, you didn't know whether they were his boss or a janitor. I mean, they were—everybody was the same. And I think that's where you get it.

Smith's Journey From Student to Teacher and School Leader

Having been an educator for 20 years, Smith looked back on his experience as a student, a positive experience overall that also taught him the importance of attending to students' needs and encouraging them to reach their potential:

> I liked school. I can honestly remember I did not take home a book to study throughout high school. I remember having Calculus in 12th grade and deciding that I wanted to be a senior and have fun instead of taking Calculus. And my parents let me out of it, which I think was a major mistake. I remember in 7th grade asking a teacher—telling her I have difficulty spelling. And she said, "Well, just look at more words," or something. She gave absolutely no help. It was really sad. But I remember going off to college and I had to learn how to study. And I had to learn how to do this, 'cause I just wasn't challenged in high school.

As Smith described it, his lack of study habits and the lack of teacher attention caught up to him in college:

> I just remember . . . I thought college was going to be like high school, where I didn't have to do a whole lot. And it was midterms and I went through freshman year, took all my midterms and I was like, "Man, I need to start studying." I need to. First of all, I need to learn how to study and I need to start studying. 'Cause I really, I thought it was just going to be a cakewalk just like high

> school. And it wasn't. But I remember, I wasn't, I commuted, so it wasn't like I was ingrained in the college atmosphere. I lived at home. I worked full-time. So it was, it was kind of like, you know my parents were just, just had enough money where I wouldn't get any money, but didn't have any money to give me for college. So it was one of those things. But I wasn't in a big hurry, and I took five years instead of four to get out.

By his telling, Smith fell into teaching as a career when he evaluated his course credits just prior to graduating college and determined he was close to having the science credits to pursue certification:

> I think I was in my last semester. I had a whole bunch of science credits. I didn't want to get into the med field. I didn't really want to touch anybody or something like that as a doctor or in the med field or dentist or anything like that. Then I started looking at a science teacher and I saw a lot of my credits fell into that and decided to go into it. So it wasn't like I was born—you know these people would say, "Yeah, I've wanted to be a teacher since I've been two," or something like that. That wasn't the case with me at all.

Once he earned his teaching certification, Smith taught first at an urban alternative high school:

> Kids had been kicked out of [their initial schools] for gun or drug offenses. It was the hardest of the hard. And there were probably 30 kids there and maybe five or six adults.

He was at the alternative school a year, and over the next 2 years, Smith taught in a suburban school and a religious school. Throughout his teaching experiences, he found fit with the culture and the values of the institution to be most important.

> Probably a couple of places that I have teached, an all-Jewish school and again I was an outsider. Taught [at] a very affluent public school right out of college where most of the kids were driving better cars than I was driving, and again you were just who you were, And now at [my school] you know what? I am a white male running basically a Black organization. But it has always been about trying . . . being who you are and respecting where you are.

Teaching in an urban school has felt right to him. At this charter school, he first taught science and physical education, and the position paid half the salary he got at the urban alternative school. But the fit was right:

> A little bit was culture. . . . I didn't want to teach in a tight, tight place. I wanted to teach in a place where I was going to be allowed to be myself and be my

> own person. And I probably, and if I would have gave [the suburban district] a chance I probably could have been that and did that kind of stuff. But I think . . . I just liked the city more. I just liked a city environment more. I still do today. I don't want to go live in the suburbs. I want to live in the city.

As a teacher, Smith was most concerned with adapting to student needs. He said this about what stood out for him when he was a teacher:

> I think learning to teach your kids not the way you were taught but the way they needed to be taught. . . . It's funny. I remember talking about external and internal fertilization. And these kids were looking at me like, "I've no idea what you're talking about." And then I actually started using some verbiage, some verbiage that probably . . . most schools would say, "You can't talk like that." But they got it! I mean, as soon as you started talking about what it was and that kind of stuff, it was like, you know then . . . you're seeing yourself.

Tied to that view is the importance of connecting with students, regardless of family wealth, urban or suburban location:

> I was up at [the suburban district] and guys who had more money, families had more money . . . , but you could tell they were just in need of attention and affection. . . . Early on I found out that no matter where you are, kids are kids, and they need you.

After teaching four years in the charter school ("not long enough," Smith said), the sponsoring organization's leaders asked him to replace the departing assistant principal. They offered to pay for his principal certification:

> Again, it was kind of like teaching, I didn't choose it. I didn't want—I didn't want to be a principal. They asked, and they were going to pay for the education, and so I said okay.

Smith served as assistant principal for the founding principal and for her short-lived replacement. Despite his relative youth, he put himself forward as a candidate for the principal position when the second principal left:

> I kind of kept this place together, "Why don't you give me a chance?" And they did, but I was 33 years old, I didn't have a doctorate degree, I was working in a place that was African American, and I am this kind of crazy white kid . . . , so I understood that they didn't want to give me that opportunity, but they did.

Succeeding as a leader has come despite some hard and challenging times. These experiences have made him a stronger leader:

> I think the hard times help you grow more than anything. I mean we won a Blue Ribbon here, we've been successful, we've got some big grants, we met AYP 11 years in a row, that kind of stuff. But with stuff I remember is . . . when Pittsburgh Public [School District] wanted to close us after 2 years, and I had to sit in an office with this old lawyer, and we kind of came up with a plan. We stayed in this office for 48 hours, just kind of writing what we needed to do to stay open when things aren't as good and you have to figure out what you're going to do.

In addition to these struggles, Smith believed that his struggles as a student have helped him understand the struggles that students face:

> I think my high school and college—just being very good at some things and not being so good at other things—I think that helps as a school leader, because I think when you're always one way or the other, like if you're brilliant at everything, I think it sometimes works against you. 'Cause you don't know, you can't understand when people struggle with things. And I can because I wasn't brilliant with everything. You know there was stuff that was hard. There were things, and then there were things that I was very good at. So it was a little bit of both.

Smith's Purposes of Education

Smith named helping develop students into being productive members of society as the most important purpose of education:

> The purpose of education is to prepare children to be productive members of society. I know kids get a little scary when we talk specifically of math and science scores and we see a little bit reading scores. I think a lot of our efforts need to be placed in our social aspect as much as academics.

Smith expanded on what he meant by the "social aspect," which translates into fostering dreams:

> I think it's preparing kids to be socially, emotionally, academically ready to be productive members of society. To try to, and I know this is an overblown term, but to try to foster dreams. I mean I run a K–8 school and more than anything else I want a kid leaving my school believing they could be anything they want to be.

Smith as a Moral Leader

In his role as a moral leader, Smith sees himself being in a position to influence others about what is right:

> My definition of leadership: someone who is willing to kind of show people a pathway that they think is right. Leadership is about believing in something. And then taking that belief, and I am not into convincing, but rather kind of giving all the facts to people and hopefully they are coming to your way of thought. You know they are moving forward that way.

True to his background, Smith is clear not to give the impression that he is putting himself above anyone else. He spoke of two elder mentors who remained connected with students and who, through their example, communicated humility and responsibility:

> This guy was like 60 or so, and he used to come down and play ping-pong with the kids, and he'd come to the Y and play basketball with the kids. And I still do that stuff today with the kids. . . . And then [the founding principal] in the middle of the lunch room she would be wiping tables. Here [she] was the founder of this school and she is wiping tables and she is picking stuff off the cafeteria floor. And if she is doing lunch duty and wiping tables and this kind of stuff, everybody else should be doing that kind of stuff. . . . She never put herself above anybody else.

Being a leader as long as he has at the school, the responsibility of leadership comes naturally to him, as does setting an example:

> I think I just do it. . . . You get to a point—and maybe I didn't did it all the time when I was 20, but now that I am 47, you know how and what to do and what the right thing to do is and that sort of thing. And you tell others. And I think being a boss for so long too . . . I kind of feel it is my responsibility to do that stuff.

The humility he seeks to portray is conveyed in his story about not wanting the assigned parking space he was offered, as he described what he considers to be the most important aspects of how he enacts equity leadership:

> I think the first one is treating everybody equal and trying to make sure that everybody treats each other that way. And some of it is the little things. Like, I work here at a nonprofit. The nonprofit owns the building and they have office space here too. And the director of the nonprofit has a parking space outside that says "executive director" . . . . "Do you want a parking spot?" I was like, "No." It's those little things, like you don't do those things, because everybody is equal. Why should I get a parking spot? If I get here on time—and I do, I get [here] before everybody else, so I get a parking spot. But it's not like I have one with my name on it or anything like that. It's trying not to do things and make yourself out, make everybody the same and in trying to treat everybody the same. We have

> a state representative's kid that goes here. But I'm not going to treat him as a parent or her as a student any differently than I treat anybody else.

Smith's humility translates into how he sees himself as a member of a collective. Smith spoke of the importance of being a good listener:

> I think one of the things [that] is important is to break down barriers for teachers, so teachers can be successful. Because I think [a leader] can break down barriers for teachers . . . not even break down barriers but rather just make things easier for teachers, make teachers more productive and make teachers happier and keep teachers that way. And I think students will be that way. I think parents would be that way. I think it is also important for me to listen to everybody involved. Listen to students, listen to parents, and listen to teachers. I mean I always talk about it in all my commencement speeches and kindergarten speeches and parent speeches. There is a triangle, and . . . it's schools, it's parents, and it's kids. And all three have to work together and get along.

As the longtime leader of a charter school sponsored by a cultural organization that has served the local community for decades, Smith is grounded in a culture with high expectations and clear commitment to the needs and interests of students.

Smith's Race-Conscious Caring Leadership

Smith's story conveys the principles that guide his race-conscious caring leadership. He has established himself as the long-term, white leader of a predominantly Black school within a larger, Black-run organization. Taking account of his distinct European ethnic identity, clear family values, and a strong religious identity, his personal story explains his approach to treating people equally but at the same time with race consciousness. His modeling of moral leadership is clearly embedded in humility taught him through family example, experience, and key role models in his personal life, and his organization. Below, we break down each aspect of his race-conscious caring leadership.

Race Consciousness. The aspects of race consciousness—culture, history, material effects, and strengths—are evident in various degrees in Smith's narrative. The significance of culture and history are evident in the existence of his school, its location in a predominantly Black neighborhood, and the culturally responsive resources in the arts, science, and technology that the school and its affiliated organizations provide to students and the community. However, Smith did not offer some of the explicit recognition of the material effects of racism and the importance of the history of racism found in some other leaders.

In Chapter 2, we characterize Smith as "respecting" race consciousness, one tier below the "responsiveness" of such leaders as Johnson. To explain more fully the distinction, Smith conveyed all the understanding of the meaning and value of racial identity but did not convey the actionable steps toward greater racial justice that Johnson and four others conveyed. Smith expressed his racial awareness when the elementary principal created an all-white leadership team:

> We went to a second building. We went over to a middle school, and we didn't have a principal over at the middle school. And it was brand new, it was the first year there. So I really thought they needed me over there. So, I went over there and I left my assistant principal, who's here for a long time, here. She was a white woman. Ahm, I did not tell her . . . how she should do everything, 'cause she had been here a long time. And it wasn't anything that she purposely did, but . . . her second in charge, her third in charge, her fourth in charge, her fifth in charge were all white. And halfway through the year, I started to get a little feedback from parents, thinking it's a pretty racist building right now . . . If you looked at it in totality the way it should be looked at, she did the right thing. She picked the people who were there that were *[voice trails off]*, but that's not the way the world works right now. Yeah, it can't be.

Attentive to the experiences of parents, Smith took the parents' concerns seriously. He also appreciated the importance of representation on the leadership team and saw the conditions of having an all-white leadership team were problematic. He understood the principal had chosen the leaders who were available, but the composition of the team was failing at race consciousness and was not defensible.

The strengths of Black students and teachers are a source of pride for Smith, who inherited a staff with strong representation. He has intentionally fostered leadership in his school that brings varied racial identities and experiences to the table:

> Last couple of years, I've really tried to promote a lot of diversity in the leadership. And I think that helps out with equity. I was sitting around on my leadership table yesterday, and . . . there were only two men, me and . . . a black male, five women—three were black, two were white. And I'm thinking, this is a pretty good group of people to sit around and listen to and just the equality at this table.

To be sure, in the individual person, Smith sees the relational capacities of teachers to be more important than racial identity:

> I think it's about the relationships, and it's individuals. I have seen where at an all-Black school, I've seen a female that weighs 102 pounds have great classroom management and the teaching skill and the passion. I have had a six-foot-six Black male that kids don't listen to, didn't respect, so again I think it comes

> down to individuals, I really do. Now I do think that kids have to see some staff that looks like them, whatever that kid is. Whatever that kid is, he should be at a place where he is seeing adults that look like that child, succeeding, being their mentors, but I don't think it should just be that.

Here Smith echoes some of the individualization of the race-evasive perspective, which highlights the need to dig more deeply when leaders call on the importance of individuals. It also highlights that Smith does not convey the responsiveness of Johnson and some of the other leaders.

Critical Caring. True to that last quotation, relational caring, narrative ethics, and collective responsibility find a home in Smith's leadership practice. Smith places relationships first and attends to the needs and interests of individuals he encounters. This relational understanding is behind his drive to treat people as equals, regardless of their social station or racial identity. For Smith, being a good person means "to do things for the betterment even if they will never be seen by others." As mentioned previously, being treated as somewhat different from his other white peers, because of his clearly European name and his family upbringing, gave him experience as an outsider of sorts that has served him well in his role in a Black organization and predominantly Black school. In the model of critical caring, Smith speaks directly to knowing students and their concerns, which is essential to relational caring. Knowing students leads directly to how he and his teachers care for each child and prepare them for future learning. Smith spoke of the importance of knowing students:

> You see a kid come into your door and you try to find out everything you can about this child. 'Cause the more things you know about a child, and you ask the parents and the grandparents, and you know instead of talking at people, you listen to people and let them tell you about your child and you can meet that child where they need to be met.

Smith's focus on relationality is evident in how he talked about his moral leadership. He emphasized how he and the organization treat people and the significance of relationships. This passage emphasizes his language about treating people:

> It comes down to how you're treating the people. How you're treating employees? How you're treating parents? How you're treating kids? All the way down to how the teachers are scheduled, who the kids have. You know there are so many things that you can [do] that can make or break that.

Smith reinforced how important relationships are in describing specific events he has led in his school designed to cultivate relationships with families and among teachers:

> All I try to do all the time is try to establish relationships. . . . We do family nights every third Thursday, and those are to establish relationships with parents and kids. . . . The first week of school before we start school, with all the teachers, the school provides breakfast and lunch for them. That's all to build relationships, and what better way to get to know somebody than to eat every meal with them for a week? . . . . And we try to make it almost like it's a camp.

Smith's sees attending to relationships as important for creating a culture of equity in a school enrolling students of differing needs. He spoke of how he wanted staff, students, and families to perceive the school:

> I hope they see someone who's trying to set up a culture of equity throughout and that they are doing it as well. Even trying to identify and getting those people to change it. . . . I can identify a few people that treat me differently because I am the CEO, and they'll talk to me one way and then I am down the hall and they talk a different way. . . . Just be yourself, be who you are. Tell me what is going on in your world. You know that sort of thing, rather than that person who does whatever you want whenever you're around, just to placate you.

Prioritizing relational development contributes to how teachers should interact with students and families:

> The one thing that I'm more cautious about is that others share that kind of value and they treat kids equally. . . . That's the big thing when you're working at a facility. If your staff doesn't look like the children, or if all your staff doesn't look like the children, I think to treat the children equally, and I always say treat children like you would treat your own. And you want to see that stuff. And if you don't, then it's time to make a change.

The result is that the school environment is caring. Smith described the environment of his school this way: "We hear it a lot: When you walk in, it's about something feels different. It feels warmer. It feels caring."

Caring was ingrained in Smith through his parents' example and his religious upbringing. His narrative makes it clear how that upbringing combined to inform his ethics. He went into greater detail about the impact of religion:

> I don't know what I would be like if I didn't go to school. I want to say, and it wasn't my parents telling me to do the right thing, they just did the right thing. I think having religion and having morality . . . ingrained in you helps.
>
> I mean I was raised [in a particular Christian faith]. And I think learning that morality in a church. And I am not saying it had to be [my religion] or even Christianity, any religion, but just having a doctrine and a kind of—yeah, there

> is a reason to be good. Not to say, if you're not religious you can't be good, 'cause you can. There are people that are. But I think that did have an effect on me.

Collective responsibility, the third element of critical caring, is evident in how Smith talks about the community that has developed in his charter school and the associated organizations the charter school is a part of. He described what he wants students to see when they arrive at school:

> I would hope you would see adults that were here for you, smiling at you. I hope you would see a clean building. I hope you would go into classrooms where you were wanted, you were needed. I hope you felt challenged—that the people, kids, and adults around you, everybody was kind of working together as a family unit.

Parents and community members need to feel welcomed at the school, something that the founder prioritized:

> I am going into my thirteenth year . . . and at the same place for 17 to 18 years and the founder before me was big on that, basically 'cause a lot of people that live in the community have been beat up by society and some things that have gone on in the public school system. So, you want to make it a place where parents feel welcomed, they feel like they are respected, kids feel welcomed. There are respectful employees. They feel welcomed.

Smith works to have his school engage in multiple opportunities for community engagement:

> I think I have a very good relationship with the community, and I think it is very important to have a good relationship. To have the kids work with the community, do things in the community, help the community come in. We have open houses for the community. We have nights for the community to see what is going on inside the school, to see what is going on with the children. We have a newsletter to the community letting them know the success of what we are doing. I think it is very important for them to keep the community informed and engaged.

While one of the downsides of that arrangement is that there might not be as much diversity of opinion about how the school should be run, he finds plenty of disagreement from parents. Nevertheless, collective responsibility involves continual listening and mutual respect.

Justice Leadership. Smith demonstrates elements of all three aspects of justice leadership: opportunity gap disposition, asset-based perspective, and principled resistance. In Chapter 4, we characterize Smith as an "evolving straddler," a leader with an asset-based approach to leadership who conveyed both achievement gap and opportunity gap orientations. Smith shuttled back and forth between the immediacy of test score pressures and the need to provide his students opportunities that students receive in other, competing settings, such as noncharter schools and nearby suburban districts. The tension between test scores and opportunity are evident in this passage:

> Our test scores have dipped the last couple of years, and I think they've dipped across the state. But, you do get people starting to say, "Don't worry about the water polo team or don't worry about this or don't worry about that. Kids need just to do math, like all day every day, and take out the music program." And you [don't] want to put [off] any of these other programs to make their lives richer and more fulfilled . . . and give them the opportunities that—again, and I know I am picking on . . . the suburban [districts]—but, when your test scores start to dip . . . then people are like, "No, you can't do any of that stuff . . . just doing math every moment of every day and math problems."

Smith's approach is to "level the playing field." That's the rationale he uses in grant applications and the approach to providing associated supports to students:

> When we go for grants and things like that, we always say to the foundations. . . . "For the money we get, what you could benefit is trying to even or level the playing field" . . . . And there are kids who come in, maybe they are packing an Oodles of Noodles over the weekend. And it's hard, it's very hard, to get on that child for not doing their homework, get on that child for not having the proper uniform on when they're trying to figure out where they are going to sleep. And figuring out what they are eating and hearing gunshots and things like that.

Smith's abstract/technical approach to test scores is evident in how he discusses the differences in test scores.

> Of course I know there is an achievement gap. The biggest thing with us is . . . we are 98% African American, and we've always tried to gauge ourselves against the best in the state and country. So, we've never gauged ourselves as the neighborhood school . . . , the street, or kids of similar backgrounds or anything else. . . . If we all did that—just tried to be [the] best students we can be—I think the achievement gap would begin to close faster than it is.

The conflict between achievement gap and opportunity comes back in this passage, where Smith spoke about how test scores are both a competition and not a competition:

> We don't look at it as an achievement gap, because we all come from the same place. So, it's more about trying to compete, but I think compete is the wrong word too. 'Cause it is a competition, but it is not. It is not a competition against the whole country. It's trying to [lift] everybody up and trying to a certain level. So, instead of competing it's more trying to work together to try to get everybody a certain knowledge base.

A similar conflict comes into play in how Smith views the assets of students. When asked to describe his students, he named assets:

> It is interesting, 'cause it is K–8 and I think you see a lot of changes in K–8. You have the kindergarteners that come in who are so ramped up for school, and that goes all the way up through. And then all of a sudden [they are] middle school kids who are too cool for school and too cool for adults. But you try to get over that and try to get through that. I think we have kids who are very intelligent, very motivated, and drive to cultivate that.

Smith described how his school uses data to identify strengths and weaknesses:

> We use that data to see where a student is excelling in a certain thing, furthering in that, or are they lacking in certain things and change that to try to address those needs. So we use it for each student to try to see where is that student and what can we do to help better adjust.

Here Smith conveyed some of the second-level strategies and initiatives that can be used to address gaps in opportunity.

Smith also offered some examples of principled resistance, including his attempts to balance the pressures associated with test scores. He said, "I have to fight battles sometimes, 'cause we always argue we're not about test scores. But then, you're about test scores." He provided an example from his science curriculum, which doesn't directly align with what the Pennsylvania State System of Assessment assesses in middle school science:

> The last couple of years our science scores have been down in the middle school and the solid three months . . . done doing science projects. And I don't think the science projects are lending themselves to the PSSAs, but I think that [in] the science projects, kids are learning amazing things. So that is a restraint, so what do you do? Okay, kids are learning how to process, to formulate, to find out how to change things, how to explore, how to hypothesize, do all these good things, but then not learn exactly what is on the PSSAs. So they are learning the skills they need for the 21st century, but they may not be learning the facts exactly. But again, I go back to [my] original statement. I don't think it is going to

> be about what you know but how. So, I think the science projects are the right thing to do. We just have to find that balance.

As another example of principled resistance, Smith thought similarly about the school's project-based learning initiative, which he expected to improve test scores eventually, but only after a time of adjustment:

> We think we are going to have some dips in test scores for a little awhile, because . . . there is going to be a kind of learning curve, and there is a little bit different and you're not teaching to the test. We never taught to the test, but project-based learning has been another step into that. But we think the learning is greater and deeper and more meaningful. And it's [a] little like the Karate Kid. You know you're teaching different parts all along the way, and the kid's not going to know that he knows it all until one day when he tries [to] use it, and then he has it all figured out. But that's tough, and it's tough watching that process as it goes along.

Here Smith articulated the principled judgment of a school leader well-grounded in a vision for student learning. He is willing to resist pressure for short-term test score gains in favor of more meaningful, long-term learning goals.

The Ethical Praxis of James Smith

Smith's ethical praxis plays out in his long-standing leadership of a charter school that positions itself as a project-based and entrepreneurially focused alternative for K–8 students throughout the area while situated within an identifiable neighborhood. Evident through this narrative analysis of his interviews is that Smith mostly fits our race-conscious leadership model, but not all aspects are represented equally. His race consciousness is unique in our sample. Growing up white but also distinctly European in his family, culture, and religion provided him both insider and outsider status in the dominant culture of schooling. That orientation was reinforced by an equitable orientation toward difference exemplified by his family and carried into his being welcomed into a Black organization to lead and grow this charter school. His race consciousness is, in other words, well grounded in his life history and his schooling context. We suspect it demonstrates capacity, sensitivity, and nuance that goes beyond the quotations shared in this chapter.

It is also very clear that critical caring is a strong aspect of Smith's leadership practice. He named relationship-building as central to the culture of the school, and we interpret his approach as relational caring. It appears central to his philosophy of education, purposes of education, leadership approaches, parental engagement, community engagement, and moral leadership. During the interviews, Smith frequently returned to the importance of caring, knowing students, and building relationships across all constituents even when responding to questions not directly related to relationships. He attributed the relational approach to the school's founding leader and named it as consistent with his career-long approach to education. Finding a caring, relational environment in an urban school has made him an authentic leader who draws from his personal background and foundational values.

More complicated is Smith's fit with our model of justice leadership. In the several interviews analyzed for this chapter, there were multiple examples of the tension between gaps in opportunity and achievement. In comparison to the leaders with a solid opportunity gap orientation, Smith did not convey the same kind of strong resistance to cultural tropes about the deficits of students of color living in poverty, overrepresented in his school. Smith did not the convey the social, cultural, and structural critiques that other leaders did. However, Smith did speak about finding students' strengths and interests and responding to their needs and interests, which is tied to his critical caring. Principled resistance is one feature of justice leadership we found in his interviews; it is part of his charter school leadership and his choice to locate himself in this particular school in this particular urban setting. With his experience, he is resolute; he knows who he is, what he is up against, and what his school stands for. His critical praxis is therefore tied to the responsibility he enacts for his students as a member of a particular kind of collective—a school chartered by a public school district and governed by a community organization with deep roots in the neighboring community.

WRITING A MORAL NARRATIVE

We encourage school leaders and those preparing to become school leaders to craft their own moral narratives as a reflective exercise to identify their areas of strength and opportunity for growth and to chart paths to developing their capacity for race-conscious caring. Numerous authors have guidance on how to write a personal narrative or a moral narrative. In this section, we provide guidance for school leaders to go through the reflective process of writing a moral narrative. This is a particular type of pedagogical activity that can be done as part of a class or study group or as a professional development exercise.

We have adopted the Nash and Jang (2016) framework specifically because they offer moral narratives as a pedagogical approach to teaching professional ethics, and they provide guidance on how to incorporate aspects of private life into public moral leadership. (The narratives in this chapter were of course not written by the respondents but pieced together by the authors from three interviews that used a semistructured interview protocol.) The following guidance does not repeat the protocols we used to interview Johnson and Smith, but the prompts are informed by those questions, supplemented with a key critical reflection question for each area. These are suggested starting places for considering the various aspects of our model and how leaders might tap into their strengths and areas for growth.

Moral identity. Explain what you consider to be your core moral commitments. Reflect on how key persons and institutions have shaped those moral commitments. Identify moral communities (family, civic, faith, etc.) that continue to guide your view of what is right and the proper way to treat people. Reflection question: *How do you incorporate your personal background beliefs and your connections to important moral communities into your leadership practices?*

Educational background. Describe in detail your experience as a student, beginning from your earliest memory of education. Consider each educational setting you attended and describe them demographically in terms of race, poverty, culture, and geographic location. Focus on how you were treated as a student, the extent of your opportunities, and any barriers you faced. Describe your experience with racial difference as a student. Consider particularly vivid memories that you carry with you as an educator and why those memories might stand out for you. Reflection question: *What meaning do you make from your experience as a student that informs who you are as an educator and leader?*

Transition to teaching. Think back to how you decided to become a teacher. Consider what role crucial others played—such as mentors, exemplar teachers, students, and family members—who may have encouraged you to pursue teaching. Recall as much as possible your reasons for becoming a teacher. Make account of the schools where you taught, what you learned from each location, and the reasons that led you to choose new teaching opportunities. Name your experiences working with students of color and students living in poverty. Reflect on how you have countered dominant deficit perspectives about poverty and children and families of color. Reflection question: *What were the key commitments that led you to choose to become a teacher and how did you imagine that as a career for yourself?*

Transition to leadership. Closer now to your current role, consider what led you to aspire to a leadership role. As you did above, consider the roles that others played in your decision to pursue leadership. Chronicle your leadership experiences and the demographics of the schools you served. Name your experiences with students of color and students living in poverty. Reflect on how you have countered dominant deficit perspectives among teachers and other school leaders about poverty and children and families of color. Reflection question: *What did you wish to accomplish by becoming a school leader?*

Purposes of education. Write out a philosophy of education, which includes a statement about the meaning and value of education, the most important purposes of education, and what you wish for your students. Incorporate your definition of educational equity, your engagement with racial difference, and the extent to which your philosophy of education considers racialization and the racial identities of students. Name barriers to enacting your philosophy of education to expand educational equity. Reflection question: *To what extent does your philosophy of education relate to equity, and how is it reflected in your professional practice?*

Moral leadership. Drawing from what you have written previously about your moral identity, build an ethical profile for yourself as a leader. At the most general level, describe what you believe it means to be a good person and name the main contributors in your life to your growth as a moral person. Transition to what it means to be a moral *leader*—the responsibilities associated with being a moral leader, the challenges you have encountered enacting your vision of moral leadership, and what you have learned about yourself as a result. Then reflect on what you do as a leader to cultivate a moral community. Reflection question: *To what extent do you lead an organization that is collectively responsible for the educational experiences for all children?*

Race consciousness. Turn now to your professional practice and how the components of your moral narrative play out in your school leadership. Provide a snapshot of your current engagement with racial difference in your school and how you are building your school's capacity to engage racial identity and the strengths, histories, and material effects of racial difference and racism in your community. Without speaking for them, locate where students of color may find sustaining engagement with racial difference in the community, personnel, curriculum, and instruction in the school. Reflection question: *What successes has your school community experienced with race consciousness, and in what specific ways does your school enact race-evasiveness?*

Critical caring. Revisiting what you described as moral leadership, consider the role that caring and relation play in your vision of yourself as a moral leader. Linking this reflection to your reflection on race consciousness above, consider the quality of relationships you have built with children, families, and communities of color in the school. Recall stories that you know about students of color and students living in poverty in your school community and consider whether those are stories primarily told by them or about them. Describe how the school community exercises its collective responsibility for the educational success of all students. Reflection question: *What successes has your school community experienced with critical caring, and in what specific ways does your school enact impersonal caring?*

Justice leadership. As much as possible from memory, describe in detail the demographics of your school, including the socioeconomic status of your students, the percentage of students who qualify for special education, multilingual learners, and the percentage of students in various racial and ethnic groups. Describe different educational opportunities, outcomes, and experiences undergone by the various groups identified (even if you are not required to report these differences publicly). Describe your responsibility and your efforts for attending to these differences. Provide examples of how you make principled decisions to enact your philosophy of education. Reflection question: *Place yourself on Figure 4.2; to what extent are you enacting justice leadership, and where is there room for growth?*

Ethical praxis. Recalling that we expect each race-conscious caring leader to enact ethical praxis in a unique way in their context and for their particular students, consider your moral leadership and the other three components of the model—race consciousness, critical caring, and justice leadership—and synthesize your leadership into a holistic practice, naming the most important aspects of your leadership, the key commitments that play through your practice, and how it is reflected in the successes of your school. Identify structural constraints that enable your work and those that you actively work against to succeed. Reflection question: *What is the best of your practice for equity leadership, and how will you continue to grow your capacity for equity leadership?*

CHAPTER 6

Professional Development for Race-Conscious Leadership

In their various roles over the last several years, Michael Quigley and Osly J. Flores have partnered with numerous schools, school districts, and other educational organizations to deliver professional development that draws from aspects of the race-conscious caring model. Through coursework and guest lecture presentations, Michael, Osly, and Mike Gunzenhauser all contribute to graduate programs that prepare school leaders at our institutions. In this chapter, we explore what we have learned from these experiences about the applicability of our model to school leadership practice. We provide several examples of professional development sessions, how school leaders and students preparing to be school leaders have taken up the work, and how much more work is still needed.

Through the reflections of our engagement with practitioners, we add dimension to our model and identify roadblocks to implementation of the model and potential pathways for capacity building. We start with a tale of two professional development settings, both for principal preparation programs, that had dramatically different dynamics and outcomes. Contrasting these experiences, we explore what we can learn and apply for the successful implementation of race-conscious caring in practice. We next look at the dynamics at play in partnerships with schools and school districts that were intended to build capacity for equity leadership and more equitable educational practices. Across these experiences are reflections on the conditions that facilitate or impede progress and the importance of leadership support. Finally, we turn to lessons learned from our work to infuse more equitable practices into our teaching practices and professional preparation programs in our schools of education, where we often encounter resistance and a lack of capacity.

A TALE OF TWO GUEST LECTURES

Over the past several years, Michael Quigley has been a guest lecturer for several cohorts of a principal preparation program. In this section, we tell the tale of two of those cohorts who had different reactions to his guest lecture. While the general population of the participants was essentially the same for these two cohorts, the specific makeup of the two groups was different, and the responses to the two lectures were markedly different. In both groups, the session was held online via Google Meet during Leslie Jefferson's class. Participants included leadership students from across Pennsylvania—some already in leadership roles and others preparing for their first leadership roles. Both groups had read materials ahead of time, and while the specific materials were different, they covered similar themes—equity leadership, race-conscious practices, and culturally responsive leadership.

Passive Resistance

In the first session, Michael presented with Angela Allie, a Black woman and longtime colleague who is a former principal and school district equity officer. They spoke about the importance of race-conscious caring and the need to understand the narratives of students, teachers, and school leaders who had experienced racial subjugation. They encountered both passive and active resistance. Some participants immediately made open comments like, "I don't get this. This doesn't make sense." One white male principal continually contested the material and gained leverage among the other participants, who began to chime in with responses like, "Well, I don't necessarily get this." The overall mood was passive-aggressive. Angela texted Michael some side comments to express her frustration and to constrain the temptation to say something unprofessional to the instigator, who was sabotaging the whole session.

Michael and Angela found themselves becoming combative, trying to convince the vocal white man of the value of the work. Besides Michael and Angela, one other Black person was in the room, a Black woman early in her career. It appeared to them she didn't feel comfortable expressing her view in the dynamic that the vocal white man had perpetrated. Professional development specialists often say that the first thing teachers ask at a session is, "I get the concept; what do I do on Monday?" With this man's continual comments, it felt that sentiment had become weaponized. With that resistance deployed, the other participants joined in. This example reveals how individuals strategically maneuver to evade discussion of concepts or theories related to race, forsaking consideration of the experiences of people of color, such as Michael and Angela, but also the experiences of the future leaders' own students. The participants further claimed they were not offered any practical way to respond to the inequities Michael and Angela described, although they indeed had offered multiple practical things leaders could apply to their practice. None of the participants took up those practical suggestions, instead picking out the most minute details and taking issue with their practicality. They wanted to know what a lesson plan should look like, rather than engaging the ideas, to undermine the premise of their inequity claims by arguing it was all impractical.

One white female student arranged an online meeting afterward with Michael. The student expressed her frustration, crying at one point, and said she did not know how to combat conversation that tries to delegitimize or avoid equity and cultural responsiveness. She did not have the language to combat it, but she wanted to. She said the only thing she could have done at that point was to burst out in tears and curse out the vocal white male. She lacked the language to resist, to tell a different story that could have challenged the dynamic of the session.

Engagement With Limited Capacity

In the more recent guest lecture session, the participants were at similar places in their careers, but the dynamics were markedly different. In this group, the practicing and aspiring principals came from several large partner school districts, including an urban district, a charter school network, and a fully virtual cyber charter school system. Compared to the previous passive-aggressive group, this group of participants appeared engaged. This group read two articles that addressed components of our race-conscious caring framework, one focused on race-conscious ethics (Gunzenhauser, Flores, & Quigley, 2021) and one focused on narrative ethics (Gunzenhauser, Flores, & Quigley, 2024). The two instructors for the course were Brian Stokes, a white male superintendent with a doctoral degree, and Leslie Jefferson, a white female faculty member and former superintendent. Stokes was engaged throughout the session, speaking about his work in his racially mixed community. Stokes is committed to racial equity work and, as a superintendent, grounds his leadership practice by doing things with students of color living in poverty in his urban school district, which also has a high percentage of students who qualify for free or reduced-price lunch.

The student dynamic was noteworthy. One of the students, Gina Crowley, is a Black female assistant principal in an urban school. Crowley felt very connected to both readings and was interested in diving into the articles and having a robust conversation in class. She also seemed to leverage the articles to make a statement to everybody else. Another student, a Black male charter school assistant principal, Andrew Steele, also used elements of the race-conscious caring framework to name and emphasize important attitudes. Steele reflected on how his school had changed over time. Founded as a charter school to provide a full, high-quality education to children of color and students living in poverty, his organization has grown into a charter school network. Steele recalled that when he first started working there, the organization was interested in developing students' critical consciousness and life skills. That is no longer the emphasis, and now he feels increasing pressure from the organization to maximize the number of students who achieve proficiency on standardized tests.

As Michael went through the material, Crowley and Steele functioned as ambassadors to the class, making connections and framing them in ways that their classmates could understand. During the lesson, Crowley referenced the Pennsylvania state leadership standards, which include a standard addressing the understanding of communities and another standard about the development of caring. Echoing our model, Crowley linked the two standards, answering the question posed to the class, "How do you care?" with the response that they should all go to the community and ask the right people the right questions so they can solve the right problems.

When the group discussed the narrative ethics article (Gunzenhauser et al., 2024), Crowley talked about the importance of understanding community cultural wealth through narrative. Drawing from her experiences doing equity work in an urban school district and recently writing a children's book, Crowley shared how educators can access and utilize the "magic" from members of the community, such as pastors, police officers, coaches, and mentors from recreational centers who meet with the kids every day in after-school programs. We take "magic" to mean the knowledge and other assets in the Black community. She talked about the wisdom of the lunch lady in the school who knows everybody and people in the community who know the kids and how important leveraging that knowledge is for educational leaders who are not from the school community. The conversation eventually shifted to questions from some white classmates on how to cultivate relationships with those knowledge bearers so they can leverage this knowledge. The discussion then turned to particular leadership actions that could facilitate those relationships, such as discipline policies, school culture, curriculum, and course content. The idea that leaders need to go to the community, get these narratives from the folks in the community, and leverage the community's cultural wealth provoked participants into telling stories about things they had done. Michael affirmed to the class that white leaders or leaders not previously connected to local neighborhoods are entirely capable of developing the knowledge and experience to become effective leaders for children of color. Furthermore, he told them, "White folks don't have the market cornered on what it means to be a racist educational leader." And as soon as he said that, Crowley chimed in about her experience and spoke that same truth.

Most of the participants were white females, seemed very connected to the work, and asked questions, especially when discussing getting into the community. They sought advice on how to identify the community's cultural wealth and to understand the circumstances from which their students come. Two white women shared that they had done similar work in urban school districts in their different areas of the state, taking trips into impoverished neighborhoods with their teaching staff as part of a professional development exercise. The two white women acted as collaborators with Michael, reinforcing the importance of the community activity. Michael found some magic in that dynamic; these two students demonstrated understanding and were interested in learning more. Even though they did not have all the answers about equity leadership, or the exposure to people of color, or all the capacity they would need to be strong equity leaders, they were willing to learn.

At the same time, their lack of capacity and understanding on how to apply and enact many of the things that they agreed on within the article was striking. This was true especially of the younger white women. Many of the participants became silent when Steele started to talk about the challenges associated with meeting students where they are but not crippling them by enabling them or being permissive—providing them with opportunities and still holding them to high standards. An ensuing conversation between Steele, the student, and Stokes, the instructor, revealed some "tough love" caring perspectives by Stokes, who spoke to the importance of holding students accountable, not just pushing them along, so they can succeed when they go out into the world. As a difference from the tough-love caring theme in Chapter 3, Stokes wants students to be equipped not only with basic math and communications skills but also with a perspective that we might call critical consciousness (although Stokes did not use that term). Despite his use of language implying a form of tough love, which (as we have seen) can be expressed in counterproductive actions, Stokes's knowledge and engagement with his school's community demonstrate a responsiveness characteristic of critical caring.

Three white male participants were in the class, and two appeared to Michael to be willing to engage in learning about racial equity. One had been an undergraduate student of Michael's, now preparing to be a principal. He seemed very interested in learning and posed questions. He talked about the pressure imposed upon him as a teacher to raise standardized test scores and students' measured proficiency rates. The third white male, who appeared hesitant to engage with the topic, was a principal, athletic director, and football coach who had little to say during the session. He made an initial introductory statement about who he was but said only one thing during the 2 hours they were together—he stated that he understood the material but provided no meaningful contribution to the conversation, as if he just wanted to make sure that he got on record, since the session was recorded. The session was at the end of the day after a full day of work, so Michael surmised this man might just have been exhausted from his day but was unsure; nearly all the other participants were likely just as exhausted but were fully engaged.

The other conspicuously quiet person was Jefferson, particularly in contrast to Stokes, her instructional partner. Jefferson has frequently tapped

Michael to provide an equity component to her coursework when required. She has asked him to visit her class or to suggest readings she can include. The invitation seems obligatory rather than substantive, reinforced by her lack of participation in the class discussion, her choice to end the session earlier than scheduled, and her subsequent disengagement with the materials and ideas that Michael offered. After Michael's presentation, Jefferson invited questions from the students; after one question, which Michael answered, and as Michael was about to ask for other questions, Jefferson asked the class to thank him and suggested he should log off the session so she could address some course housekeeping issues. Michael regards Jefferson's lack of interest and engagement as potentially generational, since the younger students were clearly interested. Jefferson, like most of the students in the first session, conveyed a lack of understanding based on a lack of exposure and experience with people of color, especially impoverished people of color.

The up-and-coming principals in the second session were interested in learning more about equitable leadership but lacked the capacity to do the work. Many indicated they were afraid to engage for fear of saying the wrong thing, which is a familiar response in education courses; on many occasions, graduate students indicated they were afraid to engage for fear of saying the wrong thing in front of a Black presenter or Black classmates. It is important to reinforce to students that the risk is necessary and worthwhile to identify areas of improvement and ultimately to build confidence and capacity to address racial inequities. Admitting these emotional responses is helpful so that tools can be developed to process and work through the reluctance.

Evidence from the second session reveals how educators when exposed to equity discussions can fall into each of the three bands in the race-consciousness model from Chapter 2. For example, Stokes, Crowley, and Steele conveyed the outer band—cultivating race consciousness—respecting and responding to the needs and interests of their racialized students. Most of the participants figured into the middle band—recognition with minimal capacity—and, for the most part, avoided the deficit perspectives emblematic of the inner ring of that middle band. The white women and the two engaged white males conveyed interest but lacked the capacity for action, so they were not yet able to enact their race recognition. Jefferson also figured somewhere in the middle band since she wanted her students to have exposure to the content, perhaps seeing it as an obligation, but she hasn't taken it on herself, perhaps from lack of experience as an educator in a predominantly white, rural setting. For his lack of participation, the stoic white male principal, athletic director, and football coach figured in the inner band—holding to color-evasiveness—essentially evading engagement in the topic and conveying little recognition.

Efficacy for Building Capacity

Across these two sessions, we draw conclusions about the efficacy of the race-conscious caring model and the challenges of its implementation. Jefferson, one of the instructors of the second session, recognized the importance of the topic of equity, whether or not her commitments align with equity in general and race-conscious caring in particular. Aware she does not have the capacity to facilitate the session herself, she invited Michael in, but there's no indication of her interest in building her own capacity. As a result, Michael and Angela were on their own during the first session. At least one student with strong interest in the material sat in frustration but lacked the language to counter the passive-aggressive response of her classmates. Clearly, leaders of change need participants to tap into some interest that helps them connect to race-conscious caring, to learn the concepts, and then to apply them to their professional practice. Resistance strategies are readily employable for the passive-aggressive deniers who either do not read or do not understand what they read or hear and refuse to engage the ideas by rejecting their practicality. Reinforcement from within the group can encourage a learning orientation for the group, especially when the content resonates with the experience of some participants. A roomful of participants without experience is a more challenging dynamic. The lack of engagement is a symptom of the systemic issues the model is trying to address, so whenever resistance in the form of disengagement occurs, it is important to address it—to find out why the disengagement is occurring. Later on, we say more about how leaders can address disengagement.

The second session was very encouraging, and the race-conscious caring model provides a framework for interpreting the varied engagement. The engagement from the majority of the class was encouraging but at the same time worrying because it was aspirational; it would require concerted action and continuous learning for all those future leaders to sustain action. Specific to the context of expanding cyber school systems in Pennsylvania, the concern is how educators working in cyber schools can get the experience of engagement in communities, especially since their students could be from multiple and varied communities, perhaps hundreds of miles apart, and the leaders would be going into those positions without experience and capacity. In response to the cyber school participants' queries about how to obtain the experience, Michael responded that he did not have clear answers, given the modality, but said that it is always important to be able to identify where their students are coming from (literally and figuratively) and what assets exist in those communities so that they can tailor the content of their teaching. Because of continuing racial and socioeconomic residential segregation, educators don't know what goes on outside their own communities, and they don't know their students' communities. They need to know how to obtain the resources available for educators, such as videos that explain the adultification and vilification of Black girls in schools and the underlying reasons behind the predictable struggles of Black and brown males in schools (e.g., see Seate, 2020).

A SINGULAR ACT OF RESISTANCE

Sometimes the resistance to engage in the work of race-conscious caring is explicit and organized. Following is a story of one such instance and what it reflects about educators' resistance to building their capacity to work with students of color. Michael and Osly worked together on a professional development contract in the Liberty School District, a suburban school district that had experienced a recent influx of additional students of color as gentrification pushed lower-income families of color out of the city limits into more affordable suburbs bordering the city. Superintendent Marcie Gibbons, a white woman, was deeply engaged in the work of preparing teachers and school staff to engage these new students and devoted considerable professional development time to the broader work of equity in the district. Gibbons specifically focused on improving the school district culture, community engagement, discipline patterns, curriculum choices, and culturally responsive pedagogy.

At one particular session, teachers and principals from across the district were in attendance, and Michael gave them a scavenger hunt assignment to complete during their lunch break. He asked them to drive to the outskirts of the district, to neighborhoods where mostly Black and mostly impoverished residents lived. He asked each person to take three pictures on their cell phones for a discussion after they returned from their lunch break: one picture that demonstrated evidence of a challenge in the community, one picture that showed a resource, and one picture that showed an asset. He gave them examples of each and explained the difference between a *resource* (such as a bank, a church, or a community center) and an *asset* (something of cultural wealth within the community that young people coming from this community can lean on and feel good about). He intended the exercise to send home the message that there is wealth in this community and that educators need to be able to tap into it. While obviously they would not be able to learn much about the community as a whole, the activity was intended as a hook to convince educators of the need to make this kind of effort to develop their knowledge and from there develop their capacity to work more effectively with their students.

Several educators grumbled about the assignment. All of them left the room, and a group of teachers gravitated toward one person, who Michael later found out was a union representative. The union representative told them that since the scavenger hunt was requested during their lunch hour, it was an encroachment on their personal time and, hence, not covered under the collective bargaining agreement; they were therefore not required to do it. So there was a cluster of teachers who did not do the assignment. Willful and intentional about their refusal, they missed the opportunity to be exposed to the reality of the neighborhoods where a lot of their racially marginalized and lower socioeconomic status students live. Some of the other teachers did the assignment, and the leaders did it (perhaps begrudgingly) since the union did not cover them. The leaders may have complied because the superintendent clearly advocated for the equity and race-conscious work, and she could hold them accountable for their participation. The PD session continued with the reflections of those who did the exercise, but within the group an opportunity for participants to more fully engage was lost.

Going further, one white woman teacher went so far as to say that even if it were covered under the collective bargaining agreement she would have refused to do it and would have filed a grievance because she grew up in a working-class community herself. On that account, she believed she knew everything she needed to know about her poor Black students' community, and she was not going to put herself in harm's way by driving through this community. To our knowledge, there has never been a midday crime wave in this community, so there is much to unpack about white fears about minoritized neighborhoods where small Black children live. According to district data, students living in these neighborhoods were typically funneled into special education classes and were overrepresented in discipline referrals, and almost all were Black.

Michael has told this story of explicit resistance during subsequent PD sessions to invite participants to imagine the motivations behind these educators' unwillingness to engage in the scavenger hunt. The contract concern is less important than the impulse to seek an official reason not to engage. It is important to surface the reluctance that mostly white educators bring to race-conscious work and to give participants an opportunity to acknowledge whatever discomfort they are experiencing in the moment.

Bringing resistance to racial equity work up for discussion acknowledges the emotions associated with race-conscious work; we can invite people to name their emotions and feelings, validate them as feelings, and then provide tools for working through their reluctance. Michael has heard similar concerns in his classes. Recently, a student wrote in a reflection paper that she wasn't sure how to have age-appropriate conversations with her Black students about their experiences. In instances like this, Michael encourages his students to worry less about initiating age-appropriate conversations with their students about their experience and instead to be prepared when students initiate conversations with them. He first encourages educators to talk with their colleagues and community members, who would gladly share their perspectives, and to use those more nuanced and sophisticated adult perspectives to pose problems and encourage discussions with their students about the race-based issues they and their communities face. This helps the students develop a critical consciousness and a connection to the teacher, who demonstrates care and concern. The dominant approach—doing nothing—instead keeps educators and their students stuck in a place of racial, cultural, and generational dissonance.

LEADERSHIP COMMITMENT WITH SCHOOL PARTNERS

Leadership commitment is vital to building capacity for race-conscious caring. Michael's work with school and school district partners demonstrates some difficulties he has encountered when trying to make his racial equity professional development work take root in schools. These challenging instances show how leaders missed opportunities to support and extend the equity work and lessened their ultimate impact on the schools' cultures. These examples demonstrate how leadership dispositions inconsistent with equity work can make it difficult to implement the components of race conscious caring leadership.

A Strained Leadership Team

In the first instance, a problematic dynamic among leaders of a high school inhibited the work. Seth Thompson, the leader of a large urban high school, contracted Michael for professional development to enhance the school's equity work. The school enrolls a diverse population of Black and white students, with many students coming from families living in poverty. Thompson, a former superintendent, has experience in many different educational settings. A teacher, Marshall Albertson, had tried implementing culturally responsive pedagogy across the school and recommended Michael to Thompson because he was having trouble gaining traction. Michael discovered why after working with the leadership team.

For the PD, leaders had the option to attend Michael's sessions with teachers, but they mostly attended sessions Michael conducted specifically for the leadership team. In addition to Thompson, there were three female assistant principals: one Black (Betty Crawford), one Latina (Lisa Martin), and one white (Wendy Vincent). Each had extensive experience in urban environments. Crawford had a rocky relationship with Martin and Vincent, who seemed more aligned with each other. Of the three, Crawford was most interested in engaging in the equity work and had multiple side conversations with Michael about what she saw as the existing barriers to that work in the school. Martin and Vincent were less engaged, which Crawford attributed to their insincere interest in making any changes. Crawford believed her two colleagues were attending the sessions merely to appease Thompson, their boss.

In relation to our model, Martin and Vincent demonstrated a tough-luck/tough-love approach to caring, a kind of "Pittsburgh tough" approach Michael attributes to their growing up in working-class white neighborhoods. Martin and Vincent felt a kind of possessiveness over their students and felt justified speaking for and about them rather than speaking with them. As explained in Chapter 3, educators who are not engaged with students or in the community often take the tough-luck/tough-love approach—they speak at students and about them. Crawford objected to this approach, but she found herself unable to challenge the other two assistant principals openly during the professional development sessions. Based on their side conversations, Michael found Crawford interested in change but, unlike Scarlett Johnson's demonstration of justice leadership, she was unable or unwilling to jeopardize her position or status. He came to understand that if she challenged her colleagues, Crawford would have exacerbated an already low-level, simmering hostility. Crawford kept it collegial, but they were neither collaborating nor working to understand one another to advance the work of equity.

During the various PD trainings, Crawford did not speak up at critical points when she had the opportunity. To make racial equity ideas work, the whole leadership team would have needed to learn from each other to then support the teaching teams to work together. They were competing rather than fostering collective responsibility. Michael suspected that it was the leadership tension that led Albertson to seek outside help; Albertson was not able to break through the tension on his own. In retrospect, Michael believes Albertson and Crawford needed more allies to build a critical mass that could effect change. Lacking this support, Crawford stayed quiet and toed the company line.

Another part to this story is Thompson's leadership. Despite his good intentions (evidenced by his support of Albertson's ideas and hiring Michael), Thompson created no urgency around improving equity and failed to manage his assistant principals' poor relationship. As principal of a large urban school, Thompson was pulled in many directions, with many external political issues to attend to. Thompson attended the trainings but routinely deferred to Michael, an external trainer, especially in the meetings with the leadership team. It is unclear how much Thompson knew about the disagreement among the leadership team and whether he attempted to address the strained and racialized dynamic. In retrospect, Thompson may have hoped the professional development would address the dynamic, but he seemed to lack the language and knowledge to make it happen. However, it is hard to imagine how the dynamic could have changed without his understanding and guidance as a leader.

Watering Down the Content

In the Wallburg School District, another district where Michael was recruited to conduct a series of PD trainings as part of a school–university partnership, we again see the absence of a critical mass of leaders and teachers determined to make change. Wallburg educators did not know what to say or how to disrupt, dispute, and challenge the current narrative about the backlash against critical race theory and wokeness. Michael met district leaders to describe the elements, cadence, sequence, and language of the PD he planned to deliver, naming the content precisely as focused on anti-Black racism in education. Following a national trend, the district leaders objected to it, wanting to avoid frank terminology and to water down the content. This was particularly frustrating since challenging anti-Black racism is the work Michael does and is known for. His white faculty colleagues were willing to acquiesce, with one arguing it was not a battle they thought worth fighting. Obeying in advance (Snyder, 2017), his white colleagues had the luxury to acquiesce, while the children of color in the school district—the ones who stood to benefit from the work—did not have that luxury.

Wallburg superintendent Kelly Mitchell was not involved in this conversation, but Michael had no reason to believe Mitchell considered the work a priority. In his prior work with Mitchell in a different school district, Mitchell neither participated nor directed any particular emphasis on race-conscious work. Mitchell's deputy superintendent, a Black female, also acquiesced and made no effort to advocate for the naming of the work in very clear antiracist terms, instead opting for a so-called "diversity and inclusion" initiative in the school district. Without guidance from the top leaders, the racial equity goals were diluted and the work lost its ability to have impact on the experiences of children of color. Michael exited that partnership in favor of partnerships with more leadership commitment.

Ego-Driven Leadership

In two other cases, different leadership limitations diminished the ability of equity professional development to take root. The two leaders displayed some common behaviors. Terrence Norman, a Black male leading an urban high school, seemed very concerned about conveying an image of dominating leadership. This image led to resistance to the content of Michael's PD. Michael refers to this form of resistance as "smartest and strongest Black guy in the room resistance." In contrast to other leadership partners who admitted their lack of knowledge and were open to learn and improve their practice, it seemed difficult for Norman to appear not knowledgeable. Concerned mostly with not being shown up by a visiting PD provider, Norman subtly challenged the content rather than substantively engaging with it. Instead of listening and learning alongside his staff, Norman asserted how processes worked in the school, conveying to everyone in the room that however they took up the work Michael was presenting, it would need to fit into the policy processes and procedures already in place. Overall, in distracting from the equity content of the PD, Norman signaled that, in his school, educators who wanted to pursue implementing the learning from the equity PD would need to bend to his will and do it his way.

This phenomenon recurred in the second case, with Marvin Robbins, the Black male superintendent of Midway School District, an urban school district. Robbins made himself conspicuously present at all of Michael's training sessions during a PD conference in Robbins's district. Michael wondered why Robbins wanted to sit in on all of his sessions, wondering if Robbins felt insecure because another Black man was providing educators at the school with a different messaging around issues of equity. In the sessions, Robbins participated a little too much. When he spoke, he did not directly contest the validity of the scholarship Michael presented, but he argued that the suggested strategies would not work with their students. Robbins reinforced the necessity to keep students in line—portraying himself more as a dean of discipline than a superintendent, much less a race-conscious caring leader. Michael felt undermined throughout. Robbins repeatedly said that the most important thing was that the district met the standards to keep the school running and not get taken over by the state. For example, Robbins said, "It's not going to be taken over, not on my watch."

The two stances shared above are noteworthy because they demonstrate school leaders placing external motivations ahead of the needs of their students—mostly external motivations for test score performance, which in Robbins's case meant eluding state takeover of the district. But also evident were the leaders' own personal motivations taking precedence. Instead of focusing on the needs and interests of students, which is what we expect of critical caring, both leaders seemed more focused on maintaining their power, leverage, ego, and job security and on maintaining order and surveillance over students of color. They did not want to appear vulnerable; paradoxically, in our view, their resistance reveals them as vulnerable because it suggests they are unwilling to engage with new and different ideas. Systemic, racialized accountability pressures exacerbate the difficulties, pitting educators against each other, and in this case, oddly incentivizing educational leaders to pit themselves against committed colleagues with whom they could build collective responsibility.

Developing capacity for race-conscious leadership is a learning process. It is primarily relational and the responsibility of all educational leaders, regardless of their race, ethnicity, gender, age, sexual orientation, disability, or other marginalized identity. At the same time, tapping into those identities should be a source of strength and a way to bridge understanding, rather than a barrier or the opportunity for a power struggle. It is important that we highlight that just because a leader holds certain identities and experiences, we cannot assume that leader to be a race-conscious caring leader. To engage the components of our framework requires work. Achieving greater equity requires replacing a controlling culture of surveillance with a pervasive culture of race-conscious care—with expansive student outcomes rather than forced test score outcomes at the expense of student interest and opportunity.

The Necessity of Leadership Commitment

The reflections on professional development partnerships in this section highlight the significance of leadership commitment to continual capacity building for racial equity. In each case, engagement with key ideas that are part of our race-conscious caring model faced nearly prohibitive challenges that prevented the ideas from coming to fruition. Simply hiring someone to do professional development is not commitment. When partnering with a school or school district to make change, the ideal situation would be for the school leader to convey a clear understanding of concepts associated with race-conscious caring, prioritize it, and hold educators accountable for engaging in a capacity-building process. Prioritizing the work may also mean engaging the larger political discourse that makes certain concepts suddenly contentious. Certain ideas may be intentionally made volatile, such as the sudden volatility in the early 2020s of equity-related theories and practices that school leaders had read about or implemented—such as *critical race theory*, *social-emotional learning,* and *DEI*—through the intentional efforts of political actors. Leaders need the language to get school boards on board with their initiatives and to defuse the noise that challenges clear priorities to serve children of color. When partnering with an individual school, district support is also important and facilitates that work. If, like Thompson, the leader is unable to convey understanding, they need to prioritize the work and be able to address whatever leadership dynamics are preventing their leadership teams from engaging in the work. Within schools, leaders need to model a learning orientation that emphasizes serving children of color rather than maintaining control of schools.

WORKING WITH FACULTY COLLEAGUES

Another significant area for enacting race-conscious caring is in professional preparation programs in higher education. As we mentioned earlier, Mike, Osly, and Michael all contribute to teacher, principal, and superintendent preparation programs in their schools and departments. In this section, we identify some barriers to and facilitators of implementing our race-conscious caring model in these settings. These experiences have continually taught us the complexity of the work and the importance of building collective efforts that work against a tide of complacency in the forms of color-evasiveness, impersonal caring, and systemic opportunity gaps.

Michael was not surprised when his faculty colleagues were willing to acquiesce to the Wallburg School District's reluctance to engage in critical race theory and the concepts associated with it. Schools of education are often slow and turgid in their efforts to incorporate more equity content into curricula. Michael and Mike were part of an initiative in 2008 to incorporate social justice into the mission of the Pitt School of Education, but that effort faltered without a critical mass of support, and it was not until 2019 that the school adopted a mission/vision centered on equity and justice under new school and university leadership. Subsequent work continued to revise teacher education and leadership preparation curricula to enact that mission/vision.

Across our institutions, teacher education curricula are driven by state certification and national accreditation standards, themselves regulated by the many large professional associations in education. The hyper-standardization of educator preparation has meant there are multiple requirements that need to be met in a field decreasing in popularity, professional autonomy, and perceived prestige. Attempts to raise standards for teacher quality run headlong into the constraints in the number of credits of an undergraduate degree (and rising tuition prices, which make graduate-level teacher education certification programs expensive). Attending to educational equity would seem to be of utmost importance, especially considering the diversity explosion in public schools, but it competes with all these other priorities. Perhaps more problematically, it comes up against education faculty's largely race-evasive perspectives toward teaching, learning, and leadership. Most colleagues lament the lack of racial representation in teaching and leadership ranks, and they are on board for recruiting more students of color into the education profession. However, they are less interested in changing their curricula.

Without commitment from a critical number of colleagues, it is difficult to imagine teacher preparation programs implementing the kind of curriculum and instruction needed to prepare students to become race-conscious caring educators and leaders. Similar to their counterparts in K–12 schools, professional education faculty in higher education are under systemic pressure to meet accreditation standards. It is challenging work to prepare teachers and school leaders in the work of equity, and it is difficult to fit in all the aspects of practice that are important to address. That state of affairs may be why advocates for stronger preparation in Pennsylvania have sought to legislate preparation requirements like those for teaching multilingual learners and students with disabilities into the state teaching standards.

The resistance to engage equity work varies from passive, with very little outward resistance, to direct confrontation, with also some clear concern about capacity and reluctance to build the knowledge and skills to do the work. When it comes to course content, the equity content often gets sequestered into elective courses or single courses, rather than being incorporated across the curriculum. The fear of offending students can outweigh an educator's commitment to equity. The result is that the equity concepts are not carried through into their logical application where we want preservice teachers and school leaders to use them, areas like teaching methods, curriculum development, leadership ethics, and strategic planning. The value judgment implied by sequestering equity content to particular courses, perhaps taught by the only faculty member of color in the program, trickles down into student expectations. They interpret the priorities fairly clearly.

At the same time, we should be clear that perfection is not the goal. It may not be possible for any one person to successfully incorporate all components found in race-conscious caring leadership. Everything can certainly be critiqued. Our own practices can always be better. Developing the capacity for race-conscious caring is a learning process and a collective responsibility. We encourage all faculty colleagues to do their part in equity work, so that equity is infused and preservice students see it as a continual focus. Racial equity, disability equity, gender equity, social class equity—we encourage colleagues to do it all, but everyone can do something.

HELPING SCHOOLS BUILD CAPACITY FOR RACE-CONSCIOUS CARING

Professional development for race-conscious caring leadership is an essential effort to expand collective capacity for expanding opportunities for all children, with special emphasis on serving children of color and children living in poverty. Working with leaders is at times very rewarding, especially when we encounter highly competent leaders who have risen to their positions because of their deep interest in making education better for children. We have worked closely with educators in our classrooms and in professional training sessions who have centered critical caring in their practice and become advocates for the most marginalized and minoritized children in their communities. Building their schools' capacity can be difficult work, and these school leaders sometimes do not succeed. In more cases than should be happening, leaders exhaust themselves and their efforts and have to move on. To counter potentially debilitating disengagement, there needs to be a critical mass of individuals for whom the work resonates. And when there is not critical mass, leaders need to start building it. Institutions cannot change for the better through the force of will of one individual leader, although they certainly can change for the worse. Leaders can expect some level of disengagement nearly any time they challenge attitudes that are taken for granted. Disengagement can signal discomfort, lack of knowledge, fear of failure, or deep-seated racist or classist beliefs. Leaders need not assume the latter is always the case, but they should name the disengagement and investigate the reasons. Passive resistance may be a strategy of avoidance, but leaders can interrupt it by bringing it into the open and taking a pedagogical approach—inviting disengaged participants to set specific learning goals. Leaders should also recognize that if disengagement is not questioned and redirected, racism will work through the disengaged—reinforcing differential power, perpetuating subjugation of students of color, and authorizing those deliberating intending to resist. Working with the recurrent resistant requires different strategies.

Addressing Recurrent Resistance

A recurring concern is the fear of alienating people. These fears lead to inaction and obedience in advance (Snyder, 2017). The work needs to remain focused on the best and most meaningful efforts to engage children of color. Watering down the content to assuage concerns that it is too critical does damage to the work—it becomes unfocused and either performative or nonperformative (Ahmed, 2012). Michael participated in a school district's extensive engagement with *Courageous Conversations* in which Glenn Singleton (2015) facilitated the professional development himself and demanded that the conversations use the critical terms that were most accurate. While Michael has sometimes directed his own work and is able to use approaches and terminology that address race consciousness directly, most often he has worked with schools and school districts who have insisted on scaling back. The most resistant leaders are consistently the most veteran white men and women leaders, who either reject the entire premise of the work or who accept race consciousness nominally and consider their work done without fundamentally changing practices.

Widespread virtual access via Zoom and other remote meeting platforms in the wake of the COVID-19 pandemic has encouraged the growth of webinars for professional development. While the technology provides some ease of access to expertise that was not available before, it is not necessarily an improvement for the work of race-conscious caring. In our experience, there seems to be more engagement and much less resistance when equity-focused professional development is offered in person rather than online. In person, presenters like Michael can engage participants in activities that encourage breaking down their barriers and forming connections with their colleagues. The distance and safety that online environments provide may encourage participants to be more vocal about their resistance, or to sit quietly and multitask rather than actually engage. At the same time, the safety of online settings provides some people an opportunity to speak up and say some things that they may not in a face-to-face session. In his work, Michael does not recall coming across a Black educator who was not ready to speak their piece—whether online or in person. In the most recent guest lecture session mentioned above, Michael encountered one of the first situations he has seen in which white women spoke out in support of the material. White superintendent Gibbons, from Liberty School District, demonstrated the strongest support of the work that Michael has encountered, participating and enforcing its importance yet keeping an appropriate distance so as not to dominate the conversation. This is, sadly, remarkable. We have found that white participants who show support typically do so in private after the session; they could have much stronger impact if they spoke out in public.

More often, Michael has observed passive participation, especially in person. He finds white educators show very little resistance in person. A notable exception was when it came from a white woman and there were tears associated with it. The white tears had a sudden nuclear effect. The tears blew up the dynamic, and everyone started to take sides. It elicited protective behavior from the white men in the group, and the Black women got angry ("How'd she get to cry?" they wanted to know). Everybody went to opposite poles, and the rest of the session was like pushing a heavy rock up a long hill. While this has not happened often in Michael's professional development sessions, we have all seen this dynamic play out in other professional development settings.

The white women (and most of the white men) in Michael's second principal cohort session broke that mold. They were very open and honest. They wanted to talk, and they wanted to learn more. It could have been because of the safety of being in front of a computer screen, or it could have been because of the dynamics of the group, with multiple others engaged and no one outwardly resisting. It is not clear if the same dynamics would have played out in person, but with the number of engaged persons across identity and gender categories, they may have felt authorized to speak up. They had some of the same concerns as those who typically resist—they were unsure how to apply the ideas in practice, since it is not a matter of taking particular steps or following a scripted protocol. In Singleton's (2015) language, it is an adaptive change. Educators need to reimagine themselves—to think about their preconceived notions and conceptualize this work as part of their responsibility, rather than just pushing to raise test scores.

Michael attempts to find the sweet spot when he does professional development to address the pressures like the ones Steele has experienced: arguments that children of color's test scores should be the leader's primary concern. Michael combines the responsible use of data with a narrative approach to connect participants with real-life experience. To do so, he often incorporates his own critical counternarrative as a biracial man experiencing race and racism. He tells them it's not abstract:

> This is me. I went through this. You're looking at the person who went through this. Oftentimes that helps. I think being biracial also helps when I tell them about the fact that my dad is a stoic Irishman. And my grandfather loved me and my sister and treated us like a prince and princess, but he was racist. And

> so when I tell these things, like my grandfather didn't want my dad to marry my mom and all this other kind of stuff. When I explain these things, I put a real face on it. So I think the narrative ethics helps, when you can tell them your story.

The counternarrative excerpt helps Michael's students and workshop participants understand the concrete importance of antiracist work. The counternarrative (a strategy with conceptual roots in critical race theory) is effective for Michael to tell on his own terms and to bring the margins to the center. Michael then couples the critical counternarrative with analysis of data. In his PDs, he shows the district data that go beyond test scores. He has them focus on the data on its disparities in discipline, the course content, the courses offered, and his classroom observations. He shares what he knows from the neighboring communities, knowledge informed by his membership in those communities. It all becomes inarguable. Michael calls this his leverage point to shift them from impersonal caring to critical caring.

Countercultural Elements of the Model

Across the concepts in the race-conscious caring model, the more difficult to convey through professional development are likely *principled resistance* and *collective responsibility*. School leaders are rare who are able to articulate the key principles that guide their practice, and it is difficult to use unanalyzed, unarticulated principles to work against the dominant pressures for test score improvement and individual resistance to equity work. Engaging standards is much easier if the standards are simply converted into curriculum (or purchased in a predigested form) rather than understood at a deep conceptual level; the former approach leads to standardization, not high standards. Collective responsibility goes against the principles of competition that ground high-stakes accountability systems. Michael sometimes begins professional development by sharing a quotation attributed to President Harry S. Truman: "It's amazing what people can accomplish when nobody cares who gets the credit." But be warned: At a professional development session at Midway School District, this sentiment did not go over well, and may be what set off superintendent Marvin Robbins, who then reasserted his power.

Many of the other components of race-conscious caring can be addressed through adding knowledge to what educators already know from their experience and then enhancing their new knowledge through practical application. We can show educators the reality of racial marginalization, impress upon them the logic of race consciousness and critical caring, then provide guided experiences so they can see how educators put the components into practice. The more difficult parts of the model place educators against the strong, dominant cultural affinity for individualism and competition. Building collective responsibility is a distinctly different approach. Even within their own schools and districts, leaders do not necessarily desire to have a shared decision-making model.

One last consideration. One of the things Andrew Steele said has stuck with Michael. Steele has talked with many parents who tell him that school did not work out for them; and for them their kids' attendance is merely compulsory; they suspect it is not going to make "a hill of beans" worth of difference once their child or grandchild graduates. "The real world is waiting for them, and they have to figure it out," Steele said. This is a far too prevalent reason why the senior prom and graduation from high school have been so important in the Black community, because families believe their student has achieved the final educational goal and as such should be ready for the real world instead of commencing to the next level of post-graduation education. Steele said he asked parents to tell him what "commence" means, and many did not know that it means to begin a journey, not complete a journey. If the whole idea of being more race-conscious and caring in our delivery of content and the way that we run schools is going to be worthwhile, we need to make sure it will make a difference in increasing graduation and matriculation into some sort of postsecondary education toward a degree or employable certification for our marginalized students of color. We need to ensure students develop a sense of self-efficacy and self-worth as global citizens, envision possibilities for themselves within and outside of their communities, have a clear-eyed and critical understanding of the world around them, find their life purpose as an asset to humanity, and walk in the fullness of that purpose.

CHAPTER 7

Carrying Race-Conscious Caring Forward

School leaders play a critical role in creating structures and conditions that promote the flourishing of all students, and it is essential to focus on the school leader as a significant center of change. In the findings of this book, we could only identify three school leaders who held all the components of race-conscious caring leadership; these three demonstrate that it is possible (see Table 7.1). Leaders reading this book may see their own leadership practices within the spectra presented, and we hope this motivates them to improve their practices or continue to push forward to create more equitable and just schools. Greater attention is needed to continue the race-conscious caring development of school leaders and to realize the crucial contribution that it can play in more equitable educational leadership practices.

In the research we have conducted with school leaders since we conducted the interviews for this book, we have seen a growth in school leaders' awareness of the distinction between *equality* and *equity*. Nevertheless, we also acknowledge that significant attention remains to be devoted to cultivating dispositions, particularly toward students who have historically experienced educational opportunity gaps. The voices of students like William Generett, J. Oliver Choo, TyNeshia Bowling, and Kalea Armstrong from Chapter 1 remind us of that. Creating more equitable schools requires work, which takes more than good intentions. Thus, a professional agenda for race-conscious caring leadership that addresses the needs of diverse communities, building upon strengths in current practice and communities, is very much needed.

In this chapter, we bring together the key contributions of the race-conscious caring model and our reflections on our subsequent practice when we have tried to put the model into place in our professional development practice and our graduate leadership courses. We first provide summary conclusions for the various components of the model. We next make recommendations for aspects of the leadership enterprise. Then we chart a particular course for the use of narrative ethics. Finally, we address implications for future work and suggest additional trajectories for extending this work to foster greater educational equity through school leadership.

Table 7.1. School Leader Characteristics and Categories in Race-Conscious Caring Model

Participant	Race Consciousness	Critical Caring	Justice Leadership	Gender, Race, Position	Type of District	Level of School	% Students of Color[1]	% Free/ Reduced Lunch[1]
Allison Edwards	Cultivating: Responsive	Critical caring	Justice Leadership	Female Black Principal	Suburban	Elementary	<5	10–15
Maya Gaffney	Cultivating: Responsive	Critical caring	Justice Leadership	Female Black Principal	Urban	Elementary	26–50	80–85
Scarlett Johnson	Cultivating: Responsive	Critical caring	Justice Leadership	Female Black Principal	Urban	Elementary	76–100	90–95
Arthur Lawrence	Cultivating: Responsive	Critical caring	Evolving Straddler	Male Black Principal	Urban	Middle/ High	26–50	60–65
Ethan Knight	Cultivating: Responsive	Caring with (minimal) responsiveness	Indeterminate Straddler	Male White Superintendent	Urban	District	51–75[3]	65–70[3]
James Smith	Cultivating: Respecting	Critical caring	Evolving Straddler	Male White Principal	Urban	Elementary/ Middle	76–100[2]	80–85[2]
Andrew Baker	Cultivating: Respecting	Caring with (minimal) responsiveness	Evolving Straddler	Male White Principal	Suburban	Elementary	<5	<5
Elizabeth Ida	Cultivating: Respecting	Caring with (minimal) responsiveness	Evolving Straddler	Female White Principal	Suburban	Middle	<5	5–10
Ella Klein	Cultivating: Respecting	Caring with (minimal) responsiveness	Achievement Gap	Female White Director	Urban	District	51–75[3]	65–70[3]

Peter Ingram	Cultivating: Developing	Color-Evasive Caring in Fortunate Communities	Justice Leadership	Male White Principal	Suburban	High	<5	10–15
Bill Roberts	Recognition: Inaction	Tough love/ tough luck	Indeterminate Straddler	Male White Principal	Urban Charter	High	51–75[2]	65–70[2]
Dennis Gable	Recognition: Deficit	Tough love/ tough luck	Indeterminate Straddler	Male White Principal	Urban	High	26–50	55–60
Emma Badell	Recognition: Deficit	Tough love/ tough luck	Achievement Gap	Female White Principal	Urban	Middle	26–50	70–75
Logan Sanders	Color-Evasive: Technical	Color-evasive caring in fortunate communities	Achievement Gap	Male Biracial Principal	Suburban	Elementary	<5	<5
Jack Maddon	Color-Evasive: Deflection	Color-evasive caring in fortunate communities	Evolving Straddler	Male White Principal	Suburban	Elementary	10–25	45–50
Scott Abbott	Color-Evasive: Deflection	Tough love/ tough luck	Achievement Gap	Male White Principal	Urban	Middle/ High	26–50	60–65
John Hall	Color-Evasive: Individualization	Caring with (minimal) responsiveness	Evolving Straddler	Male White Principal	Suburban	Elementary	5–10	15–20
Dan Gibson	Color-Evasive: Individualization	Color-evasive caring in fortunate communities	Achievement Gap	Male White Principal	Suburban	Elementary	5–10	25–30

(continued)

Table 7.1. *(continued)*

Participant	Race Consciousness	Critical Caring	Justice Leadership	Gender, Race, Position	Type of District	Level of School	% Students of Color[1]	% Free/ Reduced Lunch[1]
Laura Foster	Color-Evasive: Individualization	Color-evasive caring in fortunate communities	Achievement Gap	Female White Principal	Suburban	Elementary	<5	10–15
Paul Eaby	Color-Evasive: Individualization	Color-evasive caring in fortunate communities	Achievement Gap	Male White Principal	Suburban	Elementary	<5	<5
Kevin Labby	Color-Evasive: Unresponsive	Color-evasive caring in fortunate communities	Achievement Gap	Male White Principal	Suburban	High	<5	5–10
Michael Labette	Color-Evasive: Unresponsive	Tough love/ tough luck	Achievement Gap	Male White Principal	Urban	Middle/ High	10–25	60–65

Note: To protect the identities of participants, names listed are pseudonyms, and percentages of students of color and of students on free and reduced-price lunch are indicated as ranges.

[1]School data collected from the U.S. Department of Education Institute of Education Sciences, National Center for Education Statistics, Common Core of Data for the 2013–2014 school year.

[2]The school's state profile data are used for these two charter schools.

[3]The high school data are used to represent the district.

SUMMARY CONCLUSIONS

We have presented our argument for race-conscious caring leadership composed of four components: (1) *race consciousness,* (2) *critical caring,* (3) *justice leadership,* and (4) *ethical praxis.* Putting it all together, we define *race-conscious caring* leadership as an ethical praxis that provides a critical and reflective vision of what education can mean for children of color that is grounded in race consciousness, critical caring, and justice leadership.

The component of *race consciousness* requires educators to be mindful that race and racism have material effects on the lives of real people. When educators say they do not recognize race—ignoring patterns of differential achievement of students who identify in different racial categories—they attribute differential achievement to racial background instead of systematically considering practices and conditions that provide differential opportunities. For example, the idea that class is a more significant issue than racism in schools where there are few students of color does not mean that racism is not operating and affecting students' educational experiences. Often, school leaders who say they do not see race are caught flat-footed in being unresponsive to the needs of students of color. Consequently, we argue that school leaders need to engage with the diversity they have, seek more diversity among their staff, and engage with homes and communities through an asset-based lens. This type of mindset requires recognizing that race is a source of strength, resistance, and moral value as a component of individual and group identity. This recognition can empower leaders to create more inclusive and equitable educational environments.

The component of *critical caring* requires leaders with the knowledge, experience, and dispositions to engage students in respectful and culturally responsive relations. We have introduced four approaches to caring, representing variations in how school leaders talk about caring. Prevalent in our research was caring aligned with color-evasiveness. The mindset that one cares for all students equally or as individuals is flawed as it limits a leader's ability to think about and implement practices that can better support students of color. We propose that leaders who ground their work in critical caring bring a community-based approach to caring demonstrated by examining patterns of oppression and domination, challenging power relations and taken-for-granted practices and processes, and identifying steps for corrective action on behalf of *all* the students, families, and communities that the school serves. To enact critical caring, school leaders must be continuously aware that affirming relationships with students and families is not a given regardless of one's beliefs, social identities, and status as a school administrator. This continuous awareness and engagement can foster a sense of commitment and responsibility among leaders.

The *justice leadership* component acknowledges that students experience gaps in their schools, which are fundamentally gaps in opportunity perpetuated by structures and conditions, some within leaders' control and some reflecting large social systems. Leaders with a justice lens have an asset-based perspective for understanding the social conditions and structures that constrain children's educational opportunities. We argue that justice leaders have a clear sense of how power operates, identify how their actions affect others, especially those who are minoritized, and create conditions where the effects of power are made transparent so they can be changed and replaced. Our findings also indicate school leaders conveying the justice leadership disposition identified gaps in opportunity and spoke about a more precise notion of responsibility for student learning. Relatedly, in Table 7.1, looking at concurrences across the three components in our respondents suggests alignment between and among race consciousness, critical caring, and justice leadership.

The component of *ethical praxis* signals a contextual and historical plan of action that situates in leaders' moral narratives their concerted efforts to address differential school success. This praxis requires moral commitments and ethical responsibility instead of a managerial leadership focused on accountability. We acknowledge that taking responsibility for educational justice requires school leaders to possess courage and resiliency because they are focused on transforming adults and may have to challenge their own and staff's historical beliefs and cultural norms. An approach we suggest using is reflecting and interrogating one's moral narrative.

RECOMMENDATIONS

In this section, we provide further recommendations of how school leaders who read this book, faculty responsible for principal preparation, and district leaders can support race-conscious caring leadership. We recognize that some school contexts will incline themselves more easily to do this work, while others may require leaders to be more strategic with their actions to achieve an overall goal of educational equity. We hope readers can work toward developing their own and others' race-conscious caring leadership.

Leadership Preparation

An important site for developing race-conscious caring leadership occurs in leadership preparation programs. School leadership preparation is overdue for the integration of ethics and race consciousness. Even though national leadership standards incorporate equity, race, and caring (NPBEA, 2015), we acknowledge that colleagues in charge of leader preparation programs are working within systems and structures that create barriers for them to address issues around racial equity. At the same time, school preparation programs that do not include race-conscious practice as a central theme for their theory of action will undoubtedly continue to graduate future school leaders who are not ready to support students of color in their schools. Preparation programs must include issues of race and equity in the curriculum. This could be achieved through the inclusion of case studies, discussions with race-conscious caring leaders, and creative assignments that specifically address racial equity to challenge and transform educators' acceptance of color-evasiveness. In some instances, this will be the first time these educators engage in such conversations.

Ethical practice and a clear moral vision of the purpose of education should inform the conceptual model of any school leader preparation program. Future principals should have the opportunity, through class discussions and assignments, to engage in developing the race consciousness that will influence their critical caring. Students in leadership preparation programs must engage in the conversation about their ethical grounding in equity-based principal leadership and understand how their positionality—which refers to their personal and professional background and experiences—influences their leadership. Leadership ethics requires perpetual engagement and growth. Leader candidates need the opportunity to develop their race-conscious caring dispositions and build capacity for their leadership practice and the practices of their teachers and school communities.

Experience and community connection are not just additional factors, but crucial elements that greatly influence our ethical beliefs and professional background. A detailed account of one's life can significantly influence how we think about our existence and the ethical beliefs that ground our relationships across cultural, racial, gender, or other socially constructed identities. A school leader's positionality and background experience provide context for appreciating and engaging assets in communities and set up distinct relations of critical caring, making critical caring an embodied ethics that embraces material experience, history, and culture. It is a perpetual orientation toward work that requires humility and self-reflexivity. Principal preparation programs can have students complete the moral narrative story as part of a class activity or final paper. Moreover, we recommend students work in groups to facilitate hearing and learning from others—an application of narrative ethics. A recommended practice for school leaders is to listen to the moral narratives of other school leaders and articulate their own stories using the resources provided in Chapter 5. Modeling this practice in preparation programs should encourage leaders to continue it when they become leaders so they may continue to learn through the varied experiences of their colleagues.

Leadership preparation programs should not merely touch on but devote significant time to cultivating dispositions, particularly dispositions towards students who have historically experienced a gap in educational opportunities. Based on our respondents' experiences, personal histories, and experiences in diverse educational contexts, graduate students need to be centrally considered and should make concerted efforts to grow those dispositions in relation to other colleagues. Preparation programs can embed asset-based community trips designed to help future leaders learn about a community's historical trends and recognize the role that centers, churches, and other community organizations play in educational equity. Other issues that could be explored are the influence of housing discrimination and redlining and the existence of advocacy groups fighting against the harmful tropes that perpetuate deficit-laden dispositions.

School Leadership Practice

While all of the leaders in the study would agree that educational equity is a worthy goal, many of their foundational beliefs suggest that their capacity for race-conscious equity work is often limited, sometimes severely. Practicing leaders should be mindful of their personal histories, particularly any experiences in diverse educational contexts, and seek to develop dispositions that allow for a greater understanding of their colleagues' perspectives. This means learning from colleagues whose positionality and experiences across different backgrounds have shaped their race-conscious leadership ethics. Leaders from different communities are eager to strengthen their connections with one another, since they often experience similar challenges within and across school districts. This collegial sharing is often ad hoc and small-scale; more formal collective arrangements (with leadership coming from within the participant group) would make it even more valuable and extend it to more people. We recommend that practicing leaders seek the insights of educators, both inside and outside of schools, who have successfully engaged in critical caring. Such educators might be found in parent groups, community organizations, or among retired teachers. Leaders should not limit their search for knowledge to those holding formal educational roles.

Narrative ethics involves learning and expressing ourselves through life stories. Educators must reflect on their moral beliefs to identify areas for growth. Leaders can enhance their moral perspectives by reading stories of race-conscious caring school leaders or personally engaging with those who practice this work. However, this work must be approached cautiously. Efforts to incorporate culturally grounded ethics risk appropriation, misapplication, and erasure. There is much to learn from narrative ethics, and a respectful, learning-focused attitude must be consistently maintained. One way to enact narrative ethics is through networks of critical caring, where leaders share their experiences of antiracist work. Witnessing others' stories offers a valuable approach to learning from narratives, allowing leaders to incorporate an understanding of and connection to the lives and experiences of others. Rather than appropriating their work or insights, it is essential to center the voices and wisdom of people of color in educational settings.

Narrative ethics should not merely become a theme for professional development sessions; superficial engagement risks fostering voyeurism and reinforcing cultural and racial stereotypes. Leaders may learn from others' wisdom and rewrite their own narratives to position themselves as genuine learners and carers.

Without a race-conscious caring approach, leaders tend to rely on a vague notion of fairness and view the educational system as meritocratic. This perspective rationalizes inequities in educational outcomes based on factors like student effort, background, or family support, ultimately perpetuating racism. Equitable leadership necessitates concrete actions that lead to changes in practice, structure, and systems. While our research primarily reveals color-evasiveness, impersonal caring, and achievement-gap orientations among white leaders, it is important to recognize that leaders of color can also engage in these views across various settings. The diversity of positionalities among the school leaders discussed in this book indicates that leaders of all racial, ethnic, and gender identities can benefit from studying both theoretical and practical aspects of race consciousness. Consequently, we argue that all leaders should continue to engage with race-consciousness and explore leading practices that arise from it. School leaders ought to critically reflect on their own positionalities, recognizing the strengths and limitations they bring to their work. Once leaders acknowledge their limitations, they should seek to understand the real-life impacts of racism and other forms of oppression that students and families encounter. This understanding is crucial in ensuring that racialized and marginalized students are not subject to impersonal care.

District Leadership

School district administrators can support the creation of formal and informal principal networks that meet regularly to discuss issues. We recommend that leaders be exposed to responsive leaders from a variety of school demographic situations. School leaders in many settings are reluctant to collaborate with schools with lower achievement scores. Principals may feel vulnerable when describing their weaknesses. However, by creating more collaborative settings, district leaders can play a crucial role in building capacity across settings and minimizing the competition between building administrators. This enables the sharing of ideas and practices and fosters a culture of collective responsibility.

Another important task of school district leaders is supporting their building administrators—support that could be structural, financial, emotional, or simply readiness to protect or defend them—because any school leader who desires and is willing to make the concerted effort to transform school systems to be more equitable will experience pushback. Leaders such as Johnson who face resource issues are expected to provide educational opportunities that have been systematically denied to children of color and students living in poverty. They need the staff support, materials, and physical plant that all children deserve, even in large districts where resources tend to be distributed inequitably. Further, leaders need the language, resilience, and grounding to make it work. This grounding requires that school leaders develop principled resistance to external pressures that would harm or hinder children's educational experiences. It's crucial for school district leaders to stand firm in their commitment to equitable education, despite the challenges they may face.

MORAL NARRATIVES

We have made the case throughout the book for the significance of narrative ethics for cultivating race-conscious caring. Narrative ethics, drawing from an ancient tradition of conveying moral truths through stories told and retold, provides a less abstract approach to thinking about and developing one's professional ethics. The narratives in Chapter 5 present leaders in the context of their moral lives, explaining what is important to them and making connections to their earliest memories of school and the reasons they became educators in the first place. With the guidance of Nash and Jang (2016), we explain how leaders who are thoughtful about their professional ethics make use of multiple moral languages that take account of their personal moral lives, the moral communities they hold dear, the rules and principles that ground their public lives, and their aspirations toward membership in cosmopolitan communities. Addressing all these aspects of their moral lives helps leaders make their practice holistic and authentic to who they are as humane persons. It also helps them to distinguish among their personal moral commitments (to decide which takes priority) when they may come into conflict with public expectations. Moral reflection further helps leaders interpret situations such as the Norwin School District civil rights case (Haviland, 2024), when taken-for-granted standards within a moral community are revealed to be discriminatory toward members of that very same community.

Writing a Moral Narrative

At the end of Chapter 5, we provide a set of questions that readers may consider as a beginning framework for writing a moral narrative. Nash and Jang (2016) provide excellent guidance grounded in their extensive work with professionals in education and other human service settings, and other work by Robert Nash similarly conveys those possibilities. Readers may wonder what the author of a moral narrative is then supposed to do with that document. A leader may wish to ascertain their readiness to begin an equity leadership initiative in their school. A leader may want to pay greater attention to the needs and interests of students of color in their school, no matter how large their representation in the building, and need help on how to get started. Or a leader may want to check their own positionality in relation to race-conscious caring before engaging with like-minded colleagues interested in working together to foster greater collective responsibility for children across a community. We certainly recommend deciding on a trajectory before beginning to engage in the exercise, but it can also be helpful to identify gaps in thinking, to put onto paper thoughts a leader has not yet pulled together about how their moral commitments guide their work.

Witnessing Moral Narratives

In Chapter 5, readers are invited to witness extended moral narratives. *Witnessing* means receiving a story and receiving it on its own terms, recognizing how the narrators make meaning of their experience, and exercising moral humility—reserving judgment. Readers may feel challenged by uncomfortable, unfamiliar, or seemingly conflicting aspects of the narrative or take issue with how we have presented them. Those are expected outcomes of narratives and especially of counternarratives. In this concluding section, we highlight some features of the moral narratives that are significant for learning about race-conscious caring.

Authenticity. First, the length and detail of the stories enhance the authenticity of the narratives and invite connections. The narratives are constructed chronologically at first to portray the respondents' progression from student to teacher to leader. The narratives then turn to the respondents' philosophies of education and their views on moral leadership. The narratives end with a synthesis of how respondents fit into the race-conscious caring model. Readers will probably notice many of the connections we saw across these various aspects of their lives and make additional connections and their own interpretations. We also invite readers to consider the extended contexts shared in the narratives to determine how the stories relate to their own leadership contexts.

Counternarratives. Second, some parts of the stories can be considered counternarratives to dominant stories about education. Detail and authenticity are especially relevant for counternarratives. The narratives at times show how subjugation has worked in direct and indirect ways throughout the educational lives of Johnson and Smith, how structures and conditions of schooling both have impeded and facilitated their educational journeys, and how they have incorporated those experiences into their teaching and leadership.

True to her experiences of subjugation, support, and resistance as a Black woman growing up in Pittsburgh, Johnson's story grounds an ethical praxis of deep purpose and moral clarity. Her stories contain a multitude of meanings beyond our space limitations and our ability to interpret them.

Smith's narratives convey a distinctly different voice, grounded in his experience as a white man of European immigrant parents who often saw himself as an outsider to dominant white culture. His stories help explain why he has situated himself where he is and why he takes the stands he does, while at the same time conveying a distinctly different voice as a white leader in a Black organization.

Moral Languages. Third, readers can see the interplay of Nash and Jang's (2016) multiple moral languages in the narratives. One clear example is the role of religious faith in the lives of Johnson and Smith. Both explicitly acknowledge the influence of their faith backgrounds in the development of their moral selves, and both mention the importance of their religious beliefs to how they relate to others, their leadership, and their philosophies of education. These are strong examples of the first language of private moral spaces, and for both Johnson and Smith, they further embed those beliefs in the second language of small moral communities—for Johnson, a particular church community and for Smith, a particular denomination tied to his European heritage (Nash & Jang, 2016).

Readers need not draw the conclusion that public school leaders need a religious background or be part of a specific faith community to be race-conscious caring leaders. As Nash and Jang (2016) note, everyone converses in all four of the moral languages. Those who do not locate specific religious faith in their background beliefs still operate in those private moral and small community spaces. They can be sacred or secular or some combination. All leaders, in other words, draw on background beliefs, whether religious or secular, as sources of strength for their moral leadership.

The Challenge of Engaging Moral Narratives. Fourth, we acknowledge how rare it is for someone to integrate multiple aspects of their moral lives into the story of their moral leadership. Many people consider their moral lives private and separate from their public lives, often because they believe they should not impose their personal moral beliefs on others, especially in their public roles. Both Johnson and Smith moved seamlessly between those private moral spaces and the more public spaces. To explain their caring leadership, they integrated moral languages across private, small community, public, and cosmopolitan spaces. That makes their moral narratives clearer and more complete. They did so comprehensively, but few other respondents did.

While Johnson and Smith were the only respondents who participated in the additional interviews that went into greater detail about leaders' background experiences as students, they were asked the same questions about their moral beliefs that we asked of all respondents. This may have been because of their comfort integrating these aspects of their moral lives, or they may have been more inclined to do so after having shared their background stories. In any event, it can be uncomfortable for a leader to express their moral beliefs and how they relate to their public leadership, but we believe it is a valuable practice. It may be difficult to craft a moral narrative without specific prompting or a framework such as the one that Nash and Jang (2016) provide.

Learning From Colleagues. Fifth, we stress the importance of learning from colleagues. In our work with practicing school leaders, they have impressed on us the importance of building professional networks, especially when they become principals and no longer have peer colleagues in their buildings. In our area, most districts are fairly small. For instance, just one school district in Allegheny County has more than one high school, and while many school districts have multiple elementary schools, the number of district-level colleagues is quite small. Leaders have told us about the importance of networks across districts, especially when the state rolls out new policies or crisis situations arise.

Some of the leaders participating in Flores's (2018) dissertation study spoke of the importance of networks for doing race-conscious equity work. We strongly endorse the sharing of expertise in communities around race-conscious equity to cultivate collective responsibility for all children. We believe it especially beneficial for leaders to share narratives of moral leadership through community networks. Building race consciousness, critical caring, and justice leadership can be difficult in isolation, without guidance from someone with a different experience, perspective, and capability. It is not that the critical friend becomes responsible for their peers' learning—that happens too often already, especially for people of color in leadership roles—but so many leaders have difficulty breaking out of their limited experience. Many leaders have difficulty relating to the needs and interests of students of color and students living in poverty without adopting a deficit mindset (witness the popularity of professional development focused on the "culture of poverty").

FUTURE DIRECTIONS FOR RACE-CONSCIOUS CARING

So what does it mean for a school leader to be caring and just? What does it mean to work against the power of racism? In this book, we have shown that there is great variation in perspectives and practices when the topic turns to equity leadership, and for those who practice race-conscious caring, it is an embodied, ethical praxis that draws from all aspects of their relational experiences. As we describe in Chapter 5, it is difficult work to put into practice, especially with the numerous obstacles to engagement that are reinforced by dominant practices. However, there are strong and effective leaders who have forged a path that their colleagues can learn from. They are excellent resources.

Much work still needs to be done to understand how leaders with varied backgrounds instill their relational caring into educational practice. The research literature has given us numerous examples of success, and we hope we have added to that work to illuminate aspects of that work. More work can be done to tap into long-standing traditions in subjugated communities that built collective responsibility into structures and institutions that sustained educational spaces under enormous obstacles. Cities have their own histories to draw from as living resources. For example, more work is being done in Pittsburgh to build stronger connections between institutions, such as our universities and community organizations, recognizing that there are strengths everywhere, though often not in positions for decision-making and resource allocation.

We also wish to reiterate that the views and perspectives that leaders conveyed in our study were captured in moments of time in these leaders' development. While no doubt some have not changed at all, we have every reason to believe that most have continued to grow, particularly since we have been in contact with several of them in the intervening time, and we have seen their perspectives evolve. While we do not make claim to a developmental schema in our work—that is beyond the scope of our focus here and our particular expertise—we believe there is power in collaboration and specifically in learning from others with backgrounds different from ourselves. As we explain in greater detail in the methodological appendix, we as authors have benefited greatly from each others' life stories and the different ways we think about the work. Because our educational contexts are continually changing, there are new opportunities ahead to resist pressures that get in the way of educational equity, and always there will be new systemic opportunities to advance educational equity in the future, however hard we have to work.

We return now to the place where we started many pages ago, with the wisdom of Toni Morrison (1988/2019) and her commencement address at Sarah Lawrence College. As we close the book, we are reminded of the reason we embarked on this work—to highlight and uplift the special role of the school leader to build greater capacity for educational equity. The ethics approach we chose to focus on is clearly not easy, but it is a process worth undertaking, particularly if it can be done in collaboration with others. In that address, Morrison spoke of the importance of dreaming of something better, and we place it here to encourage all those who became educators to make a difference in the lives of all children:

> I am simply urging you to continue the dream you started. For dreaming is not irresponsible; it is first-order human business. It is not entertainment; it is work. When Martin Luther King Jr. said, "I have a dream," he was not playing; he was serious. When he imagined it, envisioned it, created it in his own mind it began to be, and we must dream it too to give it the heft and stretch and longevity it deserves. Don't let anybody, anybody convince you this is the way the world is and therefore must be. It must be the way it ought to be. (p. 72)

Methodological Appendix

The data that informs this book came from multiple sources, including two interview studies and the authors' professional responsibilities teaching and providing professional development. In this appendix, we describe how we designed the study, how our collaboration emerged, and how our interest in race-conscious caring has evolved over time. We reflect on our method and how our positionalities, backgrounds, interests, and expertise have contributed to the book. Our collaborations have helped us develop a combination of empathetic and critical analyses that we believe lead to stronger, more dialogically interesting work and more compelling implications for practice.

Our work falls within the interpretive and critical traditions in educational research. We are critical constructivists, influenced by critical theory, critical race theory, feminist research methods, and the methodological tools first popularized in educational research by Yvonna Lincoln and Egon Guba (1985). We have continually reminded ourselves that in our analysis we are analyzing interview transcripts rather than specifically the persons we interviewed. While we would agree that the narratives in Chapter 5 are likely closer and better representations of those two people, we are fully aware that our interpretations, while carefully grounded, are limited to the interview texts, which we mention as a further caveat to readers. But our goal with this book is not to represent each respondent's complete set of career and leadership abilities, but instead to explore the differing perspectives presented in the transcripts and make meaning that resonates with leaders attempting to become better at equity leadership through race-conscious caring.

The three of us have distinctly different racial and ethnic identities, different professional backgrounds, and different subfields within education. We see those positionalities as vital to the meaning generated by the research, and over the past several years, we have learned from each other as we have questioned each others' interpretations repeatedly. Mike Gunzenhauser is a white male ethicist and philosopher of education who, early in his career, worked in secondary and postsecondary schools in North Carolina. He has been a university faculty member for 26 years, the last 21 years at the University of Pittsburgh. Osly Flores is a Latino male who has previously worked as a high school teacher in Boston Public Schools and as an educational specialist at the Massachusetts Department of Elementary and Secondary Education. His collaboration with Mike began in 2013 while he was a doctoral student at the University of Pittsburgh, where Mike was his faculty advisor. Osly is an assistant professor at the University of Illinois at Urbana–Champaign. Michael Quigley is a biracial (Black/white) educational sociologist who was a student in Pittsburgh Public Schools and taught high school in the district for 13 years. He has been a faculty member for 12 years at Robert Morris University.

Most of the interview data for the book comes from an interview study with 22 school leaders interviewed in summer 2014 and summer 2015 and another study conducted in 2016–2017. The former study resulted from an initial interest expressed by Osly while a doctoral student after having read literature about the idea of the opportunity gap. The interest was a result of wondering whether there was a connection between research and practice in how practicing K–12 school leaders use the language of the opportunity gap. Working under Mike's direction, Osly and Mike designed the study from an initial project Joshua Childs developed with Mike about school leaders' use of data-driven decision making to serve the goals of equity (Childs & Gunzenhauser, 2012, 2013).

Drawing from Osly's experience and studies in educational leadership, the revised study sought to understand leaders' perspectives on gaps in achievement and opportunity, their use of data to identify and address gaps, and their moral and philosophical grounding in their efforts to address inequities in opportunity. Mike had just come off publishing his previous book on how high-stakes accountability systems had affected K–12 educators' professionalism (Gunzenhauser, 2012) and leaned into this new focus, specifically adding to the project a focus on professional ethics.

We designed the interview study by adapting the interview method of Irving Seidman (2013), a three-interview method that explores the subjective meaning that individuals make of their experiences. The three-interview design is based on some phenomenological assumptions by Seidman about where meaning comes from. Rather than securing three interviews with respondents, we combined the three components of Seidman's interview method—history, focus, and reflection—into a single interview. This adaptation de-emphasizes the history section and limits the opportunity to engage respondents in the kind of reflection that Seidman prizes in his design. We adapted to that limitation in this book by incorporating some additional data from a second study, explained in more detail below. In this main study, though, most of the time of each interview was devoted to Seidman's focus section.

Each interview was semistructured, with a script that first walked respondents through questions about their educational background, teaching experience, and relationships with students, teachers, parents, and community members. We asked them to describe their student population in terms that were important to them. The focused section got them to talk about their philosophy of education, moral leadership, and equity practices. We then asked focused questions about equity practices, such as how they use data to inform instruction of students of color, what value Black and Latina/o students bring to their school, and what skills teachers have for working with diverse populations. Interviews lasted between 50 and 90 minutes and occurred in person, typically at the leaders' school buildings.

We recruited participants initially through network and chain sampling (Merriam, 2009) in Allegheny County, the large urban county in Southwestern Pennsylvania where Pittsburgh is located. We started with K–12 principals affiliated with outreach programs at the University of Pittsburgh, the largest higher education institution in Southwestern Pennsylvania. Our recruitment email identified this focus: "to learn what educators think about the achievement gap, how they respond to the achievement gap, and how the achievement gap affects their educational practice." This method yielded 19 respondents. We recruited three additional respondents through referrals from those initial respondents. It took about a year to recruit the 22 respondents. Many school leaders did not respond to multiple inquiries.

Some of the most willing initial participants were in suburban schools, and their views about their students of color varied greatly, even in settings with similar student body compositions, so while we initially anticipated interviewing mostly leaders in schools with sizable populations of students of color, we pursued these willing participants and quickly learned their perspectives gave nuance to our focus on equity leadership. We assigned pseudonyms for all respondents, and any place names are also changed. To further mask identities, we use ranges to identify percentages of children of color and children qualifying for free or reduced-price lunch. This sample is first indicated in Table 2.2 and organized by theme. Similar tables appear in Chapters 3 and 4, and a summary table of respondents across all thematic categories appears in Chapter 7.

Osly took the lead in the analysis of the first two papers to come from the first study. Our analysis methods yielded a wealth of interesting and contradictory interpretations, and we began to appreciate how complex the phenomenon of equity leadership had become. Our first paper from the data is an earlier version of what we present here in Chapter 4. This became "Justice in the Gaps: School Leader Dispositions and the Use of Data to Address the Opportunity Gap," published in *Urban Education,* first available online in 2018 but with an official publication date of 2021 (Flores & Gunzenhauser, 2021). It appears to have come out third in order, even though it was the first written and accepted for publication. This analysis followed from our research design, which produced the most direct answers to our initial research questions.

For this first paper, our analysis followed a combination of emergent and *a priori* codes (Saldaña, 2016), followed by memo-writing and frequent meetings to discuss our interpretations. Osly made use of diagrams and maps to chart out the variations in the data. Standing out for us were the varied and compelling perspectives about the relevance of race, racial identity, and racism apparent in leaders' interviews, so our next paper explored the variation in patterns of race consciousness based both on deeply personal experiences and dramatically different school contexts. The second article, titled "The Problems with Colorblind Leadership Revealed: A Call for Race-Conscious Leaders," was published in the *International Journal of Qualitative Studies in Education* (Flores & Gunzenhauser, 2019). As suggested by the title, we first used the language of "color blindness" in our analysis (Bonilla-Silva, 2014); we later adopted the language of race-evasiveness (Annamma et al., 2017), as we explain in Chapter 2, to avoid the ableist language associated with color blindness and to explore the value of understanding the evasion of race as an active, intentional process.

The cruxes for writing a book began to emerge as we saw that ideas we were developing from the data were too big for a single journal article. We began to consider whether a book-length text would better bring together all the ideas. This was when we invited Michael Quigley to join the project. At the time, Michael and Osly were working together on a professional development project in a local school district. They were learning about how teachers and school leaders were taking up emerging ideas about equity leadership but also organizing themselves to resist their research-backed professional development. During a professional development session with the high school administration team, Osly presented findings now in Chapter 4. At the conclusion of the PD training, the high school principal, a white male, approached Osly and excitedly shared that he was a "straddler," he connected with the model, and he could see his disposition moving in the right direction. This experience also fed the impetus to write the book, because we saw that school leader practitioners were connecting with our findings.

Michael had completed his doctoral studies at Pitt with Mike in 2013 after the retirement of his initial advisor, sociologist and historian William Thomas, and at the time was a faculty member in an organizational leadership department. Having become a team of three, we restarted the data analysis process. Our next paper took on the third aspect of the initial project —the ethical underpinnings of equity leadership. This secondary analysis began with the authors participating in several meetings to review memos and articles Osly and Mike had previously written (Seidman, 2013). In initial meetings, we each familiarized ourselves with the whole dataset, established a focus for the ethics paper, and began developing the conceptual framework that would guide our subsequent analysis. To begin a collaborative coding process, the authors picked one interview transcript from the sample to independently apply a deductive coding strategy (Miles et al., 2014). The use of team coding helped to surface the distinct interpretations that each member of the team brought to the analysis of the data, to build conceptual clarity, and to establish standards for warranting interpretations in the data, which led to more effective focused coding of subsequent transcripts (Emerson et al., 2011).

The collaborative process mostly took place over Zoom, as during this time Osly moved twice to different states, and we made creative use of all the authors' positionalities, experiences, and conceptual frames. We argued over conceptual categories, word choices, and alternative theoretical explanations to arrive at the interpretations presented in the third article, "Race-Conscious Ethics in School Leadership: From Impersonal Caring to Critical Responsibility," published in *Teachers College Record* (Gunzenhauser et al., 2021).

Our initial idea received critically formative feedback from Brian Ellerbeck at Teachers College Press in Fall 2019; he encouraged us to think of the project as more than a series of articles: as, rather, a holistic project around a coherent conceptual framework. That feedback led us to resume our holistic re-analysis of the data and to develop a conceptual model that brought the ideas together in a more meaningful way. As a team, we developed a fourth article to explore in greater depth the intersection between race consciousness and critical caring, a conceptual article, "Race-Conscious Caring for Anti-Racist Leadership: A Narrative Ethics for Cultivating Communal Responsibility," published in the *Journal of School Leadership* (Gunzenhauser et al., 2024). The ideas in the fourth article rounded out our conceptual model and enabled us to write an extended book proposal for Brian and Teachers College Press, which offered us a contract in fall 2023.

To fulfill the model of race-conscious caring, specifically the notion of race-conscious as a holistic ethical praxis, we next needed to complete a systematic analysis of narratives from our respondents. Our collaborative analysis process over several years gave us a solid understanding of the interview data, even as the three of us continued to question each others' interpretations and the assumptions we relied on to make those interpretations. Nevertheless, we needed additional data and an additional form of analysis to craft the extended narratives we envisioned for the ethical praxis portion of our model. As it happens, Osly had conducted some additional interviews for his dissertation study (Flores, 2017). Using intensity sampling (Patton, 2002), Osly identified school leaders known to their peers as strong equity leaders, especially those known to support students of color and students living in poverty. Across 2015 and 2016, Osly conducted interviews with eight respondents, and coincidentally two of his participants (Johnson and Smith) overlapped with our initial sample of 22 leaders that took place across 2014 and 2015 (Flores, 2017).

Following Seidman's (2013) three-interview model more closely in his dissertation study, Osly conducted three interviews with each respondent.

Across the three additional interviews, Osly first explored the respondents' background experiences as students in K–12 and higher education, their reasons for becoming teachers, and their trajectory into leadership. He established timelines for the respondents to establish a reliable sequence of events to provide structure for their narratives. Osly then explored intensively their values, beliefs, and leadership practices associated with their advocacy for students of color and children living in poverty. The data obtained through this approach yielded coherence and connection across their student and professional lives, and for our purposes in Chapter 5, the data proved to be more than suitable for the purpose of conveying narratives.

To construct each narrative, we went through a three-tiered coding process of the original transcripts, first open-coding each transcript from scratch (this for the first time). After open-coding for the content of each line of data, we completed a second round of coding, sorting the open codes by categories we imagined would form their moral narratives, such as school background, teaching experience, leadership experience, leadership philosophy, and various aspects of leadership practice (working with teachers, working with students, etc.). This initial categorization led to a draft narrative structure that we then revised to match Scarlett Johnson's narrative. We then devised a fourth coding process that split the data into three sets: data that told Johnson's story up through becoming a principal; data that explained her leadership style; and data that mapped onto each component and subcomponent of our conceptual model. We used the original open codes to identify key meanings within each of those organizational categories to construct Johnson's narrative. We applied the same approach with Smith's transcripts. While the two narratives follow the same structure, they are not parallel in their emphasis, owing to the uniqueness of the data and reinforcing the notion that ethical praxis should look different between school leaders.

Examples in Chapter 6 came from reflections on our application of the ideas in our race-conscious caring model to our professional practice. While there has been some take-up of these ideas by students and educators we have worked with, we have also learned from the resistance that Osly and Michael have experienced in their professional development work. We use pseudonyms in this chapter (with the exception of our colleague Angela Allie, who agreed to be named and included) also to mask the identities of the participants.

As noted, the book conceptualization process took time, complicated by the COVID-19 pandemic and some job transitions for all three of us. While we continued to work on it, the project took on new urgency from the expansion of the Black Lives Matter movement after the murder of George Floyd in Minneapolis in May 2020. We all found an increasing desire, especially from emerging school leaders, to build greater capacity for race-conscious practices. The subsequent and continual backlash has only steeled our resolve to continue the work and to learn from the application of our ideas in our professional practice.

We have one final explanation about how we have presented data in the book. With the exception of Chapter 5, the quotations are as close to verbatim transcriptions of the interviews. We digitally recorded and transcribed each interview, some by a University-based transcription service and some by Osly himself. Any changes to verbatim reporting of interviews are either a substituted pseudonym, an addition or clarification [marked by brackets], or the indicated removal of one or more words by points of ellipsis. In just a few cases, a word has been substituted without the use of brackets if it makes what the respondent said clearer and it sounds enough like what is in the recording that the person could have said it.

Representing Johnson and Smith in narrative form followed a different process so that the narratives would be more readable. The quotations are longer to convey readers the personality and additional meaning. These respondents spoke freely to Osly without regard to how their words would appear in print. Working closely with the transcripts, we found it remarkable how the two had similar speech patterns (they are close in age and both from the Pittsburgh area); both respondents routinely used repeated sentence stems and the same filler words, and we systematically removed them. Both frequently added "you know," "like," and "kind of" throughout their sentences. Especially in thoughtful moments, both repeated the first two or three words of a sentence. We deleted those. If they started a sentence and drifted off in what seemed like a meaningful way, we noted that. If they started a sentence one way and restarted the sentence differently, we deleted the initial stem and put in points of ellipsis. Some things we kept verbatim to keep the narratives more natural: both deviated from standard English many times, using nonstandard subject/verb or number agreement grounded in either Pittsburgh vernacular or Black vernacular at times, often to convey emphasis. Both said "'cause" way more often than "because." Both also said, "I was like . . ." when they meant "I said . . ." It may go without saying that the respondents did not say everything in the order that it appears in the chapter. Within excerpts, however, we did not reorder any sentences.

Our desire is that practicing school leaders be able to use the findings of this book to reflect on their own practices and see areas of growth, so that they may create schools that meet the needs of all students. For those already doing the work well, we hope to inspire their perseverance. Moreover, our purpose in providing detailed notes of the study design, data collection, and analysis that supported the development of this book is to assist researchers and graduate students interested in issues of equity and school leadership research in continuing this work.

References

Ahmed, S. (2012). *On being included: Racism and diversity in institutional life.* Duke University Press.

Alcoff, L. M. (1988). Cultural feminism versus post-structuralism: The identity crisis in feminist theory. *Signs, 13*(3), 405–436.

Anderson, G. (2009). *Advocacy leadership: Toward a post-reform agenda in education.* Routledge.

Anderson, J. D. (1988). *The education of Blacks in the south, 1860–1935.* University of North Carolina Press.

Annamma, S. A., Jackson, D. D., & Morrison, D. (2017). Conceptualizing color-evasiveness: Using dis/ability critical race theory to expand a color-blind racial ideology in education and society. *Race, Ethnicity and Education, 20*(2), 147–162.

Applebaum, B. (2023). Willful hermeneutical ignorance and the "critical race theory" controversy. *Educational Theory, 72*(6), 689–702.

Aveling, N. (2007). Anti-racism in schools: A question of leadership? *Discourse: Studies in the Cultural Politics of Education, 28*(1), 69–85.

Baldwin, J. (1998). A talk to teachers. In J. Baldwin, *Collected essays* (pp. 678–686). The Library of America. (Original work published 1963)

Banaji, M. R., Fiske, S. T., & Massey, D. S. (2021). Systemic racism: Individuals and interactions, institutions and society. *Cognitive Research: Principles and Implications*, 6(82), 1–21. https://doi.org/10.1186/s41235-021-00349-3

Bass, L. (2009). Fostering an ethic of care in leadership: A conversation with five African American women. *Advances in Developing Human Resources, 11*(5), 619–632.

Bass, L. (2012). When care trumps justice: The operationalization of Black feminist caring in educational leadership. *International Journal of Qualitative Studies in Education, 25*(1), 73–87.

Bass, L. (2016). Black masculine caring in educational leadership: Introducing a masculine-centered care framework. In L. Bass (Ed.), *Black* mask-*ulinity: A framework for black masculine caring* (pp. 11–26). Peter Lang.

Bass, L. (2020). Black male leaders care too: An introduction to black masculine caring in educational leadership. *Educational Administration Quarterly, 56*(3), 353–395.

Beachum, F. D., Dentith, A. M., McCray, C. R., & Boyle, T. M. (2008). Havens of hope or the killing fields: The paradox of leadership, pedagogy, and relationships in an urban middle school. *Urban Education, 43*(2), 189–215.

Beauboeuf-Lafontant, T. (2002). A womanist experience of caring: Understanding the pedagogy of exemplary Black women teachers, *Urban Review, 34*(1), 71–86.

Beck, L. (1994). *Reclaiming educational administration as a caring profession.* Teachers College Press.

Bell, D. A. (2004). *Silent covenants:* Brown v. Board of Education *and the unfulfilled hopes for racial reform.* Oxford University Press.

Biesta, G.J.J. (2004). Education, accountability, and the ethical demand: Can the democratic potential of accountability be regained? *Educational Theory, 54*(3), 233–250.

Blackmore, J. (2010). Preparing leaders to work with emotions in culturally diverse educational communities. *Journal of Educational Administration, 48*(5), 642–658. http://doi.org/10.1108/09578231011067785

Bonilla-Silva, E., & Forman, T. A. (2000). "I am not a racist but . . .": Mapping White college students' racial ideology in the USA. *Discourse & Society, 11*(1), 50–85.

Bonilla-Silva, E. (2014). *Racism without racists: Colorblind racism and the persistence of racial inequality in America.* Rowman & Littlefield.

Bonilla-Silva, E., Forman, T. A., Lewis, A. E., & Embrick, D. G. (2003). "It wasn't me!": How will race and racism work in 21st century America. *Research in Political Sociology*, 12, 111–134.

Borrasso, J., & Smith, B. (2021, October 12). Norwin High School student calls for change after 2 other students wear Confederate flag to school. *KDKA News, CBS Pittsburgh.* https://www.cbsnews.com/pittsburgh/news/students-wear-confederate-flag-to-school-norwin-school-district/

Boykin, A. W., & Noguera, P. (2011). *Creating the opportunity to learn: Moving from research to practice to close the achievement gap.* ASCD.

Briscoe, F., & Khalifa, M. (2015). "That racism thing": A critical race discourse analysis of a conflict over the proposed closure of a black high school. *Race, Ethnicity and Education, 18*(6), 739–763.

Brooks, J. S., & Arnold, N. W. (Eds.). (2013). *Antiracist school leadership toward equity in education for America's students.* Information Age Publishing.

Brooks, J. S., & Jean-Marie, G. (2007). Black leadership, white leadership: Race and race relations in an urban high school. *Journal of Educational Administration, 45*(6), 756–768.

Caldwell, L. D., McDaniel, M. S., & Quigley, M. (2017). *Beyond plight: Defining pathways to optimal development for Black men and boys across the life course.* Association of Black Foundation Executives. https://abfe.issuelab.org/resource/beyond-plight-defining-pathways-to-optimal-development-for-black-men-and-boys-across-the-life-course.html

Carey, R. L. (2014). A cultural analysis of the achievement gap discourse: Challenging the language and labels used in the work of school reform. *Urban Education, 49*(4), 440–468.

Carey, R. L. (2019). Imagining the comprehensive mattering of Black boys and young men in society and schools: Toward a new approach. *Harvard Educational Review, 89*(3), 370–396.

Carnoy, M., Elmore, R., & Siskin, L. S. (Eds.) (2003). *The new accountability: High schools and high-stakes testing.* Routledge Falmer.

Carter, D. J. (2008). Cultivating a critical race consciousness for African American school success. *Educational Foundations, 22*(1–2), 11–28.

Carter, P. L. (2009). Equity and empathy: Toward racial and educational achievement in the Obama era. *Harvard Educational Review*, *79*(2), 387–297.

Carter, P. L., Skiba, R., Arredondo, M. I., & Pollock, M. (2017). You can't fix what you don't look at: Acknowledging race in addressing racial discipline disparities. *Urban Education, 52*(2), 207–235.

Carter, P. L., & Welner, K. G. (Eds.) (2013). *Closing the opportunity gap: What America must do to give all children an even chance.* Oxford University Press.

Case, K. I. (1997). African American othermothering in the urban elementary school. *Urban Review, 29*(1), 25–39.

Center for Race and Social Problems. (2015). *Pittsburgh's racial demographics 2015: Differences and disparities.* Author.

Chang-Bacon, C. K. (2022). "We sort of dance around the race thing": Race-evasiveness in teacher education. *Journal of Teacher Education, 73*(1), 8–22.

Childs, J. C., & Gunzenhauser, M. G. (2012, November). *Data-based decision making & ethical leadership: Implications for school leaders in the high-stakes accountability era.* Paper presented at the annual convention of the University Council for Educational Administration. Denver, CO.

Childs, J. C., & Gunzenhauser, M. G. (2013, October). *Professional ethics in the normalizing, data-driven, post-NCLB moment: Addressing the moral vacuum.* Paper presented at the annual meeting of the American Educational Studies Association. Baltimore, MD.

Choo, J. O. (2020, June 18). Black Fox Chapel students have spoken up about racism in our school district. Now students like me are no longer afraid to share our experiences. *Public Source.* https://www.publicsource.org/black-fox-chapel-students-have-spoken-up-about-racism-in-our-school-district-now-students-like-me-are-no-longer-afraid-to-share-our-experiences/

Chu, Y. (2019). What are they talking about when they talk about equity? A content analysis of equity principles and provisions in state Every Student Succeeds Act plans. *Education Policy Analysis Archives*, *27*(158), 1–30. https://doi.org/10.14507/epaa.27.4558

Code, L. (1995). *Rhetorical spaces: Essays on gendered locations.* Routledge.

Coles, R. (1989). *The call of stories: Teaching and the moral imagination.* Houghton Mifflin.

Cook, S. (2019, July 15). "Outsiders" and the Equal Access Act. *Juris Magazine.* https://sites.law.duq.edu/juris/2019/07/15/outsiders-and-the-equal-access-act/

Crenshaw, K. (1991). Mapping the margins: Intersectionality, identity politics, and violence against women of color. *Stanford Law Review, 43*(6), 1241–1299.

da Silva, C. D., Huguley, J., Kakli, Z., & Rao, R. (Eds.). (2007). *The opportunity gap: Achievement and inequality in education.* Harvard Education Press.

Darling-Hammond, L. (2010). *The flat world and education: How America's commitment to equity will determine our future.* Teachers College Press.

Darling-Hammond, L. (2013). Inequality and school resources: What it will take to close the opportunity gap. In P. L. Carter & K. G. Welner (Eds.), *Closing the opportunity gap: What America must do to give all children an even chance* (pp. 77–97). Oxford University Press.

Davis, B. W., Gooden, M. A., & Micheaux, D. J. (2015). Colorblind leadership: A critical race theory analysis of the ISLLC and ELCC standards. *Educational Administration Quarterly, 51*(3), 1–31.

Delpit, L. (2006). *Other people's children: Cultural conflict in the classroom.* The New Press.

DeMatthews, D., Serafini, A., & Watson, T. N. (2021). Leading inclusive schools: Principal perceptions, practices, and challenges to meaningful change. *Educational Administration Quarterly, 57*(1), 3–48.

Dewey, J. (1938). *Experience and education.* Touchstone.

Diamond, J. B., Posey-Maddox, L., & Velázquez, M. D. (2021). Reframing suburbs: Race, place, and opportunity in suburban educational spaces. *Educational Researcher, 50*(4), 249–255.

Diem, S., & Carpenter, B. W. (2012). Social justice & leadership preparation: Developing a transformative curriculum. *Planning and Changing, 43*(1/2), 96–11.

Dillard, C. B. (1995). Leading with her life: An African American feminist (re) interpretation of leadership for an urban high school principal. *Educational Administration Quarterly, 31*(4), 539–563.

Dumas, M. J. (2016). Against the dark: Antiblackness in education policy and discourse. *Theory Into Practice, 55*(1), 11–19.

Ellison, G. C. (2013). *Cut dead but still alive: Caring for African American young men.* Abingdon Press.

Emerson, R. M., Fetz, R. I., & Shaw, L. L. (2011). *Writing ethnographic fieldnotes* (2nd ed.). University of Chicago Press.

English, F. W. (2002). On the intractability of the achievement gap in urban schools and the discursive practice of continuing racial discrimination. *Education and Urban Society*, *34*(3), 298–311.

Fielding, M. (2001). OFSTED, inspection and the betrayal of democracy. *Journal of Philosophy of Education, 35*(4), 695–709. https://doi.org/10.1111/1467-9752.00254

Flores, O. J. (2017). *The new "eyes on the prize": School leaders' pursuit of equity* [Doctoral dissertation, University of Pittsburgh]. D-Scholarship@Pitt. https://d-scholarship.pitt.edu/32529/

Flores, O. J. (2018). (Re)constructing the language of the achievement gap to an opportunity gap: The counternarratives of three African American women school leaders. *Journal of School Leadership, 28*(3), 344–373.

Flores, O. J., & Gunzenhauser, M. G. (2019). The problems with colorblind leadership revealed: A call for race-conscious leaders. *International Journal of Qualitative Studies in Education, 32*(8), 963–981.

Flores, O. J., & Gunzenhauser, M. G. (2021). Justice in the gaps: School leader dispositions and the use of data to address the opportunity gap. *Urban Education, 56*(2), 261–288.

Forman, T. A., & Lewis, A. E. (2015). Beyond prejudice? Young whites' racial attitudes in post–civil rights America, 1976 to 2000. *American Behavioral Scientist, 59*(11), 1394–1428.

Forstadt, S. (2024, October 3). Federal education officials find Norwin educators failed to address racial harassment. *WESA.* https://www.wesa.fm/education/2024-10-03/norwin-school-district-racial-harassment

Foucault, M. (1995). *Discipline and punish: The birth of the prison* (2nd ed.) (Alan Sheridan, Trans.). Vintage Books. (Original work published 1975)

Foucault, M. (2005). *The hermeneutics of the subject: Lectures at the Collège de France, 1981–82* (Graham Burchell, Trans.). Picador. (Original work published 2001)

Fox Chapel Area School District. (2020, June 29). *Racism, diversity, equity, and the educational mission of the district.* Resolution 2020–9.

Frankena, W. K. (1973). *Ethics* (2nd ed.). Prentice-Hall.

Fraser-Burgess, S. A., Warren-Gordon, K., Humphrey, D. L. Jr., & Lowery, K. (2021). Scholars of color turn to womanism: Countering dehumanization in the academy. *Educational Philosophy and Theory, 53*(5), 505–522.

Freire, P. (1990). *Pedagogy of the oppressed* (M. B. Ramos, Trans.). Continuum. (Original work published 1970)

Frey, W. H. (2015). *Diversity explosion: How new racial demographics are remaking America.* Brookings Institution Press. https://www.jstor.org/stable/10.7864/j.ctt6wpc40

Fullan, M. (2011). *The moral imperative realized.* Corwin Press.

Furman, G. C. (2004). The ethic of community. *Journal of Educational Administration, 56*(5), 215–235.

Fusarelli, L. D. (2004). The potential impact of the No Child Left Behind Act on equity and diversity in American education. *Educational Policy, 18*(1), 71–94.

Gallagher, C. A. (2003). Colorblind privilege: The social and political functions of erasing the color line in post race America. *Race, Gender & Class, 10*(4), 22–37.

Generett, W., III. (2020, June 1). Our cities are burning, and so is the mental health of this African American teen. *Public Source.* https://www.publicsource.org/mental-health-racism-black-teen-pittsburgh-area/

Gerstl-Pepin, C., Killeen, K., & Hasazi, S. (2006). Utilizing an "ethic of care" in leadership preparation: Uncovering the complexity of colorblind social justice. *Journal of Educational Administration, 44*(3), 250–263.

Gilligan, C. (1979). Woman's place in man's life cycle. *Harvard Educational Review, 49*(4), 431–446.

Gilligan, C. (1982). *In a different voice: Psychological theory and women's development.* Harvard University Press.

Goldstein, A. (2021, August 12). Nazi salute, jeering directed at Fox Chapel school board members after approving mask mandate. *Pittsburgh Post-Gazette.* https://www.post-gazette.com/news/education/2021/08/12/fox-chapel-school-board-meeting-indoor-mask-mandate-nazi-salute-covid-19-pandemic/stories/202108120143

Gooden, M. A. (2012). What does racism have to do with leadership? Countering the idea of color-blind leadership: A reflection on race and the growing pressures of the urban principalship. *Educational Foundations, 26*(1–2), 67–84.

Gooden, M. A., & O'Doherty, A. (2014). Do you see what I see? Fostering aspiring leaders' racial awareness. *Urban Education, 50*(2), 225–255.

Green, A. D. (2004). In a different room: Toward an African American woman's ethic of care and justice. In V. S. Walker & J. R. Snarey (Eds.), *Race-ing moral formation: African American perspectives on care and justice* (pp. 55–71). Teachers College Press.

Gunzenhauser, M. G. (2012). *The active/ethical professional: A framework for responsible educators*. Continuum Press.

Gunzenhauser, M. G., Flores, O. J., & Quigley, M. W. (2021). Race-conscious ethics in school leadership: From impersonal caring to critical responsibility. *Teachers College Record, 123*(2), 1–40.

Gunzenhauser, M. G., Flores, O. J., & Quigley, M. W. (2024). Race-conscious caring for anti-racist leadership: A narrative ethics for cultivating communal responsibility. *Journal of School Leadership, 34*(1), 3–25.

Hallinger, P., Bickman, L., & Davis, K. (1996). School context, principal leadership, and student reading achievement. *Elementary School Journal*, *96*(5), 527–549.

Hank, A., Solomon, D., & Weller, C. E. (2018). *Systematic inequality: How America's structural racism help create the Black-White gap*. Center for American Progress. https://www.americanprogress.org/issues/race/reports/2018/02/21/447051/systematic-inequality/

Hannah-Jones, N. (2016, November 16). The end of the post-racial myth. *The New York Times Magazine*. https://www.nytimes.com/interactive/2016/11/20/magazine/donald-trumps-america-iowa-race.html

Hargreaves, A., & O'Connor, M. T. (2018). *Collaborative professionalism: When teaching together means learning for all*. Corwin Press.

Haviland, C. M. (2024, October 2). E-mail to Superintendent Natalie A. McCracken. U.S. Department of Education Office of Civil Rights, Region III, Philadelphia. https://ocrcas.ed.gov/sites/default/files/ocr-letters-and-agreements/03221010-a.pdf

Herring, A.-L. (2019a, April 3). ACLU demands McKeesport Schools approve Black student union. *WESA News*. https://www.wesa.fm/identity-justice/2019-04-03/aclu-demands-mckeesport-schools-approve-black-student-union

Herring, A.-L. (2019b, April 17). McKeesport students speak out after suing over stalled Black student union. *WESA News*. https://www.wesa.fm/identity-justice/2019-04-17/mckeesport-students-speak-out-after-suing-over-stalled-black-student-union

Collins, P. H. (2000). *Black feminist thought: Knowledge, consciousness, and the politics of empowerment* (2nd ed.). Routledge.

hooks, b. (1994). *Teaching to transgress: Education as the practice of freedom*. Routledge.

Horsford, S. D., & Clark, C. (2015). Inclusive leadership and race. In G. Theoharis & M. Scanlan (Eds.), *Educational leadership for equity and diversity: Leadership for increasingly diverse schools* (pp. 58–81). Routledge.

Howard, T. C. (2010). *Why race and culture matter in schools: Closing the achievement gap in America's classrooms*. Teachers College Press.

Johnson, L., & Campbell-Stephens, R. (2014). Beyond the colorblind perspective: Centering issues of race and culture in leadership preparation programs in Britain and the United States. In I. Bogotch & C. M. Shields (Eds.), *International handbook of educational leadership and social (in)justice* (Vol. 29) (pp. 1169–1185). Springer.

Johnson, R. S. (2002). *Using data to close the achievement gap: How to measure equity in our schools*. Corwin Press.

Kantor, H., & Lowe, R. (2013). Educationalizing the welfare state and privatizing education: The evolution of social policy since the New Deal. In P. L. Carter &

K. G. Welner (Eds.), *Closing the opportunity gap: What America must do to give every child an even chance* (pp. 25–39). Oxford Press.

Khalifa, M. A. (2018). *Culturally responsive school leadership*. Harvard Education Press.

Khalifa, M. A., Dunbar, C., & Douglas, T.-R. (2013). Derrick Bell, CRT, and educational leadership 1995–present. *Race Ethnicity and Education, 16*(4), 489–513.

Khalifa, M. A., Gooden, M. A., & Davis, J. E. (2016). Culturally responsive school leadership: A synthesis of the literature. *Review of Educational Research, 86*(4), 1272–1311.

Khalifa, M. A., Jennings, M. E., Briscoe, F., Oleszweski, A. M., & Abdi, N. (2014). Racism? Administrative and community perspectives in data-driven decision making: Systemic perspectives versus technical-rational perspectives. *Urban Education, 49*(2), 147–181.

Ladson-Billings, G. (2006). From the achievement gap to the education debt: Understanding achievement in U.S. schools. *Educational Researcher, 35*(7), 3–12. https://doi.org/10.3102/0013189X035007003

Ladson-Billings, G. (2013). Lack of achievement or loss of opportunity. In P. L. Carter & K. G. Welner (Eds.), *Closing the opportunity gap: What America must do to give every child an even chance* (pp. 11–24). Oxford University Press.

Ladson-Billings, G., & Tate, W. F. (1995). Toward a critical race theory of education. *Teachers College Record, 97*(1), 47–68.

Leithwood, K., Harris, A., & Hopkins, D. (2020). Seven strong claims about successful school leadership revisited. *School Leadership & Management, 40*(1), 5–22.

Lewis, A. E. (2001). There is no "race" in the schoolyard: Colorblind ideology in an (almost) all-white school. *American Educational Research Journal, 38*(4), 781–811.

Lewis, A. E. (2003). Everyday race-making. *American Behavioral Scientist, 47*(3), 283–305.

Lewis, A. E. (2004). "What group?" Studying whites and whiteness in the era of "color-blindness." *Sociological Theory, 22*(4), 623–646.

Lincoln, Y. S., & Guba, E. (1985). *Naturalistic inquiry*. Sage.

Lipman, P. (2011). Neoliberal education restructuring: Dangers and opportunities of the present crisis. *Monthly Review, 63*(3), 114.

Lopez Kershen, J. (2018). Control as care: How teachers in "no excuses" charter schools position their students and themselves. *Equity & Excellence in Education, 51*(3–4), 265–283.

Louis, K. S., Murphy, J., & Smylie, M. (2016). Caring leadership in schools: Findings from exploratory analyses. *Educational Administration Quarterly, 52*(2), 310–348.

Love, B. L. (2019). *We want to do more than survive: Abolitionist teaching and the pursuit of educational freedom*. Beacon Press.

Marino, G. (Ed.). (2010). *Ethics: The essential writings*. Modern Library Classics.

Marx, S., & Larson, L. L. (2011). Taking off the color-blind glasses: Recognizing and supporting Latina/o students in a predominantly white school. *Educational Administration Quarterly, 48*(2), 259–303.

McKinney, M. (2019, April 23). McKeesport Area School District disputes allegations in Black student union case. *Pittsburgh Post-Gazette*. https://www.post

-gazette.com/local/east/2019/04/23/McKeesport-Area-School-District-black-student-union-lawsuit/stories/201904230140

Mercado, C. I., Bullard, K. M., Bolduc, L.M.F., Andrews, C. A., Freggens, Z.R.F., Liggett, G., Banks, D., Johnson, S. B., Penman-Aguilar, A., & Njai, R. (2024). A shift in approach to addressing public health inequities and the effect of societal structural and systemic drivers on social determinants of health. *Public Health Reports*. https://doi.org/10.1177/00333549241283586

Merriam, S. B. (2009). *Qualitative research: A guide to design and implementation* (3rd ed.). John Wiley & Sons.

Miles, M. B., Huberman, A. M., & Saldaña, J. (2014). *Qualitative data analysis: A methods sourcebook* (3rd ed.). Sage.

Miller, R., Liu, K., & Ball, A. F. (2020). Critical counter-narrative as transformative methodology for educational equity. *Review of Research in Education, 44*(1), 269–300.

Mills, C. W. (1998). *Blackness visible: Essays on philosophy and race*. Cornell University Press.

Milner, H. R. (2007). Race, culture, and researcher positionality: Working through dangers seen, unseen, and unforeseen. *Educational Researcher, 36*(7), 388–400.

Milner, H. R. (2012). Beyond a test score: Explaining opportunity gaps in educational practice. *Journal of Black Studies, 43*(6), 693–718.

Milner, H. R. (2020). *Start where you are but don't stay there: Understanding diversity, opportunity gaps, and teaching in today's classrooms* (2nd ed.). Harvard Education Press.

Miranda, H. P., Mokhtar, C., Tung, R., Ward, R., French, D., McAlister, S., & Marshall, A. (2014). *Opportunity and equity: Enrollment and outcomes of Black and Latino males in Boston Public Schools*. Center for Collaborative Education and Annenberg Institute for School Reform.

Mordechay, K., & Orfield, G. (2017). Demographic transformation in a policy vacuum: The changing face of U.S. metropolitan society and challenges for public schools. *The Educational Forum, 81*(2), 193–203.

Morrison, O. (2020, June 9). Fox Chapel district investigates racist videos as students and alumni call it to embrace Black Lives Matter movement. *Public Source*. https://www.publicsource.org/fox-chapel-students-call-for-change-as-the-district-investigates-racist-videos-black-lives-matter/

Morrison, T. (1992). *Playing in the dark: Whiteness and the literary imagination*. Vintage Books.

Morrison, T. (2019). Sarah Lawrence commencement address. In T. Morrison, *The source of self-regard: Selected essays, speeches, and meditations* (pp. 67–73). Alfred E. Knopf. (Original text published 1988)

Murphy, J. (2003). *Re-culturing educational leadership: The ISLLC standards ten years out*. National Policy Board for Educational Administration.

Murphy, J., & Shipman, N. (1999). The interstate school leaders licensure consortium: A standards-based approach to strengthening educational leadership. *Journal of Personnel Evaluation in Education, 13*(3), 205–224.

Nash, R. J., & Jang, J.J.J. (2016). *Teaching college students how to solve real-life moral dilemmas: An ethical compass for quarterlifers*. Peter Lang.

National Center for Education Statistics (2019). *Achievement gaps*. https://nces.ed.gov/nationsreportcard/studies/gaps/

National Policy Board for Educational Administration. (2015). *Professional standards for educational leaders 2015*. Author.

Niederberger, M. (2019, March 19). New data shows racial achievement gaps at more than half of Allegheny County school districts. *Public Source*. https://www.publicsource.org/how-new-state-data-has-revealed-institutional-racism-in-pittsburgh-area-school-districts/

Niederberger, M., Hacke, S., & Vicens, N. K. (2019, March 19). Allegheny County schools with reported racial achievement gaps. *Public Source*. https://www.publicsource.org/allegheny-county-schools-with-reported-racial-achievement-gaps/

Noddings, N. (1984). *Caring: A feminine approach to ethics and moral education*. University of California Press.

Noguera, P. A. (2001). Racial politics and the elusive quest for excellence and equity in education. *Education and Urban Society, 34*(1), 18–41.

Oakes, J. (2005). *Keeping track: How schools structure inequality* (2nd ed.). Yale University Press.

Oakes, J. (2008). Keeping track: Structuring equality and inequality in an era of accountability. *Teachers College Record, 110*(3), 700–712.

Oplatka, I. (2014). The place of "social justice" in the field of educational administration: A journals-based historical overview of emergent area of study. In I. Bogotch and C. M. Shields (Eds.), *International handbook of educational leadership and social (in)justice* (pp. 15–34). Springer.

Orfield, G. (2013). Housing segregation produces unequal schools: Causes and solutions. In P. L. Carter & K. G. Welner (Eds.), *Closing the opportunity gap: What America must do to give all children an even chance* (pp. 40–60). Oxford University Press.

Orfield, G., & Frankenberg, E. (2014). Increasingly segregated and unequal schools as courts reverse policy. *Educational Administration Quarterly, 50*(5), 718–734.

Orfield, G., & Jarvie, D. (2020). *Unequal public schools makes affirmative action essential for equal opportunity*. UCLA Civil Rights Project. https://escholarship.org/uc/item/3hb1h0z7

Paris, D. (2012). Culturally sustaining pedagogy: A needed change in stance, terminology, and rhetoric. *Educational Researcher, 41*(3), 93–97.

Patterson, J. A., Gordon, J., & Price, P. G. (2008). The color of caring: Race and the implementation of educational reform. *Educational Foundations, 22*, 97–116.

Patton, M. Q. (2002). *Qualitative research & evaluation methods* (3rd ed.). Sage Publications.

Quigley, M. W., & Allie, A. (2021). Woke leadership: Why critical race consciousness matters for educational leaders. In R. Shankar-Brown (Ed.), *Bending the arc toward justice: Equity-focused practices for educational leaders* (pp. 49–72). Information Age Publishing.

Quigley, M. W., & Mitchell, A. B. (2018). "What works": Applying critical race praxis to the design of educational and mentoring interventions for African American males. *Journal of African American Males in Education, 9*(2), 74–102.

Reardon, S. F., Grewal, E. T., Kalogrides, D., & Greenberg, E. (2012). *Brown* fades: The end of court-ordered school desegregation and the resegregation of

American public schools. *Journal of Policy Analysis and Management, 31*(4), 876–904.

Ritter, M. (2008). The significance of finding a witness in liberatory education. In B. Stengel (Ed.), *Philosophy of education, 2007: Proceedings of the annual meeting of the Philosophy of Education Society* (pp. 359–366). University of Illinois.

Rivas-Drake, D., Seaton, E. K., Markstrom, C., Quintana, S., Syed, M., Lee, R. M., Schwartz, S. J., Umaña-Taylor, A. J., French, S., Yip, T., & Ethnic and Racial Identity in the 21st Century Study Group. (2014). Ethnic and racial identity in adolescence: Implications for psychosocial, academic, and health outcomes. *Child Development, 85*(1), 40–57. https://doi.org/10.1111/cdev.12200

Rivera-McCutcheon, R. (2021). *Radical care: Leading for justice in urban schools.* Teachers College Press.

Roseboro, D. L., & Ross, S. N. (2009). Care-sickness: Black women educators, care theory, and a hermeneutic of suspicion. *Educational Foundations, 23*, 19–40.

Rutan, D. Q., & Glass, M. R. (2017). The lingering effects of neighborhood appraisal: Evaluating redlining's legacy in Pittsburgh. *The Professional Geographer, 17*(3), 339–349.

Ryan, J. (2003). Educational administrators' perceptions of racism in diverse school contexts. *Race Ethnicity and Education, 6*(2), 145–164.

Saldaña, J. (2016). *The coding manual for qualitative researchers* (3rd ed.). Sage Publications.

Schofield, J. W. (2010). The colorblind perspective in school: Causes and consequences. In J. A. Banks & C.A.M. Banks (Eds.), *Multicultural education: Issues and perspectives* (7th ed., pp. 259–284). John Wiley & Sons.

Seate, M. (Writer, Director, & Producer). (2020). *Childhood lost: The adultification of African American girls* [TV documentary, online video]. WQED Pittsburgh. https://www.pbs.org/video/childhood-lost-the-adultification-of-african-american-girls-nbtzti/

Seidman, I. (2013). *Interviewing as qualitative research: A guide for researchers in education and the social sciences* (4th ed.). Teachers College Press.

Sergiovanni, T. J. (2009). *The principalship: A reflective practice perspective* (6th ed.). Pearson.

Shapiro, J. P., & Gross, S. J. (2013). *Ethical educational leadership in turbulent times: (re)solving moral dilemmas* (2nd ed.). Routledge.

Shapiro, J. P., & Stefkovich, J. A. (2011). *Ethical leadership and decision making in education: Applying theoretical perspectives to complex dilemmas* (3rd ed.). Routledge.

Shields, C. M. (2004). Dialogic leadership for social justice: Overcoming pathologies of silence. *Educational Administration Quarterly, 40*(1), 109–132.

Shoho, A., Merchant, B. M., & Lugg, C.A. (2011). Social justice: Seeking a common language. *The SAGE handbook of educational leadership: Advances in theory, research, and practice* (2nd ed.) (pp. 36–54). Sage Publications.

Singleton, G. E. (2015). *Courageous conversations about race: A field guide for achieving equity in schools* (2nd ed.). Corwin Press.

Sirotnik, K. (Ed.) (2004). *Holding accountability accountable: What ought to matter in public education.* Teachers College Press.

Snyder, T. D. (2017). *On tyranny: Twenty lessons from the twentieth century*. Crown.

Solomon, P. (2002). School leaders and anti-racism: Overcoming pedagogical and political obstacles. *Journal of School Leadership, 12*, 174–197.

Solorzano, D. G., & Bernal, D. D. (2001). Examining transformational resistance through a critical race and Latcrit theory framework: Chicana and Chicano students in an urban context. *Urban Education, 36*, 308–342.

Solorzano, D. G., & Yosso, T. J. (2001). Critical race and LatCrit theory and method: Counter-storytelling. *International Journal of Qualitative Studies in Education, 14*(4), 471–495.

Solorzano, D. G., & Yosso, T. J. (2002). Critical race methodology: Counter-storytelling as an analytical framework for education research. *Qualitative Inquiry, 8*(1), 23–44.

Starratt, R. J. (1991). Building an ethical school: A theory for practice in educational leadership. *Educational Administration Quarterly*, *27*(2), 185–202.

Starratt, R. J. (2004). *Ethical leadership*. Jossey-Bass.

Starratt, R. J. (2014). Ethics and social justice: Strangers passing in the night? In I. Bogotch & C. M. Shields (Eds.), *International handbook of educational leadership and social (in)justice* (pp. 67–80). Springer.

Stefkovich, J., & Begley, P. T. (2007). Ethical school leadership: Defining the best interests of students. *Educational Management and Leadership, 35*(2), 205–224.

Stovall, D. (2004). School leader as negotiator: Critical race theory, praxis, and the creation of productive space. *Multicultural Education, 12*(2), 8–12.

Strike, K. (2006). *Ethical leadership in schools: Creating community in an environment of accountability*. Corwin Press.

Tarca, K. (2005). Colorblind in control: The risks of resisting difference amid demographic change. *Educational Studies, 38*(2), 99–120.

Tatum, B. D. (1998). What do you do when they call you a racist? *NASSP Bulletin, 82*(602), 43–48.

Tatum, B. D. (2017). *Why are all the Black kids sitting together in the cafeteria? And other conversations about race*. Basic Books.

Taylor, E. (2006). Toward a coherent theory of race in the education of school leaders: Fly fishing across the racial divide. *Race Ethnicity and Education, 1*(2), 225–239.

Theoharis, G., & Haddix, M. (2011). Undermining racism and a whiteness ideology: White principals living a commitment to equitable and excellent schools. *Urban Education, 46*(6), 1332–1351.

Thompson, A. (1998). Not the color purple: Black feminist lessons for educational caring. *Harvard Educational Review*, 68(4), 522–555.

Thompson Dorsey, D. N., & Roulhac, G. D. (2019). From desegregation to privatization: A critical race policy analysis of school choice and educational opportunity in North Carolina. *Peabody Journal of Education, 94*(4), 420–441.

Thorndike, E. L. (1914). *Education: A first book*. The Macmillan Company.

Todd, S. (2004). Teaching with ignorance: Questions of social justice, empathy, and responsible community. *Interchange, 35*, 337–352.

Touré, J., & Thompson Dorsey, D. N. (2018). Stereotypes, images, and inclination to discriminatory action: The white racial frame in the practice of school leadership. *Teachers College Record, 120*(2), 1–38.

Trotter, J. W., & Day, J. N. (2010). *Race and renaissance: African Americans in Pittsburgh since World War II.* University of Pittsburgh Press.

U.S. Census Bureau. (2020). *Profile of general population and housing characteristics, Allegheny County.* Accessed January 8, 2025 from https://data.census.gov/

Valencia, R. R. (1997). Conceptualizing the notion of deficit thinking. In R. R. Valencia (Ed.), *The evolution of deficit thinking: Educational thought and practice* (pp. 1-12). The Falmer Press.

Valenzuela, A. (1999). *Subtractive schooling: U.S.-Mexican youth and the politics of caring.* State University of New York Press.

Venzant-Chambers, T. T. (2009). The "receivement gap": School tracking policies and the fallacy of the "achievement gap." *The Journal of Negro Education, 78*(4), 417–431.

Walker, V. S. (1996). *Their highest potential: An African American school community in the segregated south.* University of North Carolina Press.

Walker, V. S. (2018). *The lost education of Horace Tate: Uncovering the hidden heroes who fought for justice in schools.* The New Press.

Walker, V. S., & Snarey, J. R. (2004). *Race-ing moral formation: African American perspectives on care and justice.* Teachers College Press.

Walker, V. S.., & Tompkins, R. H. (2004). Caring in the past: The case of a Southern segregated African American school. In V. S. Walker & J. R. Snarey (Eds.), *Race-ing moral formation: African American perspectives on care and justice* (pp. 77–92). Teachers College Press.

Watson, W. (2018). We got soul: Exploring contemporary black women educators' praxis of politicized care. *Equity and Excellence in Education, 51*(3–4), 362–377.

Welch, S. D. (1990). *A feminist ethic of risk.* Westview Press.

Welsh, R. O. (2019). Ebbs and flows: Revisiting the relationship between student mobility, segregation, and neighborhoods. *Peabody Journal of Education, 94*(5), 493–520. https://doi.org/10.1080/0161956X.2019.1668210

Welton, A. D., Diem, S., & Holme, J. J. (2015). Color conscious, cultural blindness: Suburban school districts and demographic change. *Education and Urban Society, 47*(6), 695–722.

White, A., & Young, C. (2016). *Positive racial identity development in early education: Understanding PRIDE in Pittsburgh.* University of Pittsburgh Office of Child Development.

Witherspoon, N., & Arnold, B. M. (2010). Pastoral care: Notions of caring and the black female principal. *The Journal of Negro Education, 79*(3), 220–232.

Yearby, R., Clark, B., & Figueroa, J. F. (2022). Structural racism in historical and modern US health care policy. *Health Affairs, 41*(2), 187–194.

Yosso, T. J. (2005). Whose culture has capital? A critical race discussion of community cultural wealth. *Race Ethnicity and Education, 8*(1), 69–91.

Index

The letter *f*, *n*, or *t* after a page number refers to a figure, note, or table, respectively

About the Authors

Michael G. Gunzenhauser is a professor in the Department of Educational Foundations, Organizations, and Policy and senior associate dean in the School of Education at the University of Pittsburgh. He is a philosopher of education and qualitative research methodologist who studies ethics and epistemology in relation to social justice in education. His work includes the book *The Active/Ethical Professional: A Framework for Responsible Educators* (Continuum, 2012). Before becoming a faculty member, he served in several professional administrative roles, including residential counselor at the North Carolina School of Science and Mathematics and coordinator for precollege programs at Duke University.

Osly J. Flores is an assistant professor in the Department of Education Policy, Organization, and Leadership at the University of Illinois at Urbana–Champaign. His research focuses on two main areas: race-conscious leadership in K–12 schools and the persistence of graduate students of color in navigating higher education. In the first area, he explores three themes: equitable leadership practices, leadership ethics, and the experiences of school leaders of color. In the second area, he uses critical frameworks to highlight the successes and resilience of graduate students of color. His work has been published in various journals, including *The Urban Review, Urban Education, Teachers College Record, Journal of College Student Development, AERA Open,* and the *International Journal of Qualitative Studies in Education.*

Michael W. Quigley is an associate professor at Robert Morris University with joint appointments in the Department of Education and the Department of Communication and Organizational Leadership. He conducts research on educational leadership, critical leadership, and youth leadership. He is the coauthor, with Anthony B. Mitchell, of "'What Works': Applying Critical Race Praxis to the Design of Educational and Mentoring Interventions for African American Males" (2018); "Woke Leadership: Why Critical Race Consciousness Matters for Educational Leaders" (2021), with Angela Allie;

and *Beyond Plight: Defining Pathways to Optimal Development for Black Men and Boys Across the Life Course* (2017), a framework for improving life outcomes for Black men and boys, with Mark McDaniel and Leon Caldwell, for the Association of Black Foundation Executives.